Psychological Evaluations & Case Plans

A Handbook for Referring Professionals

John Kayser

LOVE PUBLISHING COMPANY®

Denver • London • Singapore

Dedication

To Dan and Holden

Published by Love Publishing Company
P.O. Box 22353
Denver, Colorado 80222
www.lovepublishing.com

Library of Congress Catalog Card Number 2007939930

Copyright © 2009 by Love Publishing Company
Printed in the United States of America
ISBN 978-0-89108-334-4

Contents

About the Author

John Kayser is a professor of social work at the University of Denver. Currently he teaches courses on clinical social work theory and practice, mental health interventions with children and adults, and adult development and aging. He received the MSW in 1975 and the Ph.D. in 1990. Prior to joining the faculty, he practiced as a licensed clinical social worker in a university-based children's day treatment center, and served as the director of social work and the director of child and adolescent treatment services in a private, nonprofit psychiatric hospital system.

He is the lead author of the 2000 *Child Welfare* article, "Teaching Social Workers To Use Psychological Assessment Data," and has developed training curricula and conducted numerous workshops in Colorado, with a psychologist colleague, on using psychological assessments in case planning. In addition, he has received several funded grants to develop interprofessional curricula and training opportunities for social workers, psychologists, educators, early childhood interventionists, and nurses at the master's and doctoral levels.

Chapter 1

Psychological Assessments and Case Planning

*When referring. . .for testing,
follow these guidelines:
have a specific reason for
referring a client; explain to
the psychologist what questions
you want answered, provide
information you have collected
to the psychologist; prepare the
client for what to expect at the
psychologist's office; do not have
unrealistic expectations of what
the testing will provide—testing is
only one tool for assessing the
client; and ask the psychologist to
explain any limitations of the
specific test that your client has
been given.*

(Jordan & Franklin, 1995, p. 151)

This chapter exam-
ines the contribu-
tions that psychological

OVERVIEW

evaluations can make to the case planning or treatment planning process
and identifies the competencies needed by referring professionals in other
disciplines who seek to become knowledgeable consumers of psychological evaluations. Consumers have a working knowledge about the
strengths and limitations of psychological assessment data and are able to
apply that information competently in designing and implementing appropriate, effective case planning decisions with their clients.

The Case Planning Process

For conceptual purposes, helping professionals divide into distinct phases
of work the processes and tasks by which they assist clients in effecting
change in their lives. Different disciplines and different fields of practice
use different terms to describe this process:

> *case planning*—used in case management and social services
> *treatment planning*—used in mental health
> *lesson planning*—used in education
> *medical orders*—used in medicine and nursing
> *judicial orders*—law

Although each of these terms has its own unique meaning, they all
describe a similar process. This is the period between data gathering/
assessment and implementation of the intervention phase in which desired
goals and objectives are specified in advance and the intervention techniques, procedures, methods, and/or programs are designed, planned, prescribed, and/or ordered to accomplish the outcomes sought. In this text the
terms *case planning* and *treatment planning* are generic descriptors that
refer to this process. As summarized in Table 1.1, case planning addresses
a series of important steps and questions.

TABLE 1.1   The Case Planning Phase

PLANNING TASKS	PLANNING QUESTIONS
Prioritizing problems	How should problems be prioritized? Out of all the global concerns or problems identified in the assessment phase, which one is the *starting place for work*? Which are the most severe or complex? Which are easiest to change? Which are clients most motivated to work on and change?
Selecting a focus for change	What aspect of the client system and/or social environment could be the target of professional intervention? Can more than one intervention be planned with different parts of the client system or environment?
Ascertaining capacities, present functioning, problem areas, and strengths	What are the client's present functioning, achievements, and capacities? What types of problems or impairments interfere with the client's functioning? What strengths and resources do clients have that can be used in designing interventions?
Selecting a modality of intervention	What modality of intervention should be used (i.e., individual, family, couple, small group)?
Selecting goals and objectives	What are the immediate, intermediate, and ultimate goals of the intervention? What are specific objectives to accomplish these goals?
Selecting an intervention	Which intervention approaches are likely to be the most effective and efficient in effecting change? What specific interventions will be made?
Contracting	What do clients have to do to effect change? Will the contract be oral or written?
Determining cultural considerations	What intra-cultural or cross-cultural factors between clients and professionals have to be taken into account in undertaking a culturally appropriate intervention?
Determining collateral contacts	What other extended family members, helping professionals, external systems of care, or other collateral parties have to be involved?
Determining length of and timing of interventions; and estimating the degree of change anticipated	How much time is available to work with clients? Will the intervention be short- or long-term in duration? What is the timing or order of interventions over the course of time? What type of change can be anticipated over the course of the intervention?

Adapted from *Child Welfare*, by V. Brown, 2002, Boston: Allyn & Bacon; *Exploring Child Welfare*, 2nd edition, by C. Crosson-Tower, 2001, Boston: Allyn & Bacon; *Empirical Clinical Practice*, by Jayaratne & Levy, 1979, New York: Columbia University Press; and *The Use of Psychological Testing for Treatment Planning and Outcome Assessment*, by M. Maruish, 1994, Hillsdale, NJ: Erlbaum; and *Diagnosis and Treatment Planning in Counseling*, by L. Seligman, 2004, New York: Kluwer Academic/Plenum Publishing.

Although conceptualized in a sequential manner, in actual practice assessment, case planning, and intervention phases typically occur concurrently, with each phase influencing the others (Crosson-Tower, 2001). That is to say, case planning is an ongoing process, constantly changing as new information is obtained regarding the nature of clients' problems and strengths, and how they have responded over time to the interventions.

The Contribution of Psychological Assessments to Case Planning

Psychological assessment is a comprehensive process of synthesizing and deriving meaning from multiple sources of data, to achieve a broad but detailed understanding of individuals and the reciprocal interactions between their behaviors and environments (Reynolds, Gutkin, Elliot, & Witt, 1984). Psychological assessments can play a significant role in the treatment planning process by helping to answer some of the case planning questions outlined above.

Assessments may focus on answering referral questions regarding conceptualizing a current pattern of behavior; identifying probable causes of the behavior; prognosticating about the likelihood of changes that might take place over time; suggesting ways in which problematic behavior can be modified and/or ways in which strengths can be enhanced and supported; and pointing out areas of delay, deficit, or dysfunction (Brems, 2000). Yet, according to Maruish (1994), opinions have varied on the usefulness of these psychological assessments. Table 1.2 summarizes the positive and negative views regarding the contributions of psychological assessments to the treatment planning process.

In the remaining chapters, each of these positive and negative points are considered in greater detail. Matarazzo (1990) points out the contributions that psychological assessments can make in identifying clients' problems and strengths:

> Psychological assessment of intelligence, personality, and type or level of impairment is a highly complex operation that involves extracting diagnostic meaning from an individual's personal history and objectively recorded test scores. Rather than being totally objective, assessment involves a subjective component. Specifically, it is the activity of a licensed professional, an artisan, familiar with the accumulated findings of his or her young science, who

TABLE 1.2	Positive and Negative Views Regarding the Contributions of Psychological Assessments to the Case Planning Process

POSITIVE VIEWS	NEGATIVE VIEWS
• Psychological assessments can provide timely and cost-effective information about clients' personality structure, educational and psychological needs and/or functioning at the time of the assessment, and possible diagnosis.	• Psychological assessments do not yield as much valuable information as a good face-to-face clinical interview with clients.
• Psychological assessments can help clients find out more about themselves, particularly regarding thoughts and feelings outside their conscious awareness.	• Test-based psychological assessment may be counterproductive and off-putting to clients, creating barriers to rapport building and collaboration, and interfere in the treatment process.
• Psychological assessments provide crucial information about symptom severity, problem complexity, and clients' readiness to change, which are not always readily obtainable from clinical interviews.	• Test results emphasize deficits and impairments, and thus may be dehumanizing to clients because the pathology, rather than the person, becomes the object of attention.
• Psychological assessments can identify unforeseen obstacles to treatment, as well as identify areas of potential growth for clients.	• Test results may bias practitioners negatively in their expectations about clients' ability to change.
• Psychological assessments permit a comparison of individual clients' problems, functioning, and performance against a normative frame of reference, which may help to answer questions about severity of symptoms as well as expected prognosis.	• Results from psychological assessments do not translate readily into intervention or treatment plans.
• Psychological assessments can link assessment results with intervention approaches that have the highest likelihood of success.	• Psychological tests are culturally biased against clients of color and other minority groups, and their results typically exaggerate client problems and minimize client strengths.
• Psychological assessments can provide information about clients who are not easily interviewed (e.g., oppositional clients).	• Psychological tests have the potential to become political tools of oppression, by forcing people to be tested against their will and/or by using information against them.

Source: Adapted from *A Practical Guide to Psychodiagnostic Testing*, by L. Katz, 1985, Springfield, IL: Charles C Thomas Publishing; and *The Use of Psychological Testing for Treatment Planning and Outcome Assessment*, by M. Maruish, 1994, Hillsdale, NJ: Erlbaum.

in each instance uses tests, techniques, and a strategy that, *whereas also identifying possible deficits, maximizes the chances of discovering each client's full ability and true potential* (p.1000) [italics added].

Psychological assessments are based on a broad array of information, not just test score results. The questions asked and information provided by other helping professionals (i.e., medical records and health histories, psychosocial histories, client observations, clinical interviews) serve as collateral sources of data that an evaluator must integrate with existing testing data. Finally, the clinical judgment of psychologists plays a critical role not only in *selecting* the appropriate assessment tests, techniques, or evaluation strategies, but also in *interpreting* the results to derive meaning (or greater understanding) about the clients' present functioning—strengths and problems—as well as identifying underutilized potential and future areas of growth.

Collaboration Between Referring and Evaluating Professionals

Psychological assessments make their most important contribution to case planning decisions when their information is "triangulated" with the data arising from other evaluation sources so that a comprehensive picture of clients' strengths and weaknesses is obtained (Kaufman & Lichtenberger, 2002). A good psychological evaluation provides "added value" to case planning decisions, particularly when clear referral questions have been posed and other case history information has been provided to the evaluating psychologist.

But conducting a psychological evaluation simply for the sake of doing so, when it is unclear how such an evaluation will add to understanding the client, clarify a case planning decision, or serve to formulate intervention recommendations, is to be avoided at all costs. The intent of this book is to encourage professionals from other disciplines to use psychological evaluations more effectively in their treatment and case planning decisions, and to be able to decide when they might request such evaluations to augment their existing information about clients.

Barriers to Using Psychological Assessments in Case Planning

Professional consumers from other disciplines face numerous barriers to developing competence in understanding and applying information from psychological assessments to their clients' case plans. Consider the following scenario, a composite of many examples shared in various workshops by social workers and other professionals regarding their difficulties in using psychological assessment data.

The case scenario is typical of the complicated cases that frequently appear in social services and in a variety of other human service systems as well. And dedicated professionals who are not psychologists frequently encounter numerous barriers in effectively incorporating the psychological assessment information about clients into their case planning decisions. A closer inspection of these barriers suggests the following dimensions of the problem.

Lack of Knowledge About Psychological Evaluations

Referring professionals from other disciplines often lack familiarity with the principles of psychological assessment. Curricula in their undergraduate and graduate training typically do not contain core or elective courses covering psychological testing. As a result of this lack of training, the caseworker in this scenario is unaware that *all* the evaluations contain crucial information that is directly relevant to case planning decisions regarding whether to pursue family reunification or to seek termination of parental rights. The caseworker's overall lack of familiarity with the principles of psychological assessment and nature of tests prevents her from recognizing the implications of key pieces of data contained in the various reports.

Further, the agency supervisor was uninformed about psychological evaluations because the county department of social services provided no training in this area. Some supervisors naively assume that practitioners can pick up a working knowledge of psychological assessments just by being "on-the-job."

Lack of Access to Evaluators

Access to evaluating psychologists varies enormously, by agency and by geographic region. Professionals and agencies in large urban areas may

Case Scenario 1.1

Carla Jimenez, recently hired as an ongoing caseworker by the county department of social services, has begun reviewing the case file of Billy Jordan, an African-American child, age 9, to develop an expedited permanency plan. Among the documents in Billy's file are reports from a variety of professionals in the community, including four different types of psychological evaluations:

1. A clinical psychological evaluation was requested by the Department of Human Services to provide the court with information about Billy's emotional health and developmental needs following severe physical abuse from his father, and to offer an opinion regarding the capacity of Billy's mother to bring him up in an appropriate, safe, and healthy manner. Various assessment procedures were used in the evaluation (i.e., clinical interviews with mother and child, standardized intellectual and personality testing and projective testing with Billy, and observation of mother–child interactions).

   The psychologist's report describes Mrs. Jordan as being "guarded, mistrustful, and uncooperative" during the evaluation process. According to this evaluator, the clinical interviews with mother and observations of parent–child interactions suggested a pattern of emotional abuse and parental neglect. Based on Billy's poor performance on standardized testing measures, the evaluator concluded that the course of his development was being adversely affected by his father's abuse and his mother's inability to provide adequate protection.

2. A *school psychology evaluation* of Billy took place at the beginning of this school year. For some time, Billy's school performance has been characterized by significant delays in reading, spelling, and comprehension, and currently he is functioning considerably below his expected grade level. The school psychologist's report drew particular attention to the results of intelligence testing, which indicated a significant difference between his above-average verbal reasoning abilities and his below-average nonverbal reasoning abilities.

   In addition, projective tests and observations of his emotional and social functioning in the school suggest that Billy has considerable anger and resentment toward adults and peers, which occasionally erupt into verbal and physical aggression. The evaluator recommended that Billy be placed in a self-contained special education program for children with emotional and behavioral disturbances.

3. A *disability psychological evaluation* of Billy's mother was conducted by a psychologist working for vocational rehabilitation, to determine whether

(continued)

she was capable of obtaining employment. After reviewing her medical history, the results of standardized neuropsychological testing, observation of simulated work tasks, and a clinical interview, the evaluator's report attributes Mrs. Jordan's problems with organization and memory retention—which have interfered markedly with her past jobs and current employability—to a suspected closed head injury received from repeated episodes of physical battering by her husband. Although the report does not address issues other than Mrs. Jordan's capacity for work, Ms. Jimenez, the caseworker, wonders if the effects of the closed head injury also have negatively impacted the mother's parenting abilities and household management.

4. A *forensic psychological evaluation* of the father was completed by a prison psychologist after the father's incarceration for child abuse and domestic violence. Based upon clinical interviews with Mr. Jordan, as well as the results of a standardized, multidimensional personality inventory, the prison psychologist described the father as deeply ashamed of his violent behavior. Having recently converted to Islam in prison, Mr. Jordan is determined to prove himself to be a worthy husband and father, and expresses a strong desire to reunite with his family upon his release. Noting that the father's previous violent outburst occurred only when he had been abusing drugs and alcohol, this evaluator recommended that the father receive ongoing drug and alcohol treatment and domestic violence counseling when he returns to the community.

With the father's prison sentence scheduled to end in the next few years, Ms. Jimenez wonders which of the information in these reports is relevant to the decision facing her about this case. Should a reunification plan be developed for Billy with the mother alone, or with the mother and father, or should the Department move toward a recommendation to terminate parental rights? Given the concerns about the adequacy of the mother's parenting abilities, would the father's return to the household create further strains on the family, or would a nonviolent, sober father actually act as a stabilizing influence in the home? Ms. Jimenez also wonders about the extent to which the evaluators took into account the family's African American heritage and other cultural factors.

Unfortunately, Ms. Jimenez was unfamiliar with the assessment measures, technical terms, and meaning of the test results used in these various evaluation reports. Because she was not able to reach any of the evaluating psychologists to clarify her questions, she decided to consult with her casework supervisor, Mrs. Jones. The supervisor advised her not to worry about the technical information in the body of the report, and suggested that she skip to the last section of each report—the psychologist's conclusions and recommendations.

have direct access to a host of psychological evaluators who are available for consultations or conferences concerning the clients they have evaluated. In contrast, counties in remote and rural areas may have few local psychologists available to them, and/or little direct contact with the evaluators they do have. When consumers from other professions lack access and skills in seeking consultation from examining psychologists, they clearly will have difficulty in effectively utilizing psychological assessment data in case planning decisions.

Problematic Written Reports

Psychologists want to communicate clearly the results of their evaluation in an effective and helpful manner, but their reports may be laden with unexplained technical terms or emphasize quantifiable test scores with little accompanying narrative or explanation. Generally, these types of evaluation reports have little utility (Wodrich & Kush, 1990), especially because the main consumers of psychological reports are overwhelmingly nonpsychologists (clients, parents, judges, lawyers, social workers, teachers, probation officers, employers, nurses, etc.).

Psychologists' Unfamiliarity with Certain Service Systems

Psychological evaluators themselves may have little understanding or orientation to the specific helping systems in which referring professionals work. For example, psychologists employed by county departments of social services or the courts usually have not received formal training in the parameters of the child welfare system. As a result, the psychologists may have limited experience in working with other professionals in collaborative case planning. Further, as Maruish (1994) notes, clinical and other applied psychologists actually receive very little training about "how test results can assist in planning treatment or assessing the impact of treatment" (p. xiii). Rather, the emphasis of their educational courses and internship experiences typically is on symptom identification, descriptions of personality, and diagnostic appraisals.

Whatever the contributors, the end result is that referring professionals often lack understanding of the assessment data and test results being reported and interpreted by psychological examiners. In extreme cases, referring professionals even may resort to the shortcut offered by the casework supervisor in the case scenario—skipping the information in the body of the report and reading only the recommendations and interventions.

Needless to say, this practice is extremely unwise (not to mention unethical), and it is fundamentally harmful to clients, in that case plans and interventions are being formulated based on data that are poorly understood by nonpsychologist professionals whose decisions and recommendations will greatly affect the life trajectories of children, parents, and family members.

Case Planning Considerations: Becoming Informed Consumers

Imagine that Ms. Jimenez had developed specific competencies as a knowledgeable, informed consumer of psychological evaluation reports. What would be different about her case planning decisions now?

Understanding the Principles and Methods of Psychological Assessment

Having acquired a basic understanding of the principles of psychological assessment, Ms. Jimenez would have a working knowledge of the major objective and subjective evaluation approaches that psychologists typically employ. Further, she would have a working familiarity with the major cognitive, adaptive, and social-emotional tests and protocols used in client assessment. In addition, she would understand the distinction between *clinical* evaluations and *forensic* evaluations. Most important, she would be in a position to make an informed choice about whether additional assessment or testing for the various family members is necessary to clarify points of confusion or contradiction.

Understanding the Psychologist's Education and Training

As an informed consumer, Ms. Jimenez would understand that the four psychologists conducting these evaluations had markedly different specialty areas, training, and education. She would know that clinical psychologists, school psychologists, and neuropsychologists differ in specialty training, and in specific skills in assessing child, adult, and family mental health functioning, cognitive and learning abilities, vocational abilities, drug and alcohol abuse, and potential for dangerousness. Understanding the general background and training of each psychologist would help her know more about who is conducting the evaluation, as well as the specific purposes for an evaluation.

Understanding Cultural Competencies

The caseworker would understand the cultural competencies that psychological evaluators need in working with her clients from diverse cultural backgrounds. Among these competencies are:

- evaluators' knowledge of cultural values, beliefs, practices, and communication styles affecting clients;
- evaluators' self-awareness and understanding of themselves as cultural beings; and
- the selection, administration, and interpretation of assessment procedures and tests that are nonbiased.

Specifically, Ms. Jimenez would be able to examine the various reports for an appraisal of evaluators' familiarity with the Jordan family's African American cultural background, and whether family members were evaluated accurately within the context of their own cultural background.

Understanding the Referral Question

Ms. Jimenez would know that when psychological evaluations are requested or ordered, clear referral questions should be stated. The four psychological evaluations in her case file differed and were done for vastly different purposes. Each evaluator had different referral questions to answer, which, in turn, led to the selection of *different methods of assessment*. Ms. Jimenez would know that the results and findings from those methods have varying degrees of reliability and validity, and she would understand the empirical evidence upon which the opinions, conclusions, and recommendations of the psychologists are based.

Understanding the Role of Client Preparation

The four evaluation reports differ in their account of how cooperative or mistrustful Billy and his mother were with the various examining psychologists. The caseworker would know that undergoing a psychological evaluation is stressful for many clients, who may be fearful of being judged or labeled as somehow dysfunctional. The caseworker would look to the evaluation report for clear descriptions about what steps the evaluator took to build rapport, whether the evaluator explained the purpose of the evaluation and how the assessment information would be used, and whether the evaluator felt successful in the efforts to reduce the client's anxiety and maximize performance.

Understanding Relevance of the Report to the Case Planning Decision

Ms. Jimenez would know that *all* of the evaluation reports contain relevant information for the case plan decision on what direction the permanency plan should go. For example:

1. Billy's low nonverbal reasoning score described in the school psychologist's report suggests that he may need considerable help in deciphering nonverbal social situations and interpersonal interactions. His above-average verbal reasoning abilities, however, indicate an important strength—the capacity to process verbal information about himself and the world. These findings, in turn, have significant implications for the type of therapeutic interventions that might be undertaken. For example, social skills training, behavior therapy, and cognitive-behavioral therapy seem to be appropriate methods to deal with Billy's misperceptions of the social environment, impulsiveness, and aggression. In addition, "talking therapy" may be helpful in teaching him ways to verbalize and resolve his feelings of anger and sadness. Based on this information, the caseworker could play a key role in facilitating close coordination between the special education program and the outpatient therapist treating Billy.

2. The school psychologist's report highlights the discrepancy between Billy's strong verbal reasoning skills and his below-grade academic performance in reading, spelling, and comprehension. The family conflicts and unresolved emotions that Billy has experienced over the years likely have interfered markedly with his learning—further exacerbating his learning disabilities. If individual and family therapy can resolve some of these issues, he may begin to achieve greater school success.

   The caseworker can use these data in working with Billy's teacher and school social worker to find ways to increase his motivation for learning and to strengthen his academic skills. The psychologist's report may provide the teacher with ideas about new instructional strategies that might aid the transfer of learning of course material. In addition, the caseworker may facilitate the foster parents' greater school involvement by initiating and monitoring a behavioral reward system at home to reinforce Billy's improved academic performance.

3. The clinical psychologist working for the court judged the mother to be a neglectful parent because of her difficulty in monitoring and supervising Billy's daily activities. The psychologist's report for vocational rehabilitation, however, indicates that Mrs. Jordan's organizational and tracking difficulties may be neurologically based, possibly the result of a closed head injury rather than an indicator of parental neglect or emotional detachment. Although the information in the two reports seems to be contradictory, further interviewing of the mother by the caseworker and other professionals involved in the case should clarify the nature of mother's parenting difficulties, which would help determine the appropriate treatment interventions. Whatever the etiology of her difficulties, both reports suggest the necessity of helping the mother provide more structure, monitoring, and support in her parenting.

4. The prison psychologist's evaluation of Mr. Jordan provides an optimistic view of the father's functioning: When he is not abusing drugs or alcohol and if he remains firmly committed to Islamic religious principles emphasizing responsibility to Allah for the care of self, family, and community, the father may be motivated to maintain nonviolent and nonabusive relationships with his wife and son. The caseworker would have a working knowledge regarding the effects of alcohol and legal and illegal drugs on the client's functioning, and would understand the importance of triangulating the findings from this prison psychologist's report with additional information obtained through direct observation over time and in different settings about the father's interactions with others, to assess his capacity for self-control or potential for violence. The report would help the caseworker generate several relevant case planning questions, such as:

- If the father reunites with the mother and remains in the home, would this be a safe environment for Billy?
- Can the father maintain his motivation for sobriety and nonviolence outside of a prison structure? Can the father be actively supported for his religious conversion and acceptance of responsibility, even if mother and son do not share the same religious faith or practices?

- What type of safety plan should be developed for the mother and son if the father returns home?
- Can a monitoring plan for the father's drug- and alcohol-related behavior be developed in conjunction with his probation officer and prospective employers?
- What would be the impact on Billy if the social service department were to seek to terminate parental rights, with the rationale that neither parent can protect him adequately from additional harm?

Failing to consider the implications of the above points derived from the four psychologists' reports is likely to lead the caseworker to develop an inaccurate view of the child and family, as well as an unsuccessful permanency placement plan. Ultimately, the risk to this family would be considerable, particularly if the county department of social services were to decide to petition the court for termination of parental rights, based on the mother's failure to comply with a treatment plan that ignored important information about family members.

Obtaining Consultation

Having developed new competencies as an informed consumer, Ms. Jimenez would have acquired more skill in engaging evaluating psychologists in follow-up case consultation and treatment planning. The psychologists in our scenario each evaluated different family members and addressed different family issues. Whereas clinical and school psychologists are likely to view as their primary client the person being evaluated (or parent or legal guardian, in the case of a child), the prison or forensic psychologists may view the court, correctional system, or the client's attorney as their primary client, rather than the individual being evaluated.

These latter psychologists proceed with very different understandings about clients' rights to confidentiality, and also with differing expectations regarding their role in case planning. Forensic evaluators may see their role as primarily rendering opinions to the court, with little responsibility for how the report's information is disseminated to plaintiffs and respondents, or used in subsequent case planning decisions. In contrast, other evaluators, such as those in schools or clinical settings, may seek a collaborative role with social workers or other practitioners, and be willing to clarify the report information or to provide input into formulating the social service plan. Ms. Jimenez would have developed competencies in how to negotiate with both systems and evaluators regarding obtaining appropriate case consultation.

Understanding What Constitutes an Informative Evaluation Report

Ms. Jimenez would be in a better position to judge adequacies and deficiencies in each evaluator's report as a result of understanding professional standards of good report writing. She would know that when a psychological report is done in isolation from other relevant sources of information, the evaluation may provide a less accurate picture of the client's functioning. Because most psychological evaluations occur in a time-limited, structured office setting, evaluators must incorporate information gained over longer periods of time and in other contexts, such as the naturalistic settings where clients live and work. The informed consumer would develop an appreciation for the importance of *multiple sources of information* in contributing to the psychologist's evaluation.

Additional Resources

Several national psychology organizations have available information for the general public on a variety of practice issues, such as frequently asked questions (FAQs) about psychological assessments. Websites for the American Psychological Association (APA) [www.apa.org] and the National Association of School Psychologists (NASP) [www.nasponline.org] provide general information about psychological assessments and tests. For example, the document *Finding Information about Psychological Tests* can be accessed through the APA website. Many state psychology organizations also have information on psychology practice.

Numerous online testing services can be found on the Internet, where clients can have a variety of psychological tests rapidly administered, scored, and interpreted over the computer for a fee. At first glance, this may seem like an attractive option, particularly in areas where few psychologists are available. A major caution about using or referring clients to online services, however, is the difficulty in finding out where these online testing services are located and whether any previous complaints have been made to the local state regulatory agency or state board of psychology examiners.

According to a statement released by the APA (1997), the ethics code for psychologists does not specifically address services such as Internet testing or telephone or teleconferencing therapy. Thus, no practice standards currently exist to evaluate the appropriateness of Internet-based psychological services. Nonetheless, these online psychological evaluators are bound by other provisions of the ethical code, such as those pertaining to professional and scientific relationships, boundaries of competence, the basis for scientific and professional judgments, avoiding harm, fees and financial arrangements, and standards governing advertising.

Conclusion

Psychological assessments can make an important contribution to case planning decisions, particularly when psychological data and evaluation data from referring professionals are used in conjunction with each other. For this to happen, professionals from other disciplines and evaluating psychologists must recognize the barriers to and boundaries of interdisciplinary collaboration. Referring professionals from other disciplines must develop specific competencies as informed consumers of psychological assessments. This will enable them to understand and incorporate appropriately psychological assessment information into their case planning.

Chapter 2

The Qualifications, Ethics, and Practice Standards of Evaluating Psychologists

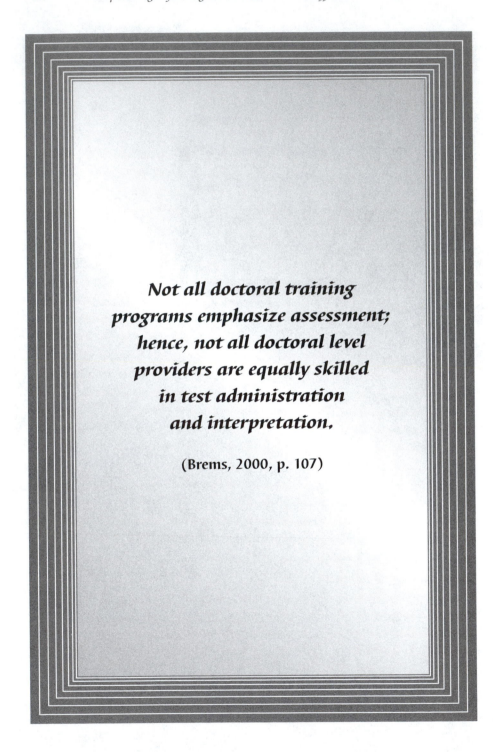

Not all doctoral training
programs emphasize assessment;
hence, not all doctoral level
providers are equally skilled
in test administration
and interpretation.

(Brems, 2000, p. 107)

As informed consumers, referring professionals must have a working knowledge of the qualifications of psychologist examiners, whether the referring professionals are able to choose the examiner or whether they are making referrals to a psychologist who is already employed or is under contract with an agency or program to perform evaluations. In this chapter we examine the distinctions and typical practice features among the various branches of psychology, the types of education and training of different psychologists, and the ethical principles and practice guidelines under which evaluating psychologists practice. An illustrative example provides a context to examine the problems that can arise when this information has not been clarified at the outset of the evaluation.

This chapter also explores the controversies among different professional groups as to who is qualified as an examiner to administer and interpret psychological instruments. Ethical standards and practice guidelines developed by national psychology organizations regarding psychological evaluations and testing are reviewed. Case planning considerations are discussed in terms of where to get further information about the qualifications of individual psychologists.

Qualifications of Evaluating Psychologists

In the comedy-fantasy movie *Ghostbusters* (Medjuck & Reitman, 1984), the celluloid citizens of New York were faced with a recurring question whenever they had to get rid of ghostly ectoplasm: "Who ya gonna call?" This question is similar to the one that real-life referring professionals typically have when they require psychological evaluations for case planning decisions. They have to know not just *who* to call, but also *what kind* of psychologist should be called. In addition, the professional consumer of psychological evaluations should have a working knowledge of the ethical codes and practice standards to which evaluators must adhere in their practice of psychology. Finally, beyond just knowing something about

psychologists' credentials, it is important to ascertain the cultural competencies and personality traits which contribute to a psychological evaluator's skillful assessments.

To illustrate the need for social workers and other referring professionals to become knowledgeable regarding the specific type of education and training of psychological evaluators, consider the following
case scenario involving a challenge to the credentials of an evaluating
psychologist:

Case Scenario 2.1

Marge Cassidy, RN, director of a community health clinic, secured a
contract with a local public school district to develop a new program in an
inner-city high school serving teenage mothers and their babies. Because of
the growing number of infants and young children who showed difficulty in
developing secure attachments to their mothers, she felt fortunate in hiring
Dr. Irene Quiros, a developmental psychologist, whose professional background included basic and applied research on normal attachment and
bonding. Dr. Quiros was employed to perform clinical evaluations of the
teen mothers and to design a parenting program that would improve the
bonding experiences between the teen parents and their children.

Indeed, Dr. Quiros was known for her careful and detailed observations
of parent–child interactions and the subsequent inferences she drew regarding the quality of attachment between teen parents and their children.
Nonetheless, her evaluations increasingly became a source of controversy
within the teen parenting program itself and with other helping professionals in the community. Professionals involved with the teen mothers and
their children in social services and mental health agencies began to disagree
with Dr. Quiros's inferences and conclusions.

Their criticisms centered on two complaints: (a) that Dr. Quiros's evaluations were based solely on the observations gathered in the teen-parenting program and failed to include the ecological data of parent–child interactions reported by these other observers; and (b) that Dr. Quiros's
evaluations were largely negative in nature and did not reflect the apparent
strengths and nurturing capabilities the teen mothers were observed to display at home and in various community settings.

Inevitably, this controversy emerged in court, when the parents of one
of the teen mothers sought custody of their granddaughter, and Dr. Quiros
was subpoenaed to testify. During the *voir dire* process (the legal procedure
for certifying the credentials of an expert witness called to give testimony in

(continued)

a deposition or trial), Dr. Quiros admitted that her training did not include a clinical internship or mental health practicum in child and family assessment. When asked why she currently was not licensed as a psychologist in the state, Dr. Quiros stated that because she worked for the community health clinic rather than the school district, she was not required to be licensed to perform her duties.

Because her professional education did not include specific training in clinical assessments of child and adult psychopathology, the court did not admit the findings of Dr. Quiros as evidence. Other challenges soon followed, and Dr. Quiros eventually left the teen-parenting program under a cloud of controversy. The health clinic had not considered her training and licensure status carefully in evaluating this psychologist's qualifications.

The case scenario suggests that referring professionals must have an informed understanding of the background, training, and professional credentials of the psychologists who are called upon to evaluate children and adults. Simply assuming that all psychologists have the appropriate training in this area can be problematic and may result in unusable evaluation results in certain contexts.

Because the profession of psychology is broad, no single psychologist can be an expert in all aspects of human behavior or mental processes. As a result, psychology has developed several specialty areas. Psychologists typically are united within a common base of general knowledge about psychological principles and methods and by their adherence to a professional code of ethics, but they typically become specialized in terms of education, training, career interests, and work activities. For example, the American Psychological Association (APA), the largest national organization of psychologists in the United States, has more than 50 divisions. Each division represents a different specialty field or field of practice, which suggests something about the rich complexity and scope of this profession.

Education, Training, and Professional Credentials

When selecting psychological evaluators for child, adolescent, and adult clients, the following four parameters should be considered:

1. specialty area of psychology in which evaluators have been trained;
2. typical practice features of that specialty area;

3. licensure requirements for unsupervised practice; and
4. relative emphasis given to training in child, adolescent, adult, or family mental health and functioning.

An additional parameter—the cultural competence of evaluators—is a major consideration in selecting psychologists and making referrals. This parameter is examined in Chapters 3 and 4 within the context of a larger set of issues regarding psychological assessments of multicultural clients.

Table 2.1 presents a description of the typical practice features, licensure status, and training emphasis of the specialty areas in psychology that are most relevant to the evaluation of children, adolescents, and adults. As the table indicates, the specialty areas vary considerably in the type of mental health training that psychologists receive in work with child, adolescent, and adult clients. Clinical psychologists, counseling psychologists, and school psychologists all have specialty training in mental health, but the training of clinical psychologists tends to be oriented heavily toward adult assessment and treatment. Clinical child psychologists and school psychologists typically have more training in the assessment and treatment of child and adolescent emotional and behavioral disorders and learning problems.

In addition, the conceptual framework (e.g., cognitive theory, behavior theory, psychoanalytic theory, humanistic theory, existential theory) and research interest (e.g., psychopathology, neuroscience, test construction) of psychologists often are important considerations in shaping their clinical expertise. Also, educational psychologists and developmental psychologists, who in some instances work directly with people, usually do not have clinical training in child, adolescent, or adult mental health disorders. As the case example illustrates, competence in one specialty area of psychology does not imply competence in another specialty area.

It should be apparent, then, that "psychologists" may do similar types of diagnostic or treatment work, work in the same settings, have identical job titles and academic degrees, yet come from very different types of educational and training backgrounds. When requesting psychological evaluations, referring professionals have to be sensitive to these different areas of specialization. As seen in the earlier case example, courts have the advantage of determining the competence of an expert to provide opinions through the *voir dire* process. But nurses, social workers, physicians, educators, and other professionals usually do not depose a psychological evaluator beforehand. Thus, some general knowledge of psychologists' educational training and background will help the professional consumer

TABLE 2.1   Specialty Areas of Psychology

SPECIALTY	TYPICAL PRACTICE FEATURES	DEGREE, TRAINING, AND LICENSURE*	EMPHASIS
Clinical Psychology	Diagnosis and treatment of emotional and behavioral disorders, and other mental health problems; also may conduct research on personality, particularly the study of abnormal behavior; may develop and evaluate new psychological tests.	*Degree:* Ph.D., Psy.D., or Ed.D. *Clinical training:* Full-time internship; 1 or 2 years post-degree supervised experience. *Licensure:* Yes.	Often primarily adult-focused; heavy emphasis on mental health.
Child Clinical Psychology	A subspecialty of clinical psychology; does all of the above but specializes in the problems of children and adolescents.	*Degree:* Ph.D., Psy.D., or Ed.D. *Clinical training:* Full-time internship; 1 or 2 years post-degree supervised experience. *Licensure:* Yes.	Primarily child- and adolescent-focused; heavy emphasis on mental health.
Neuro-psychology	A specialty of clinical psychology that focuses on brain–behavior relationships; emphasizes the role of neurological and other physiological systems in normal and aberrant behavior.	*Degree:* Ph.D., Psy.D., or Ed.D. *Clinical training:* Full-time internship; 1 or 2 years post-degree supervised experience; specific coursework and internship in neuropsychology. *Licensure:* Yes.	May be child-focused or adult-focused; emphasis on brain-behavior relationships.
Counseling Psychology	Therapeutic work with individuals and groups in schools, agencies, or hospital settings.	*Degree:* Ph.D., Psy.D., or Ed.D. *Clinical training:* Full-time internship; 1 or 2 years post-degree supervised experience. *Licensure:* Yes.	Often is adult- or family-focused; emphasis on psychotherapeutic interventions.

(continued)

TABLE 2.1   (continued)

SPECIALTY	TYPICAL PRACTICE FEATURES	DEGREE, TRAINING, AND LICENSURE*	EMPHASIS
School Psychology	Diagnosis and treatment of children's learning and behavior problems in schools; direct work with children, parents, and teachers to enhance achievement, child mental health, and social adjustment; psychological and educational assessment.	*Degree:* Ph.D., Psy.D., Ed.D., or Ed.S.** *Clinical training:* Full-time internship; 1 or 2 years post-degree supervised experience. *Licensure:* Yes.	Child- and adolescent-focused; emphasis on learning and mental health.
Educational Psychology	Study of educational processes, including learning, motivation, methods of instruction, curriculum development; and testing of abilities.	*Degree:* Ed.D. *Clinical training:* Usually training has no clinical component. *Licensure:* Usually not.	Basic or applied research; program evaluation.
Developmental Psychology	Study of growth and change over the life-span; some developmental psychologists specialize in infancy, child, adolescent, or adult development; some also specialize in a specific area, such as perception, social development, or cognitive development.	*Degree:* Ph.D. *Clinical training:* Usually training has no clinical component to training. *Licensure:* Usually not.	Basic or applied research; program evaluation.

Adapted from "Teaching Social Workers To Use Psychological Assessment Data," by J. Kayser & M. Lyon, in *Child Welfare, 79,* 197–222. Adapted with permission of the Child Welfare League of America.

* In most states a doctoral degree (Ph.D., Psy.D., or Ed.D.) in an appropriate specialty of psychology, completion of a full-time internship, completion of a specified period of postdoctoral supervision, and passing a written, standardized exam and/or oral exam is required to obtain licensure for unsupervised practice. Licensure requirements vary by state.

**In some states the private practice of school psychology is authorized for those who hold a specialty degree (Ed.S., CAGS) or its equivalent, and appropriate licensure from a state department of education.

appraise the quality of the evaluation and usefulness of information provided. Obviously, the background, education, training, and work experience of a psychologist contribute to both the objective and the subjective components of the psychological evaluation.

Personality Traits of Skilled Evaluators

In addition to their education, training, and professional credentials, a number of "ideal" personality traits go into making a skilled evaluator. These include (Katz, 1985; Kaufman & Lichtenberger, 2002; Zuckerman, 1995):

- the capacity for detective work in sleuthing out diagnostic clues and organizing data from diverse sources into a coherent framework of meaning;
- the capacity to establish rapport with the person relatively quickly, as most assessments are done on a time-limited basis;
- the capacity to motivate clients to provide a performance that is representative of their typical capacities in non-testing environments;
- the capacity for cognitive flexibility, to be able to look at data from an variety of points of view and to develop alternative hypotheses about the data;
- a sense of creativity in oral communications and written reports that synthesize information from diverse sources into a picture of the whole person;
- interpersonal sensitivity in understanding the impact of results of a psychological evaluation on a person; and
- the ability to produce quality written reports in a timely manner.

Referring professionals might have their own list of additional "preferred" personality traits or qualities in the evaluating psychologist with whom they work. Although these preferences have nothing specifically to do with the professional competence needed to conduct psychological assessments, referring professionals, when possible, should look for well-rounded, well-grounded psychologists with whom they can develop a collegial relationship, while respecting psychologists' need for objectivity in doing their job. The point here is that the rapport and respect between referring professionals and evaluating psychologists can be important in how referrals are made and whether evaluation findings and recommendations ultimately are incorporated and implemented in the case planning process.

Forensic Versus Clinical Psychological Assessments

Referring professionals must understand the distinctions between *forensic* and *clinical* psychological assessments. Melton, Petrila, Poythress, and Slolbogin (1997) observed that in clinical evaluations

- individuals usually are seen on a voluntary basis;
- diagnostic questions about their functioning and the development of treatment plans usually are a central focus;
- clients may have more input into the selection of assessment procedures and objectives;
- psychologists strive to understand clients' perspectives or unique points of view about their problems;
- psychologists employ empathy, trust, and caring to build a therapeutic relationship with clients; and
- evaluations can proceed at a more leisurely pace.

By contrast, in forensic evaluations

- diagnostic and treatment issues often remain in the background because the assessment focuses more narrowly on the legal issues before the court;
- clients usually are involuntary;
- the objectives of the evaluation are determined by the statutes or case law relevant to the legal dispute;
- understanding clients' viewpoint is secondary to arriving at an accurate, objective appraisal of clients' functioning, because there is a far greater possibility that clients will deliberately falsify or distort key information obtained in forensic assessments;
- typically, there is greater emotional distance between forensic evaluators and clients because of the adversarial nature of the legal proceedings; and
- the pace of evaluations is dictated by the court as to when evaluations must be completed and psychologists' opinions and recommendations must be finalized.

Psychologists who perform forensic mental health evaluations in criminal, civil, or juvenile justice systems need advanced clinical competencies beyond their basic psychology education and training. Forensic psychologists must be familiar with the legal system in which they work; forensic assessment instruments and techniques; legal doctrines regarding the admissibility of mental health evaluations; research on a variety of psychological conditions and phenomena not typically covered in basic psychological training; and the demands of being an expert witness. Similar to the above point, competence in one area of forensic work does not imply competence in another area (Dyer, 1999; Melton et al., 1997).

Licensure

Regulation of the practice of psychology varies greatly from state to state. Some states issue a single *generic license* covering all specialty areas, whereas other states issue *specialty licenses* for distinct areas of psychology practice. Most states license psychologists only at the doctoral level (i.e., Ph.D., Psy.D., Ed.D.) In some states that issue generic licenses, developmental psychologists and educational psychologists can obtain licensure if they complete additional appropriate clinical training. Masters-level graduates in professional counseling are licensed in many states as Licensed Professional Counselors (LPCs) or as Marriage and Family Therapists (MFTs).

The training of doctoral-level psychologists and masters-level professional counselors differs considerably in practice and scope. Historically, professional counseling emerged from the fields of psychology and education, but now it is considered to be a separate profession, with its own body of knowledge, ethical principles, and licensing regulations (Seligman, 2004).

State regulation may be through a state board of psychologist examiners or, in the case of school psychologists, through a state department of education, or through both. Licensure requirements set forth the *minimum standards* for competent psychologists. As will be discussed later in the chapter, professional associations of psychologists have developed ethical codes of conduct and practice guidelines that set forth principles and standards to ensure the highest quality of professional services.

Controversies about Evaluator Qualifications

Are psychologists the only professionals qualified to conduct psychological testing? Overlapping of roles and competencies among different disciplines or competing groups may result in blurring of professional boundaries. This makes it difficult for referring professionals to sort out what type of evaluation and/or whose expertise is required or is most appropriate. A number of areas of confusion are discussed next.

"Psychological" or "Psychiatric"

One area of confusion results from failing to distinguish between a *psychological* and a *psychiatric* evaluation. Psychiatrists are physicians who diagnose and treat mental disorders using a variety of methods. An evaluation conducted by a child and adolescent psychiatrist might include

- clinical interviews with parents, child or adolescent, and family;
- developmental, health, school, and medication histories;
- psychosocial and mental health history of each parent, including a marital history; and
- mental status exam of the referred child or adolescent.

Interventions may include psychotherapy and prescribing psychotropic medications. Typically, however, psychiatrists are not trained to administer and interpret psychological tests, such as intelligence tests, projective tests, or objective measures of personality functioning. Those evaluation tools are the province of psychologists, who may do all of the above evaluation procedures as well as additional psychological tests designed to address specific referral questions.

Although there has been a push within psychology to obtain medication privileges, generally psychologists do not have legal authority to prescribe medications for clients. At the time of writing this chapter, New Mexico and Louisiana were the only states allowing prescription privileges for psychologists (Bradshaw, 2004 January/February; 2005, May/June). Psychiatrists and psychologists, however, both may have expertise in understanding neurological/biological factors affecting behavior and/or learning.

Most of the time, psychiatrists and psychologists work in a complementary manner. Knowing the scope of practice of the two disciplines, however, can avoid some confusion or "turf wars." For example, managed-care companies frequently employ psychiatrists as gatekeepers guarding access to client services, because they determine the "medical necessity" of treatment. In an effort to hold down utilization and costs, psychiatrists in some managed-care companies have taken the position that psychological evaluations do not add any information beyond what can be obtained during the course of clinical interviews. Referring professionals should regard such statements cautiously. If the psychiatrist has *no specific education or training in psychological tests and evaluation procedures*, these pronouncements cannot be considered as a qualified expert opinion because the statement is formed outside the typical competence of psychiatrists.

Psychologist Versus Other Types of Professional Evaluators

A variety of other professional groups claim to have the required education, training, and experience to administer certain educational and psychological tests, even though their graduate degree may be in a field other than psychology. For example, professional associations representing a broad array of groups such as vocational and mental health counselors, art and music therapists, and a variety of masters-level clinicians assert that, by virtue of their education, training, experience, and license, they should be allowed to purchase, select, administer, score, and interpret test instruments to evaluate current functioning, diagnose, and make interventions or referrals. Many of these groups have banded together to form the National Fair Access Coalition on Testing to fight what they believe are unnecessary restrictions imposed by state psychology licensing boards regarding who is qualified to conduct psychological assessments (www.fairaccess.org)

These claims are strongly disputed by national psychological organizations, such as the APA and the National Association of School Psychologists (NASP), which hold that only psychologists are qualified to do psychological testing. Interested readers are referred to these organizations' policies on test-user qualifications and for further discussion and debate on these issues.

My strong recommendation is that, at all costs, referring professionals should avoid using evaluation findings and test results from persons who are not qualified or licensed to practice psychology. This recommendation in no way discounts the fact that other disciplines do contribute important knowledge about clients and their situations, based on their own methodologies and areas of expertise. The discussion under Case Planning Considerations, later in the chapter, provides guidance and direction on where to obtain information about who is qualified to administer psychological tests and where to seek a psychological evaluator.

Ethical Standards and Practice Guidelines

Referring professionals also should be familiar with the *governance structure* in psychology, which consists of mandatory ethical principles and codes of conduct, as well as voluntary practice guidelines. The role of each is described below.

Ethics

Ethical standards and codes of conduct have been developed and periodically revised by national organizations of psychologists such as the American Psychological Association (APA) and the National Association of School Psychologists (NASP). APA's first ethical standards were developed in 1953, and its most recent revision became effective in 2003 (APA, 2002a). These standards are mandatory, enforceable rules for the professional conduct of psychology covering a wide variety of professional and scientific behaviors of psychologists, such as establishing and maintaining professional competence; human relations; interruption of psychological services; advertising and other public statements; record keeping and fees; education and training; research and training; assessment; and therapy.

The ethical code also sets forth procedures for handling ethical complaints. In cases of emerging practice where no specific ethical standard has yet been established, psychologists are guided by the principle of "do no harm" and the requirement to take reasonable steps to ensure the competence of their work.

Because one purpose of ethical codes is to gain the public's trust, adhering to the ethical principles and code of conduct usually requires *a higher standard of behavior* for psychologists than existing laws or policies. Although these ethical standards are binding specifically on members of the promulgating organizations, they also may be adopted by organizations or agencies that employ psychologists. The standards do not govern the private, non-work related behavior of psychologists. Also, ethical violations do not necessarily overlap with violations of state laws regulating the practice of psychology.

The ethical standards that are most relevant to the assessment and treatment planning process are summarized briefly below (APA, 2002a).

1. *Basis for making an assessment.* All of the statements in a psychological report such as opinions, recommendations, and diagnoses, are based on information and techniques sufficient to substantiate their

findings. The evaluation is founded on established scientific and professional knowledge in psychology. Psychologists conduct evaluations only within the boundaries of their competence, in conformance with their education, training, supervision, consultation, study, and/or professional experience. Psychologists' evaluation of clients is based upon on an examination that is adequate to support their statements or conclusions. When an examination is predicated on limited assessment information, psychologists clarify the impact the limitation may have on the reliability and validity of their opinions. Psychologists state the source of the information underlying their recommendations and conclusions.

2. *Use of assessments*. Assessment techniques such as tests, interviews, or other instruments must be up-to-date and properly administered, scored, and interpreted in an appropriate manner, consistent with their intended purpose. Clients are assessed using instruments that have established reliability and validity for the population(s) of which clients are members. When psychologists use instruments whose reliability and validity have not been established for the population(s) of which the client is a member, the strengths and limitations of the assessment findings must be described clearly. Clients are assessed according to their language preference and competence, unless their fluency in another language is part of the reason they are being evaluated.

3. *Obtaining informed consent*. Informed consent is obtained from clients when they participate in an assessment. Clients should be informed, both orally and in writing, about the nature and purpose of the assessment, cost of the evaluation, involvement of outside parties, and any limits to confidentiality. Clients should have an opportunity to ask questions about the evaluation. Exceptions to confidentiality (e.g., when clients are mandated for services, cases of suspected abuse, or imminent danger to self or other) are clearly explained in the informed consent form. When clients' capacity to give informed consent for testing is unknown or uncertain, as well as in situations in which clients are mandated for testing, psychologists should provide an explanation about the purposes and use of the evaluation, using language that is understandable to the individuals being evaluated. In addition, when linguistically different clients require the use of an interpreter, clients must give informed written consent. Psychologists are responsible for ensuring that test results remain confidential, and for keeping test results and reports secured.

4. *Releasing test data.* Test score data (raw and scaled scores), interview responses, and psychologists' notes or recordings pertaining to the evaluation are not released to others unless they receive clients' permission, or receive a court order, or are otherwise required by law. Psychologists may decide not to release the information in situations where release of test data would substantially harm a client, be misused, or be misrepresented. Federal law, such as the *Health Information Portability and Accountability Act* of 1996 (HIPAA), as well as state laws or regulations regarding privileged communication between psychologists and clients, establish the limits of confidentiality and govern the release of test data.

5. *Interpreting results.* Interpretation of test results is based on the purpose of the assessment and various test factors, such as the testing situation and the characteristics of the individuals being evaluated (including their cultural and linguistic differences). Psychologists describe any significant limitations of interpretations, judgments, or accuracy of their findings.

6. *Test scoring and interpretation services.* Psychologists are responsible for appropriate interpretation of results, whether they score tests themselves or use automated services. Use of test scoring and interpretation services considers the evidence of validity of their procedures. The scoring and interpretation services should provide accurate information about their purpose, norms, reliability, validity, applications, and special qualifications for their use.

7. *Explaining assessment results.* Reasonable steps are taken to ensure that assessment results are explained to the persons being evaluated or designated representatives. When the nature of the relationship or purpose of the assessment precludes this (such as in a forensic evaluation), it is explained ahead of time to the persons being assessed.

8. *Test security.* Reasonable steps are taken to ensure that the integrity and security of test materials and techniques are maintained.

Although similar in scope to the APA standards, the NASP ethical standards were developed specifically to govern the professional conduct of school psychologists (NASP, 1997a). Among the NASP ethical standards that are relevant to psychological assessments in schools is the requirement to secure parental participation and support in the evaluation process, such as providing an explanation on why a psychological evaluation was requested, who will receive the information, and possible outcomes. In addition, school psychologists are required to explain any provision of services by psychological interns or practicum students and obtain parental agreement.

Practice Guidelines

APA, NASP, and other groups also have developed nonbinding practice guidelines to govern the conduct of psychologists in performing their professional roles and duties (APA, 1992, 1994, 1998a, 2002b, 2002c; American Psychology-Law Society, 1991; NASP, 1993, 1997b, 1999a, 1999b). These guidelines are position statements regarding *best practices*, or descriptions of what constitutes the hallmarks of quality, or recommendations regarding the specific professional behavior that psychologists should follow in specific areas of practice. Guidelines differ from ethical standards in that ethical standards are both mandatory and enforceable, whereas practice guidelines are largely advisory and voluntary. Their goal is to promote development of the profession and ensure a high level of competence in specific practice arenas.

A variety of practice guidelines have relevance to referring professionals, depending on the organizational auspices and client population with whom they work. Although it is beyond the scope of this chapter to review all the practice guidelines that might be relevant to professional consumers, those pertaining to psychological evaluations in child maltreatment cases and in disputes in divorce proceedings regarding parenting time and decision making warrant additional elaboration (APA, 1994, 1998).

As noted by Dyer (1999), one major difference between these practice guidelines is that in custody evaluations, psychologists are asked to determine which of the divorcing marital partners is better able to make appropriate childrearing decisions, whereas in child-protection evaluations, psychologists often are asked to determine whether parents have so harmed their children that it is in the children's best interests to have the relationship with their parents terminated.

In either case, the practice guidelines emphasize that, in conducting these complex evaluations, psychologists require specialized competence over and above their general clinical training in evaluating children, adults, and families. Education, training, experience, and supervision are essential in areas such as

- child and family development;
- child and family psychopathology;
- impact of abuse, neglect, and/or divorce on children's adjustment and subsequent development;
- current functional abilities of parents and their fitness to parent;
- impact of separation on the child;
- nature of various types of child abuse and neglect;
- role of human differences; and
- the nature of forensic practice.

In addition to the above areas, psychologists increasingly are asked to evaluate the impact of psychological and physical trauma on learning and academic achievement. The psychologist's role in these evaluations is to maintain an unbiased, objective stance. This means that psychologists must avoid dual relationships, such as being both evaluator and therapist.

The NASP practice guidelines (1997b) for psychological evaluations in schools emphasize the role of evaluations in providing information on ways to maximize student achievement, potential, educational success, psychological adjustment, and behavioral adaptation. School psychologists often are called upon to perform evaluations of students to determine whether they have an educational handicap as defined under the Individuals with Disabilities Education Act (IDEA) and qualify for special education services. This type of assessment is educational and/or clinical rather than forensic in nature. The NASP guidelines emphasize the autonomy of school psychologists in deciding on the type, nature, and extent of the assessment techniques used in evaluations, as well as determining the content and nature of their reports.

Case Planning Considerations

To refer back to our question at the beginning of the chapter—"Who ya gonna call?"—a variety of resources may be consulted when selecting a psychologist to conduct an evaluation or, if not in a position to select a psychologist, to learn more about the professionals with whom you are dealing. Had the director of the community health clinic in Case Scenario

2.1 been an informed consumer of psychological evaluations, one or more of the following steps would have been taken.

1. Ask evaluators directly for information about their specialty area, education, and training. Agencies that employ or contract with psychologists for evaluations should have on file psychologists' curriculum vitae or resume containing information about their professional education, training, credentials, work history, areas of specialization or expertise, and licensure status. In addition, professional consumers may refer to the psychologists' *mandatory disclosure form* that many states require to be given to clients at the outset of treatment. This form provides concise information about psychologists' degrees and training. Although this procedure is part of the informed consent process for clients, the general principle can be adapted for use when psychologists collaborate with helping professionals from other disciplines.

2. Whenever possible, seek evaluations only from licensed psychologists. If an unlicensed psychologist is used, it is important to learn if he or she is supervised, as well as the name, credentials, educational background, and clinical training of the licensed psychologist providing the supervision.

3. Contact individual state boards of psychology examiners for information on whether a psychologist is currently licensed and whether the psychologist ever received a disciplinary action. Most state regulatory agencies disclose information to the public regarding disciplinary sanctions against psychologists licensed in that state, such as the nature of the grievance and disciplinary actions taken. These boards investigate complaints, and, when appropriate, discipline psychologists who have been found to be in violation of the provisions of the state's psychology practices act. The licensure status of the psychologist becomes relevant to the professional consumer because of the seriousness of case planning decisions and the potential impact of psychological evaluations on the life trajectories of child, adolescent, or adult clients being evaluated.

   For example, educational testing for intelligence and academic achievement typically has a significant bearing on a child's or adolescent's educational placement and the kinds of special education services or gifted placements that are subsequently provided. Likewise, a clinical or forensic evaluation bearing on fitness to parent, family reunification, termination of parental rights, or determination of mental competency requires the expertise of a licensed psychologist.

4. Contact the ethics committees of the state organization of psychologists to ascertain if ethical complaints have ever been made against a psychologist who may be a member of that organization.

5. Contact referral services for psychologists that are operated by several organizations. At the national level, APA has a toll-free number (1-800-964-2000) to make referrals to psychologists who are members of that organization. Individual state organizations of psychologists also may have referral services for member psychologists. The APA website has links to individual state organizations. The Association of Black Psychologists (ABPsi) has a state-by-state listing of its members and their areas of expertise, which may be consulted when making referrals. Website: www.abpsi.org. Address: Association of Black Psychologists, P.O. Box 55999, Washington DC, 20040-5999. Phone: 202-722-0808.

6. Consult the *National Register of Health Service Providers in Psychology*—a national database of psychologists—to obtain further information about psychologists' qualifications. The *National Register* provides summary information for more than 14,000 psychologists in the United States, including their degree, training, licensure or registration status, theoretical orientation, current practice setting, target populations served, and areas of expertise. The *National Register* is updated annually and is available in both print form (National Register of Health Service Providers in Psychology, 1120 G Street, NW, Suite 330, Washington, DC 20005) and online (www.nationalregister.com). The standards for inclusion in the *National Register* may be higher than the individual state licensing requirements.

7. Ask clients to contact their insurance carrier or managed-care company for a list of psychologists on the insurance panel. Keep in mind that these providers may be asked to operate under severe limitations imposed by the managed-care companies that could significantly limit the kinds, quantity, and quality of psychological services offered.

8. Contact the local community mental health centers that may have clinical psychologists on staff to conduct a variety of psychological services, including psychological assessments.

9. Contact local university or college departments or graduate schools of psychology that may run their own assessment and treatment clinics as part of their training program for clinical, counseling, or school psychology students. Typically, students work under the supervision of an experienced psychology faculty member. Some clinics have the

ability to negotiate with low-income or uninsured clients on a sliding fee-for-service basis. This resource may be suitable for uncomplicated cases that call for clinical or educational evaluations and treatment but usually are not appropriate for complex clinical or forensic cases.

Additional Resources

The summary information in this chapter on ethical standards, codes of conduct, and practice guidelines are not intended to substitute for the complete texts of documents produced by national psychology organizations such as APA and NASP. The APA ethical standards, code of conduct, and various practice guidelines can be obtained from the American Psychological Association, 750 First Street, NE, Washington, DC 20002-4242. They also are available on-line from the APA website: www.apa.org. The search function on the APA home page can be used to locate the practice guidelines on child custody and divorce, child protection, working with multicultural and gay, lesbian, and bisexual clients, and the rights and responsibilities of test takers.

The NASP ethical standards, codes of conduct, practice guidelines, and position papers can be obtained from the National Association of School Psychologists, 4340 East West Highway, Suite 402, Bethesda, MD 20814. They also are available online from the NASP website: www.nasponline.org.

The APA practice guidelines regarding providing psychological services to culturally and linguistically diverse client populations as well as gay, lesbian, and bisexual clients are examined in greater detail in chapter 4. The APA guidelines regarding the rights and responsibilities of test takers in clinical, school, or industry settings are examined in Chapter 8.

Conclusion

Effectively incorporating psychological assessment information into case planning decisions starts with selecting the appropriate evaluator. This chapter provides information about the scope of psychology—its specialty areas, practitioner education and training, personal characteristics, legal regulations, ethical standards and practice principles—that are most relevant in the clinical or forensic assessment of children and adults. This information can serve as a helpful guide to professionals from other disciplines in considering where to seek appropriately trained and credentialed evaluating psychologists.

One final thought: A psychological evaluation is only as good as the quality of the evaluating psychologist (Brems, 2000).

Chapter 3

Psychological Assessments and Tests: An Introduction

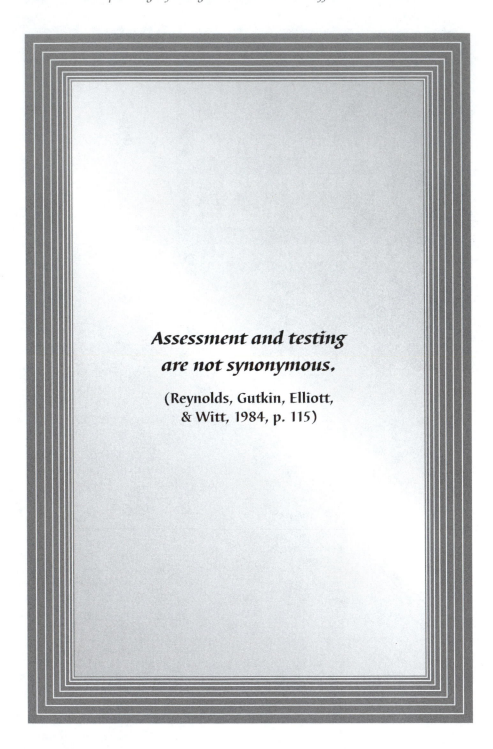

***Assessment and testing
are not synonymous.***

**(Reynolds, Gutkin, Elliott,
& Witt, 1984, p. 115)**

Informed consumers must have a working knowledge of the major

OVERVIEW

principles, concepts, and methods used in psychological assessments and tests. Because the central focus of this book is on referring professionals' needs in the case planning process, the examination of test design and theory in this chapter is kept purposefully at a descriptive and nonmathematical level. My aim is to convey something of the key conceptual issues, strategies, contributions, and controversies in which psychologists have been engaged over the years regarding the development and use of psychological tests as a major component of psychological assessments.

In addition, the chapter covers the construction, selection, administration, scoring, and interpretation of psychological tests and examines the steps psychologists actually use when evaluating test-takers. This chapter introduces the topic of psychological testing of those from culturally diverse backgrounds, and this is examined more extensively in chapter 4.

Differentiating Assessments and Testing

Psychological testing is one subset of a *larger, more comprehensive process* of psychological assessment. As noted in the case scenario, the difference between these two concepts initially can be confusing to referring professionals.

In the case scenario, part of the teacher's difficulty stems from confusion over the distinction between *assessment* and *tests*, as well as confusion about the meaning of the different types of tests.

Assessment

Psychological assessment is a process of "deriving meaning from data, achieving a broad but detailed description and understanding of individuals, behaviors, environments, and reciprocal interactions among these elements" (Reynolds et al., 1984, p. 115). A psychological or educational

---

Case Scenario 3.1

Shawn Banks is an English as a second language (ESL) teacher who works frequently with the children and adolescents of refugee families. Many of his students have incurred multiple traumas and losses in their country-of-origin, and have had significant adjustment difficulties in relocating to a new country. Over the years Mr. Banks has made several helpful referrals for psychological evaluations, when students' difficulties are the result of factors such as language and communication difficulties in learning spoken and/or written English; academic delays or deficits, such as might occur when school attendance in the home country was disrupted because of war or armed conflict; past psychological traumas; neurological processing problems caused by injury or disability; cultural clashes between students' culture-of-origin and those of the dominant American society; and the stresses and strains of normal adolescent development.

One barrier that Mr. Banks has encountered in trying to utilize information from psychological evaluations in his work with students is the confusing ways in which psychologists describe their assessment and testing procedures. As a teacher, Mr. Banks is familiar with *cognitive assessments*, knowing that psychologists typically employ a variety of tests to assess students' intelligence, achievement, or aptitude. He is less knowledgeable of (and less comfortable with) information contained in *personality assessments*, which involve evaluating nonacademic aspects of students' functioning including extent of psychopathology, unconscious motivations, cognitive distortions, self-esteem, and so forth.

Part of the confusion arises in that some of the personality evaluations use the standardized, paper/pencil test format with which he is familiar from the cognitive assessments, whereas other personality assessments use "projective tests," which on the surface do not really seem like tests at all. Although intuitively knowing that each of these types of assessments and tests provides something different about students' abilities and functioning, Mr. Banks is not entirely certain how to weigh their relative merit and determine relevance to the educational interventions he must plan with his students.

---

assessment encompasses "any systematic method of obtaining information from test and other sources, used to draw inferences about the characteristics of persons, objects, and programs" (American Educational Research Association, American Psychological Association, & National Council on Measurement in Education, 1999, p. 172).

Assessments are used to generate and test hypotheses about various aspects of individuals' functioning or concerns, as well as to develop intervention strategies. Assessments also may be conducted to monitor their progress, evaluate programs, and conduct a program of research (Hersen, 2004; Hood & Johnson, 2002).

Typically, psychological assessments synthesize *multiple sources* of relevant information about the person, employ *multiple methods of data collection*, and evaluate *multiple domains* of client functioning. Depending on the purpose of the assessment, these sources and methods might consist of (Brems, 2000; Hood & Johnson, 2002; Merrell, 1994):

- obtaining or reviewing developmental, educational, occupational/ vocational, marital, family, symptom and treatment histories, or other relevant biographical information;
- gathering observational data in a controlled and/or naturalistic setting;
- obtaining data from clinical interviews, physiological tests, rating scales, and individuals' self-report measures, and integrating the results from one or more psychological and educational tests, which might include standardized objective tests, projective techniques, and other types of assessment instruments or clinical protocol.

The multiple domains of individuals' functioning that might be the focus of psychological assessments include

- intellectual functioning; learning styles and information-processing abilities; academic achievement;
- vocational interests and aptitudes;
- extent of integration that individuals have achieved between an indigenous culture-of-origin and a dominant culture within society-at-large; and
- personality characteristics and presence of psychopathology (i.e., paranoia or other psychosis, depression, anxiety, personality disturbance, potential for harm to self or others, and dimensions of self-esteem).

The comprehensive nature of these multiple data sources helps evaluators develop a broad view of the individual and his or her presenting concerns and can also serve to corroborate the results of one assessment method by comparing it to the findings of a different assessment method (Hood & Johnson, 2002). Assessments help answer questions such as how *chronic*, how *severe*, and how *extensive* the individual's problems and concerns are, as well as identify the person's *strengths and resources* within their environments (Kayser & Lyon, 2000; Merrill, 1994).

Conducting assessments is only one of many professional services that psychologists provide during a typical workweek. Psychologists in mental health settings and state mental health hospitals typically devote about 15% to 18% of their time to assessment activities. School psychologists, neuropsychologists, and psychologists conducting forensic assessments generally expend more time in conducting assessments (Hogan, 2003; Kaufman & Lichtenberger, 2002).

Tests

Psychological tests are "standardized, repeatable procedures used to elicit and measure samples of human behavior" (Megargee, 2000, p. 47). According to Gregory (cited in Brems, 2000), integral to all psychological tests are the standardized procedures for sampling behaviors and assigning behaviors to categories or numbers, which subsequently can be used to compare, contrast, and predict a person's performance. Characteristics of psychological tests include uniformity, quantification, and objectivity (Wodrich, 1997).

Hogan (2003) has described four key assumptions underlying psychological testing:

1. People have distinct but overlapping characteristics or personality attributes—referred to as *traits*—that can be observed.
2. The differences between these traits can be quantified (i.e., traits are operationalized as variables to be measured).
3. The traits are relatively enduring and stable across time, place, and space.
4. The results of measures of these psychological traits can be generalized to shed light on a person's actual behavior in real-life situations.

Some traits frequently measured by psychological testing are cognitive abilities, academic achievement, psychological disturbances and pathology, and vocational interests.

According to Brems (2000), psychological testing typically focuses on five primary areas:

1. classification (i.e., determining eligibility for services; screening, placement);
2. diagnosis and treatment;
3. self-knowledge;
4. program evaluation; and
5. research.

Literally thousands of psychological tests have been developed over the years, only a fraction of which have been published, and used much less widely. Psychologists cannot learn, much less master, all of the tests. More commonly they become experts with a small number of tests that they use frequently, and then expand or supplement those tests with other tests and/or additional clinical tools, protocols, or assessment procedures, as necessary, depending on the purpose of the evaluation and the specific referral question they are seeking to answer (Katz, 1985).

Classification of Psychological Tests

The various ways in which psychological tests are labeled can be confusing, and perhaps even intimidating, to referring consumers. Because authors in the area of psychology categorize tests differently, a brief explanation of selected terms is given in Table 3.1.

Measures of Abilities, Achievement, and Aptitude

Abilities tests, achievement tests, and aptitude tests appraise individuals' cognitive performance. They are best thought of as existing on a continuum that "represents the extent to which *specific training* influences test performance" (Hogan, 2003, p. 446, italics in original). In the past, abilities and achievement tests sometimes were differentiated in that abilities tests were thought to assess learning potential or ability uncontaminated by experience, whereas achievement tests were thought to assess the extent of past learning based on the products of previous experience. This differentiation largely has given way, in part because of the recognition that there is no way to assess abilities independent of experience (Kaufman & Lichtenberger, 2002; Wodrich, 1997). In actuality, the constructs and content of abilities and achievement tests often are quite similar, and abilities tests and achievement tests both might best be subsumed under the term "measures of accomplishment" (Megargee, 2000).

Mental Abilities Tests

The best known of all the abilities tests are the *mental abilities tests* (otherwise known as *intelligence tests*), such as the *Stanford-Binet Intelligence Scale* and the *Wechsler Intelligence Scales*. The Stanford-Binet is an American adaptation of an intelligence scale originally developed in

TABLE 3.1   Categories, Description, and Examples of Psychological and Educational Tests

CATEGORY	DESCRIPTION	EXAMPLES
Abilities Test	Abilities tests are designed to assess the capacity to learn material and profit from instruction. (Mental abilities tests are the most widely used of these).	Stanford-Binet Intelligence Scale Wechsler Intelligence Scales
Achievement Test	Achievement tests are used to assess how well individuals have mastered the subject matter in a course of instruction.	Wechsler Individual Achievement Test (2nd edition) Woodcock-Johnson Tests of Achievement (3rd edition)
Aptitude Test	Aptitude tests measure the ability to acquire a specific type of skill or knowledge.	SAT, ACT (college entrance exams)
Objective Personality Test	Objective personality tests are paper/ pencil tests scored according to criteria independent of the judgment of the examining psychologist.	Minnesota Multiphasic Personality Inventory II Beck Depression Inventory
Subjective (also called Projective) Personality Test	Subjective tests assess clients' perceptions using the presentation of ambiguous stimuli. Traditionally, interpretation of client responses has relied heavily on examining psychologists' clinical judgment and theoretical orientation in making inferences. More recently, some widely used projective tests have developed objective scoring criteria and norms to aid in interpreting client responses.	Rorschach Inkblot Test Thematic Appreception Test
Neuropsycho-logical Test	Neuropsychological assessments focus on functioning of the central nervous system and brain in relation to indi-viduals' learning capacities and style of information processing.	Halstead-Reitan Neuropsychological Test Battery Luria-Nebraska Neuropsychological Battery

(continued)

TABLE 3.1   (continued)

CATEGORY	DESCRIPTION	EXAMPLES
Paper/Pencil Test	Paper/pencil tests present clients with written items as multiple-choice, true/false, or other type of structured question-and-answer response.	Group tests of cognitive abilities and achievement Objective global personality inventories, specific-trait objective measures of anxiety, depression, etc.
Performance Test	Performance tests ask clients to do something or to produce something.	Nonverbal reasoning subtests on an intelligence test (identifying missing pieces of a picture; copying designs while being timed; arranging a series of pictures in a logical order; and using blocks, objects, symbols, and mazes) Gordon Diagnostic System (a measure of attention and distractibility)
Norm-Referenced Test	Norm-referenced tests are standardized tests that compare individuals' performance on a test to a representative comparison group of similar individuals, whose group scores are used as a means of interpreting the performance of individuals who subsequently are being tested.	Objective measures of intelligence, achievement, and aptitude Objective measures of personality
Criterion-Referenced Test	Criterion-referenced tests are standardized tests that compare individuals' performance on a test to a defined content area, body of knowledge, or set of behaviors that individuals are expected to have mastered.	Teacher-made tests (e.g., spelling tests, math quiz) State educational proficiency tests

Adapted from *Dealing with Challenges in Psychotherapy and Counseling*, by C. Brems, 2000, Belmont, CA: Books/Cole: Thomson Learning, *Psychological Testing: A Practical Introduction*, by T. Hogan, 2003, New York: John Wiley & Sons; and *Children's Psychological Testing: A Guide for Nonpsychologists* (3rd ed.), by D. Wodrich & S. Kush, 1997, Baltimore, MD: Paul H. Brookes.

France by Alfred Binet in 1905. Currently it is in its fourth edition. During the first part of the 20th century, it was *the* primary measure of intelligence, designed to assess mental abilities in individuals from age 2 to adulthood.

The Wechsler Intelligence Scales (the first of which appeared in 1939) have eclipsed the Stanford-Binet in use and popularity, and subsequently have come to dominate the field of intelligence testing. The Wechsler scales also have undergone periodic major revisions, and now separate versions are available for children ages 2½ to 7 (*Wechsler Preschool and Primary Intelligence Scale, Third Edition*—WPPSI-III); elementary and high school children, ages 6 to 16 (*Wechsler Intelligence Scale for Children, Fourth Edition*—WISC IV); and adults, ages 16 to 89 (*Wechsler Intelligence Scale for Adults, Third Edition*—WAIS III) (Hogan, 2003; Kaufman & Lichtenberger, 2002; Ryan & Smith, 2003).

Intelligence tests measure broad reasoning skills, or general intelligence, that are applicable to solving a wide variety of problems and are not dependent upon a specific course of instruction. Because of their importance to psychological theory and test construction and their relevance in assessing clients and making and case planning decisions, intelligence tests are discussed in more detail later in this chapter (in the discussion of psychological theory, constructs, and evidence underlying testing).

Aptitude Tests

In contrast to measures of general intelligence, *aptitude tests* measure specific cognitive abilities—verbal abilities, mathematic abilities, musical abilities, spatial abilities, and many others. The term "aptitude" has lost favor in some circles because it mixes the constructs of ability and attainment (Kline, 2000), and because it implies a biologically determined trait that is "inborn and personal" (Kaufman & Lichtenberger, 2002, p. 19). The SAT (originally called *Scholastic Aptitude Test* but later renamed *Scholastic Assessment Test*) and *American College Test* (ACT) are well-known aptitude tests that measure the potential of high school students to perform well in college.

Achievement Tests

Achievement tests measure previous learning in a variety of school and academic content areas such as reading, writing, mathematics, science, vocabulary, and comprehension, among others (Brems, 2000). Achievement tests focus on the "products of academic instruction, rather than the processes underlying learning" (Wodrich, 1997, p. 163). More achievement tests have been developed than any other type of psychological tests.

Both group and individual achievement tests have been developed. Examples of group achievement tests are educational achievement tests—mandated in many states and/or by the federal government. Another example is the licensing examinations that many professional consumers take during the course of their career to obtain a state license or certification as social worker, professional counselor, or teacher; or to the medical boards to practice medicine; or to pass the bar to be able to practice as an attorney. Well-known individual achievement tests are the *Wechsler Individual Achievement Test* (2nd edition) and the *Woodcock-Johnson Tests of Achievement* (3rd edition) (Hogan, 2003).

Objective and Subjective (or Projective) Tests

Although almost all psychological tests could be classified as objective in the sense that they typically generate numeric scores, the terms "objective tests" and "subjective tests" have particular meaning in the assessment of personality characteristics.

Objective Tests

An *objective personality test* is one that can be scored according to criteria independent of the judgment of the examining psychologist. Typically, the format of objective tests is multiple-choice, in which the test-taker chooses from a fixed set of responses (Hogan, 2003).

Objective tests have been developed to assess normal and abnormal personality functioning or characteristics, either in specific domains (e.g., self-concept, gender role identity, depressive thoughts) or in a more comprehensive personality inventory that assesses many aspects of personality at one time. Kline (2000) refers to objective personality tests as *nomothetic* tests, which means that the tests are concerned with studying individual differences in people as measured against some common traits or dimensions that are assumed to be present in all people. Objective personality tests are predicated on the assumption that most people will answer accurately to direct questioning about their thoughts, emotions, and behaviors.

A noteworthy feature of many objective personality tests is their ability to assess clients' "atypical" responses (those rarely endorsed by others, which may be an indication of highly unusual thinking or behavior, such as by someone who is experiencing paranoia or psychosis). Objective tests also may reveal when test-takers are attempting either to present themselves as better than they are (known technically as *social desirability*, or colloquially as "faking good"), or are attempting to present themselves as worse than they are (*malingering*, or "faking bad"). The scoring profiles of some objective tests are so sophisticated that they can detect test-takers who are answering the test randomly or capriciously.

The best known and most widely used objective measure of personality is the *Minnesota Multiphasic Personality Inventory* (MMPI), first published in 1943, and subsequently revised and restandardized in a second edition in 1989 (MMPI-2). A close second to the MMPI in popularity is the *Beck Depression Inventory* (BDI), a specific-trait objective measure measuring depressive thoughts. It was first published in 1961 and subsequently revised in 1996 (Hood & Johnson, 2002).

Subjective Tests

Subjective tests, in contrast, are so labeled both because they assess clients' subjective perceptions (wishes, fantasies, preoccupations, motives, fears, and desires), including those that may be out of their conscious awareness, and because interpreting the meaning of individuals' responses traditionally has relied heavily on the examining psychologists' clinical judgment and subjectivity in making inferences about the data (Hogan, 2003; Hood & Johnson, 2002; Kline, 2000).

Subjective tests are referred to more commonly as *projective tests* because in their usual format they present individuals with some form of ambiguous stimuli, such as being presented with a series of sentence beginnings to which the test-taker is asked to complete the ending; being shown a series of evocative pictures or drawings about which the test-taker is asked to generate a story; or being shown a series of inkblot cards to which a test-taker is asked, "What might this be?" (Allen & Hollifield, 2003).

Ambiguous stimuli have no inherent or predetermined meaning. Rather, the responses are assumed to be based on a process of unconsciously projecting their basic personality, needs, and wishes onto the ambiguous stimuli, and thereby revealing deeper aspects of themselves than is possible with objective tests. Further, test-takers' responses are unstructured; they are not choosing from a predetermined response set but, rather, are free to respond in any manner they choose (Brems, 2000). Kline (2000) refers to projective tests as *ideographic* measures, which means that they are concerned with "measuring what is unique and individual to a person—all those aspects of personality not shared with anyone else" (p. 277).

Two well known and widely used projective tests are the *Rorschach Inkblot Test* (Hogan, 2003) and *The Thematic Apperception Test* (Murray, 1943). Some projective tests, such as the Rorschach, can detect test-takers' highly unusual responses. For example, a test-taker interprets the form or color or some other aspect of an inkblot card (or portion of it) as an extremely violent image, in contrast to the more usual benign or neutral image that others see. Thus, the former response would be regarded as atypical, and potentially suggest the individual's aggressive predilection, especially if similar images on the cards were to evoke the same response repeatedly.

Projective tests are predicated on the assumption that most people have limited ability to respond accurately to direct questioning about their thoughts, feelings, and behaviors, particularly those out of their conscious awareness. Thus, indirect means of questioning are employed, using ambiguous stimuli and open-ended responses. Hence, projective measures make it difficult for test-takers to deliberately present as better than or worse than they really are.

It is not an exaggeration to say that the world of psychologists can be divided into two groups: those that are highly skeptical of the value and use of projective tests (Wodrich, 1997), and those that consider projective tests as providing a unique set of data not obtainable through other sources and methods of assessment (Allen & Hollifield, 2003; Haak, 2003; Katz, 1985). Academic and research-based psychologists generally do not like projective measures (many would not even call them "tests") because of their low reliability and validity compared to objective tests (Hogan, 2003). Clinical and counseling psychologists, however, continue to use projective tests in their assessment practices because these tests are perceived as capturing information about clients that usually is not obtainable from objective measures (Chandler, 2003; Kline, 2000).

In forensic assessments, where major legal issues usually are at stake (e.g., termination of parental rights, competency to stand trial, and mental status at the time of offense), the projective measures may not be used at all, or used only as a supplement to well-standardized objective personality tests, because of potential challenges to the clinical inferences made by the evaluating psychologist (Dyer, 1999; Melton, Petrila, Poythress, & Slobogin, 1987, 1997).

A number of objective scoring systems and standardized methods of administration have been developed for projective measures. Among them is the Exner Comprehensive System for the Rorschach, which has improved its reliability and validity over other scoring methods (Allen & Hollifield, 2003). But much debate in psychology still surrounds the appropriateness of projective measures, particularly in classifying clients' functioning as either normal or abnormal. Their use as clinical tools in exploring clients' underlying or unconscious dynamics seems to be more widely accepted (Chandler, 2003; Dupree & Prevatt, 2003).

As noted in chapter 2, psychologists must have extensive training in the use of objective tests and projective instruments (i.e., courses on testing, practice experience in testing clients in a supervised internship or practicum). In addition, the use of projective tests requires advanced clinical assessment skills, because test-takers' responses on projective tests can be construed to refer to a wide variety of personality traits and can be interpreted in a number of different ways (Kline, 2000).

Neuropsychological Tests

Neuropsychological assessments address "the functioning of the central nervous system, especially the brain" (Hogan, 2003, p. 8). Both ability and achievement tests may be employed, as well as other specialized tests, to examine a variety of cognitive functions such as visual-motor speed, memory for verbal and pictorial material, cognitive complexity, style in which information is processed, and capacity for abstract thinking (Brems, 2000; Hogan, 2003). Neuropsychological testing may be conducted for conditions such as suspected brain injury and organizational difficulties, problems with frontal lobe activities (i.e., executive functions), learning disabilities, and nonverbal learning disorders (Wodrich, 1997).

Two well-known groups of neuropsychological measures are the *Halstead-Reitan Neuropsychological Test Battery* and the *Luria-Nebraska Neuropsychological Battery* (Brems, 2000). Administration, scoring, and interpretation of these measures usually requires advanced coursework and training in neuropsychology.

Norm-Referenced and Criterion-Referenced Tests

Norm-referenced tests and *criterion-referenced tests* are two different ways of answering the question, "Compared to what?" As used in psychological and educational assessments, norm-referenced and criterion-referenced tests help to put an individual's scores or responses in the context of a comparison group or some other frame of reference so meaning can be derived from the individual's test results (Hood & Johnson, 2002). Without such a comparison, it would be impossible to know what a person's score on a given test means because there would be no way of ascertaining whether the individual scores on a given test were better than, worse than, or about the same as the scores of others who took the test, or were reflective of absolute mastery of content, as determined by some external standard.

Wodrich (1997) notes that "the creation of a norm group is a key distinguishing feature of standardized psychological tests" (p. 4), because it provides more precision and objectivity in determining how an individual performs on a test compared to a broadly representative sample of similar peers. As is covered more extensively in the discussion of test construction, normative groups (also called a *standardization sample*) are used widely in developing tests of intelligence, academic achievement, and objective measures of personality. Some projective tests also have developed normative groups for comparison, although with less success than normative groups developed for objective tests.

Of the many different types of norms, the most widely used norm-referenced psychological tests employ *national norms*. For example, a children's intelligence test would be constructed using a randomly selected comparison group that is broadly representative of the population of children in the United States, based on current U.S. census data. Such a comparison group is considered representative if it empirically demonstrates close approximation to the U.S. population of children in terms of characteristics such as the percentage of age ranges, ethnicities, geographic region of the country, and parents' education levels that are included in the sample (Wodrich, 1997). Use of normative groups provides a basis for examining the *reliability* and *validity* of standardized tests. These two important concepts are addressed in the discussion of test construction later in the chapter.

In contrast to norm-referenced tests, criterion-referenced tests compare a person's score on a test with "an absolute score established by an authority" (Hood & Johnson, 2002, p. 40). The comparison is not made between a person taking a test and others who took the test but, instead, to some external standard or criterion of performance. Typically, the person or group developing the test determines what that standard or criterion should be. For example, a school district may want to know whether its existing elementary school curriculum helps children acquire a predetermined level of academic proficiency expected at each grade level.

Teachers or educational psychologists then might construct criterion-referenced tests, using as the criterion the number or percentage of math problems solved correctly, words spelled correctly, reading material comprehended, science facts learned, and the like, that the school board expects children to master at each elementary school grade level (e.g., students passing 80% of the items correctly are determined to be "proficient" learners).

Robertson (2003) provides a useful way of differentiating norm-referenced and criterion-referenced tests (p.30):

> Norm-referenced interpretations report an individual's rank within a specified norm group (e.g., "Ramon spelled as well as or better than 65% of the third graders tested nationally"). Criterion-referenced interpretations report performance on a set of clearly defined learning tasks (e.g., "Ramon spelled 65% of the words on the third-grade word list correctly").

Criterion-referenced tests are used more commonly in educational assessments and are rarely found in clinical or forensic assessments. According to Wodrich (1997), two major disadvantages of criterion-tests are that they do not allow comparisons between individuals and that they often ignore the issues regarding reliability:

> Unfortunately, because of the informal nature of criterion-referenced tests, many educators assume reliability is unimportant. Teacher-made tests must be sufficiently long, possess unambiguous items, and be consistently administered if minimum standards of reliability are to be assumed. (p. 165)

Performance and Paper/Pencil Tests

Tests of intelligence usually have a combination of *paper/pencil* and *performance* subtests that examinees must complete. Objective tests of personality are almost always paper and pencil tests, based on a structured response format such as multiple-choice, or true/false answers.

An example of a widely used, well standardized performance test is the *Gordon Diagnostic System*. This is a portable computerized device with built-in software that is used frequently in assessing suspected Attention Deficit/Hyperactivity Disorder (ADHD). It assesses the performance of individuals in terms of their ability to focus and sustain their attention and concentration, screen out distractions, and control their impulses (Wodrich, 1997).

Theories, Constructs, Assumptions, and Evidence Underlying Testing

Some understanding of the conceptual and pragmatic foundations of psychological testing is necessary for referring professionals to become informed consumers of psychological assessment information. To cover all of the relevant topics in this chapter is not possible, but the domain of intelligence testing provides an illustrative example of some of these issues.

The appraisal of intelligence has occupied an incredibly large place in the world of educational and psychological testing, and has shown itself to have many pragmatic applications, such as predicting school performance, vocational performance, and the capacity to benefit from treatment (Katz, 1985; Kaufman & Lichtenberger, 2002). The main point is that psychology is a changing and dynamic discipline. Sometimes these theories, constructs, assumptions, and evidence about intelligence have converged with the development of specific intelligence tests, and sometimes they have not (Flanagan & Ortiz, 2001; Valencia & Suzuki, 2001). This process reflects the ongoing work of psychologist researchers, test developers, and practitioners as they engage dynamically in building and critically examining the major tenets, evidence, and practices of their profession.

Early Theories of Intelligence

The philosophy of science underlying psychological testing originally was based on *logical positivism*, "the belief that it is possible to find incontrovertible truth[s] about people that apply to everyone equally, and on the idea that science is the only and best way to accumulate such knowledge" (Brems, 2000, p. 115).

The first studies of intelligence in England in the late 1800s arose from this model of science. As an extension of Charles Darwin's evolutionary theories, these early investigations essentially moved from the study of how physical attributes were inherited to the study of how mental abilities were inherited (Suen & French, 2003). The first European and American intelligence tests were developed from a belief that differences in mental abilities among people could be measured objectively and scientifically. Intelligence was assumed to be determined largely by heredity, and was seen as a fixed, unchanging commodity throughout the lifespan. Also, intelligence or mental abilities were assumed to be largely independent of experience (Wodrich, 1997).

Intelligence as a Variable, Construct, Measure, and Data

Within this logical positivist model of science, intelligence is conceptualized as a human trait that varies among people. These human traits, which are innumerable, are called *variables*, lest we forget that they vary! Hogan (2003) describes a variable as having three levels of generality:

1. as a *construct* (a verbal definition and description of the phenomena under study);
2. as a *measure* (the operational definition of what is to be observed and how it is to be observed, as specified on the test); and
3. as *raw data* (the specific numbers or scores resulting from the administration of the test).

For example: As a construct, intelligence might be defined as general problem-solving ability. As an operational definition, intelligence would be measured by an intelligence test structured to generate an overall composite index of intelligence (i.e., intelligence quotient or Full Scale IQ), as well as to generate separate indexes of verbal and nonverbal reasoning skills (i.e., Verbal and Performance IQ), as well as other indices (i.e., working memory, perceptual organization, processing speed). As raw data, intelligence would be defined as the number of correct responses on the various subtests of an intelligence test.

Hogan (2003) claims that the real interest of psychologist researchers is at the construct level. An individual's responses on specific tasks (subtests) in an intelligence test are not of primary interest but, rather, what those responses might indicate about the person's general intellectual ability, conceptualized broadly (Kaufman & Lichtenberger, 2002).

Current Controversies about Intelligence and Intelligence Tests

In perhaps what may surprise many referring professionals, psychologists have not reached consensus among themselves about the construct of intelligence (Valencia & Suzuki, 2001). Within the profession of psychology, vastly different, competing ideas about the nature and structure of intellect have been developed and debated over the years. For example, some investigators, based largely on the relative high degree of statistical association among various intelligence subtests, have theorized that in actuality intelligence tests measure only *one generalized mental ability*.

Other investigators have assumed just the opposite—that the degree of statistical association among subtests is low enough to suggest that the intelligence tests are assessing a *set of distinct, primary mental abilities*, largely separate from each other, with only a small generalized mental abilities factor present. Still other investigators have proposed a variety of complex hierarchical models of intelligence, attempting to reconcile the theories of differentiation of generalized versus specific mental abilities, or have anchored their theory in other ways, such as in information-processing models or biologically based models of brain functioning (Hogan, 2003).

Application

What is the practical relevance of all this theorizing, research, and conceptual debates about the nature of intelligence? Referring professionals should care about this because these debates go to the heart of what intelligence tests actually measure. The position of some psychologists and test developers is that *the vast majority of current intelligence tests do not adequately assess the complete range of broad abilities of the various distinct mental abilities*, and that the only way to do this is to employ a testing strategy in which subtests from several different intelligence scales are administered in a "cross-battery assessment" (Flanagan & Ortiz, 2001).

Other psychologists disagree with this view (Glutting, Watkins, & Youngstrom, 2003), emphasizing that the assessment of intelligence should not be based primarily on the desire to measure all of the separate mental abilities in a theoretical or statistical model about the structure of intelligence but, rather, "the goal of any meaningful assessment [of intelligence] is to *target assessment to the specific cognitive processes underlying the clinical issue for which the [individual] was referred*" (Weiss, Saklofske, & Prifitera, 2003, p. 143, italics added).

Referring professionals should be alert to these controversies and debates, even though they rarely will be explicit in psychologists' reports. In particular, terms such as "Full Scale IQ" may lead consumers to believe mistakenly that the results of intelligence tests objectively and conclusively reveal the full extent of how intelligent clients are or how intelligent clients act in the real world. Rather, intelligence tests (and for that matter, all psychological tests) are best thought of as simply *one sample of behavior, gathered in a standardized manner*. As Kaufman and Lichtenberger (2002) wrote: "The global IQ in any test, no matter how comprehensive, does not equal a person's total capacity for intellectual accomplishment"

(p. 20). When a client's verbal and nonverbal functioning differ significantly, a global or Full Scale IQ is not considered to be a meaningful measure of the individual's intelligence.

In reading an assessment report of clients' intelligence, it is important to recognize that the test developers' theory of intelligence may or may not be the same as the examining psychologists' theory of intelligence (as evidenced by the strategies selected to assess clients' cognitive functioning), and these, in turn, may be different from the notions of intelligence held by referring professionals themselves (e.g., teachers, special education personnel, early childhood interventionists, forensic practitioners, probation officers, clinical social workers, attorneys, and judges) who are using the assessment data and recommendations to make case planning and programming decisions.

Rather than concentrate exclusively on the numeric scores from intelligence tests (i.e., Full Scale IQ, Verbal IQ, Performance IQ), referring professionals should look to psychologists' narrative report for meaningful information regarding the breadth and depth of clients' accumulated knowledge (which has been termed *crystallized knowledge*) and their capacity to process information, form concepts, recognize patterns, draw inferences, engage in deductive and inductive reasoning, and develop conclusions (termed *fluid knowledge*) related to the specific clinical, educational, vocational, or forensic questions for which clients originally were referred for psychological assessment (Hogan, 2003; Ryan & Smith 2003).

For example, intelligence testing of neglectful or abusive parents could shed light on parents' general fund of knowledge about the world and about their general problem-solving abilities. This information, in turn, could be integrated with other assessment measures and procedures (e.g., clinical interviews, observations of parent–child interactions, objective and/or projective personality tests, and self-report measures on parents' attitude toward the child) and subsequently applied to specific assessment concerns about the current adequacy of their parenting skills.

Thus, understanding these types of psychological concepts and methods of assessment more fully will help consumers better answer key case planning questions such as, "Do these parents have adequate knowledge of appropriate parenting roles/responsibilities and child development?" and, "Can parents use their problem-solving and reasoning abilities to consistently promote children's growth and development as well as ensure their safety?"

A final word about the construct of intelligence: Referring professionals should realize that subsequent studies of intelligence have recognized that intelligence has a large heritability component (perhaps as much as 50%) and also that the social environment plays a key role in determining how malleable mental abilities are over the lifespan (Kaufman & Lichtenberger, 2002). Thus, it is of great practical interest to learn how individuals' immediate environment and broader social-cultural contexts reinforce their general and specific mental abilities.

Test Construction

The importance of developing working knowledge of how psychological and educational tests are constructed is best illustrated by an example. A severe criticism often made against psychological tests in general, and intelligence tests in particular, has been that they are biased against members of racial/ethnic minority groups, or other culturally different groups (Dana, 1993; Georgas, Weiss, van de Vijver, & Saklofske, 2003; Jones, 1988; Samuda, 1998; Valencia & Suzuki, 2001). The type of criticism has been made both against *specific items* on a test that were alleged to, or gave evidence of, either favoring or penalizing one cultural group over another, and against the construction of normative groups that were said not to be representative of the individuals being tested but whose individual scores nonetheless were being compared to those of the normative group.

These criticisms arose because the norms in some early tests of intelligence and personality were based on standardization samples that included only Caucasians, omitting altogether representatives of other races and ethnicities and/or not including minority-group representation in proportion to their distribution in the U.S. population (Reynolds & Kaiser, 2003). Since the late 1940s and early 1950s, however, the construction of new psychological and educational tests has become much more rigorous (Anastasi, 1954, 1995; Cronbach, 1949; Gulliksen, 1950). Currently, the principles and best practices of test construction have been consolidated into a comprehensive set of guidelines, *Standards for Psychological and Educational Testing,* which was developed and published jointly by three professional associations (American Educational Research Association, American Psychological Association, & National Council on Measurement Used in Education, 1999).

Nonetheless, many referring professionals continue to have lingering doubts about whether psychological tests are constructed in an unbiased manner. This concern is particularly likely to surface when referring professionals—or family members—refer individuals who are members of cultural different groups for psychological evaluation and/or when these individuals do not perform as well as the referring agents expected them to do on tests of cognitive abilities or academic achievement.

Indeed, test construction is a complex, highly technical, lengthy, and expensive process. At the risk of great oversimplification, there are a discrete number of steps for constructing psychological and educational norm-referenced tests (Hogan, 2003; Robertson, 2003; Sapp, 2002). Norm-referenced tests are those in which an individual's scores are compared to those derived from a carefully drawn comparison group. [See Hambleton and Zensky (2003) for a discussion on advances in the construction of criterion-referenced tests.]

1. Determine the purpose of the test.
2. Specify the content of the test, develop test items, conduct test tryouts, and analyze results.
3. Determine the reliability and validity of the test; revise as necessary.
4. Standardize the administration, scoring, and interpretation of the test (i.e., writing test manual; recruitment of comparison group, and construction of norms).
5. Publish the test and testing manual; conduct follow-up studies.

Determining the Purpose of the Test

Tests are usually developed either to meet a practical need or to validate theoretical constructs. Continuing with the theme of intelligence tests as an illustration, the developers of two well-known intelligence tests—Alfred Binet in France and David Wechsler in the United States—developed their measures of intellectual abilities because each was faced with an urgent pragmatic task. Binet wanted to learn which children could profit from regular instruction in school and which required specialized instruction. Wechsler wanted a better instrument to assess the intelligence of adults who had been hospitalized for psychiatric treatment (Hogan, 2003; Kaufman & Lichtenberger, 1999; Tulsky, Saklofske, & Ricker, 2003). Later measures of intelligence have been developed focusing more explicitly on specific theories about the nature of intelligence (Flanagan & Ortiz, 2001; Kaufman & Lichtenberger, 2002).

In formulating the purpose of a test, developers begin by specifying the need for a new test, the traits or target variables the test is intended to measure, and the population for which the test is designed, then begin to consider a number of preliminary design issues, such as the test's length, format, method of administration, type of scoring, and amount of training required for examiners (Hogan, 2003). In addition, at this stage, test developers and test publishers are concerned with ascertaining the marketability of a new test, particularly if the new test is to compete against an existing instrument (Robertson, 2003).

Content Specification, and Item Development, Tryout, and Analysis

Once the purpose and preliminary design issues have been settled, developers specify the content of the test, such as, for example, whether the test is intended to measure intellectual abilities, academic achievement, or some other personality characteristic or trait of interest (Robertson, 2003). Then a large number of test items is written, edited for clarity, often reviewed by panels of experts for potential cultural bias, and tried out on individuals in a series of formal and informal trials (Hogan, 2003). Subsequently, test items are modified based on the feedback obtained from individuals taking the preliminary versions of the test (Sapp, 2002).

Eventually, a revised version of the test typically retains fewer test items, based on evidence of the items' ability to measure accurately the trait(s) the test is seeking to evaluate. Various of statistical analyses are conducted in this phase to determine the ease or difficulty in passing a given item, as well as the item's ability to distinguish individuals who have more of the trait from individuals who have less of the trait (Hogan, 2003). This is usually the step in which test developers investigate whether items are biased toward members of culturally different groups, such as racial and ethnic minorities (Robertson, 2003).

Determining Reliability and Validity

Test developers, either as a separate step or concurrently with the next step of test construction (test standardization, described below), then undertake a series of studies to ascertain the *reliability* and *validity* of the test. Because these two properties are of central concern in test construction, they require elaboration. Both reliability and validity are based, in part, on statistical procedures measuring the degrees of association and variance among a whole set of variables, such as between the individual items on a test, between different sets of test scores, and between test scores and some type of external criterion. Test developers use a variety of statistical procedures to ascertain how much test score variation can be accounted for by "true score performance" and how much can be attributed to "error variation."

Reliability

Although reliability can be ascertained in a number of ways, reliability for the purposes of test construction means determining the *stability of the test over time* and *internal consistency* (Kline, 2000). Ascertaining stability—technically, *test–retest reliability*—addresses the question of whether individuals who take the same test on two or more occasions obtain similar scores. Internal consistency refers to the extent to which the items on the test are associated with each other, or how well the items on the test are working together, technically termed *item homogeneity*.

Knowing these two facets of a test helps developers estimate, with some degree of precision, the amount of error involved in measurement of the attribute under study. Stated another way, determining reliability through various statistical computations (i.e., reliability coefficients, standard error of measurement) helps psychologists state the degree of confidence they have that the "obtained score" an individual achieves on a test falls within a band or interval that reflects the "true score"—the hypothetical score they would achieve if the test were to measure with 100% accuracy and no error. "Error," as used here, does not refer to mistakes or bias but, rather, to random variations in individuals' test scores that might be attributable to a host of nonspecific factors including client factors (e.g., luck, fatigue, illness, lack of attention), environmental factors (e.g., distractions in the test setting), and examiner factors (e.g., giving ambiguous or confusing test instructions) (Kline, 2000; Sapp, 2002; Wodrich, 1997). Test developers want their tests to be as reliable as possible.

Validity

Determining the validity of test scores is the most important facet in test development (Hogan, 2003). Validity refers to the overlap between tests and the underlying constructs or traits the tests intend to measure. There are several different types of validity, involving both computation of a variety of complex statistics and, ultimately, test developers' subjective judgment that there is sufficient evidence to conclude that the test scores are valid *when used for the particular purpose for which the test was designed.* Although the ideal is to have a large overlap between tests and the underlying constructs, this is rarely achieved in reality; hence validity is a matter of degree, not an all-or-nothing property (Hogan, 2003).

When new tests are first published, developers usually report initial findings on the validity of a test. Much of the information about a test's validity, however, accumulates only after the test has been in use for a number of years, as subsequent studies are conducted (Robertson, 2003).

In the construction of different types of psychological and educational tests, certain types of validity are more important than others.

- *Content validity*: the overlap between the content on a test and a "well-defined domain of knowledge or behavior" (Hogan, 2003, p. 176); particularly relevant in the construction of educational achievement tests and employment tests. The key issues in content validity are whether the test items broadly *match* and are *representative* of the types of knowledge or behaviors that individuals are expected to have attained in the specific content area being measured by the test.
- *Criterion validity*: the relationship between performance on a test and a criterion (i.e., a standard) that is taken to be an important indicator of the construct being measured (Hogan, 2003); particularly relevant in the construction of measures of intelligence and personality. The criterion selected may be the relationship between test scores and an individual's status at some *future* point in time; hence it is called *predictive validity*. Or the criterion may be the relationship between test scores and an individual's status at the *current* time; hence, called *concurrent validity*.

  For example, criterion (predictive) validity of an intelligence test might be demonstrated if it accurately foretells how well students subsequently will perform in school (as measured by their grade point average). Criterion (concurrent) validity of a newly developed intelligence test might be demonstrated if its scores correlate highly with an existing measure of intelligence known to have high reliability and validity, or with the scores of groups known to differ markedly in intellectual abilities (e.g., students in a gifted and talented classroom would be expected to differ from students in a special education classroom for individuals with significant intellectual delays or retardation).

  Similarly, predictive validity of a new measure of mental health disturbance/psychopathology might be demonstrated if its scores successfully predict which individuals subsequently will need mental health treatment. Concurrent validity of a newly constructed measure of depression would be demonstrated if its scores correlate highly with the individual's scores on an existing measure of depression known to be reliable and valid, or with the scores of individuals known to differ in terms of whether they are depressed or not.

- *Convergent and divergent validity:* Two special forms of criterion-related validity, essentially opposite sides of the same coin. Convergent validity means that the scores of a new test are correlated highly with the scores on another established measure of the *same construct.* Divergent validity means that those same test scores are not highly correlated with the scores of another established measure of a *different construct.* Thus, a new measure and an existing measure of self-esteem should demonstrate a high degree of association with each other, while also demonstrating that the new measure of self-esteem has a low degree of association (or no association) with a measure of a completely different construct, such as one measuring oppositionality and negativity. Convergent and divergent validity are particularly relevant in the construction of personality tests (Hogan, 2003).

Test Standardization

Standardization refers to test developers' writing specific guidelines and protocols regarding how the test is to be administered and scored in a uniform, objective manner, and to their constructing a "standardization sample"—the normative group that will serve as the basis of comparison for individual clients' scores (Robertson, 2003).

Kaufman and Lichtenberger (2002) suggest that the use of standardized procedures for administering and scoring tests is analogous to conducting a fixed experimental procedure that must be reproduced exactly with each individual taking the test. This helps to ensure that evaluating psychologists do not use testing procedures that vary from one person to the next; inadvertently teach them the tasks, skills, or knowledge being measured; give hints or feedback to test-takers about how they are performing; or change the conditions of the test from one focused on ascertaining clients' *typical performance* to one focused on ascertaining their *maximum performance.*

Constructing normative comparison groups involves complex methods of randomly sampling groups whose demographic characteristics closely match U.S. census targets on variables such as gender, race/ethnicity membership, socioeconomic status, and geographic region of the country (Robertson, 2003). Sample size is important, because larger samples have a higher probability of achieving the goal of being broadly representative of the characteristics of the larger population from which the samples were drawn. Obtaining large sample sizes is expensive and time-consuming, though, and test developers often have to make trade-offs between the ideal of achieving large sample sizes and the pragmatic considerations of the cost, time, and effort in doing so.

The raw data from individuals or groups participating in the standardization sample are then converted through a variety of statistical procedures into *norm-referenced scores* that allow meaningful comparisons between an individual's score and that of the comparison group. Although a variety of ways are used to convert raw scores into comparison scores, such as age or grade equivalents, the preferred method of constructing norm-referenced scores is to convert the raw scores into *standard units of measurement*, such as *percentages* (i.e., an individual's rank in a comparative group of 100) or, more commonly, *standard scores* (Robertson, 2003; Wodrich, 1997).

Standard scores, also called *scaled scores*, are based on the idea that most human traits are "normally distributed" in the population. This means that, if you were able to obtain a sufficiently large sample of people and measure them on some common trait, slightly more than two-thirds of the sample would have scores that cluster together, indicating they had (more or less) an average amount of the trait. Those having very low or very high scores would be much fewer, indicating either a negligible or a prodigious amount of the trait, respectively.

Usually, this distribution pattern is represented graphically in the well-known "bell-shaped curve," in which the large cluster is in the middle, around either side of the average (graphically, the hump in the middle, or the top of the bell), and those with amounts of the trait markedly above or below the average are toward the diminishing edges of the curve. Standard scores are calibrated in such a way as to have a common numeric reference point for the central cluster (technically, the *mean*), as well as common numeric reference points for measuring departures from the central cluster (technically, *standard deviation units*). These departure points have plus (+) or minus (–) signs in front of them, signifying whether the departure indicates having more of the trait, as signified by the + sign, or having less of the trait, as signified by the – sign.

Different psychological and educational tests employ different ways of calibrating standard scores. For example, intelligence scales use deviation

IQ standard scores. The Wechsler Intelligence Scales have a mean of 100 and standard deviation units of ±15. The Stanford-Binet intelligence test has a mean of 100 and standard deviation units of ±16. Many personality tests and behavioral rating instruments use a T scale, which is calibrated with a mean of 50 and standard deviation units of ±10.

Once the mean and standard deviation of the standardization group's test scores are known, an individual's standing relative to others on the construct or trait in question can be determined easily. Standardized tests make use of the normal distribution to aid in interpreting such scores. Scores within ±1 standard deviation are considered to be within the *average range* of performance. Scores between ±1 and ±2 standard deviations from the mean are considered to be *significant departures* from typical performance on the construct in question, and scores more than ±2 standard deviations from the mean represent *statistically rare occurrences*.

Special interpretive significance, therefore, often is attached to scores that reach ±2 or more standard deviations from the mean. (Scores between ±2 standard deviation units account for 95% of the normal distribution.) For example, scores on intelligence tests that are more than 2 standard deviations below the mean are used, in part, to diagnose mental retardation. Similarly, scores on many personality tests that are elevated more than 2 standard deviations above the mean may suggest serious problems or psychopathology.

Test Publication and Subsequent Studies

The final step in test construction is to write the test manual, which contains, at a minimum, information about the purpose of the test, the process of constructing items, initial data on the reliability and validity of the test, recruitment of the standardization sample, development of test norms, and the procedures used for administration, scoring, and interpreting the test.

As the test comes into use, additional studies are likely to be conducted. Whether the test becomes widely used or not depends, in large part, on whether it continues to demonstrate adequate psychometric properties of reliability and validity and also whether the test proves to be useful in practice. In addition, subsequent studies often shed light on whether tests are unbiased and fair in assessing culturally diverse groups (Reynolds & Kaiser, 2003).

The interpretive scheme of standardized tests must prove to be clear, parsimonious, and *clinically useful*. That is, the investment of psychologists' and test-takers' time and effort in taking, scoring, and interpreting the test should be justified by the results obtained, and their potential for addressing specific referral concerns. Incumbent on the evaluator is the task of translating test results into practical and meaningful recommendations for treatment or intervention planning. Therefore, tests with good psychometric properties (e.g., acceptable standardization samples, reliability coefficients, and validity data) must be chosen in these cases, as results from the tests will be used to make critical decisions about clients.

Test Selection

Selecting the specific procedures, clinical protocols, and psychological and/or educational tests for examining psychologists to use with clients is based on several interrelated factors (Beutler, Wakefield, & Williams, 1994; Goldman, L'Engle Stein, & Guerry, 1983; Wodrich, 1997):

- the *specific referral question* being posed or *purpose* for which the evaluation is being conducted (discussed further in Chapter 7);
- the psychologist's *theoretical orientation, training, and experience* with testing instruments;
- the *setting* in which the evaluation is being conducted (e.g., school, mental health, legal, medical, vocational); and
- the psychologist's *professional judgment* regarding which tests or procedures are likely to offer the best source of information regarding the type of case planning decision being contemplated

In addition, some *external forces* may impinge on the psychologist's test selection; for example (Hersen, 2004; Katz, 1985; Werthman, 1995):

- an agency's admission policies; state and federal law governing such things as special education placement or disability determination; and
- third-party organizations such as managed care or insurance companies, which may limit reimbursement to only certain types of psychological test procedures as part of an evaluation.

Test selection should be individualized and tailored to meet the specific needs of the individual who is the focus of the psychological assessment. In addition, Beutler et al. (1994) suggest that test selection of personality tests be based on the measure's psychometric properties of *reliability*, *sensitivity* (ability to distinguish accurately those with higher amounts of the trait from those with lower amounts); *specificity* (ability to accurately identify those who do not have trait being measured from those who do); and *predictive validity* (the ability to accurately identify those who will benefit from differential types of treatment interventions).

Test Administration

Psychological and educational tests typically are time-consuming to administer, and test developers and examining psychologists alike have a great interest in finding ways to increase the efficiency and effectiveness of test administration. Three major issues that consumers should know about in test administration are: (a) individual- versus group-administered method of administration; (b) computer-assisted administration; and (c) the use of psychological assistants who may administer and score tests, but do not interpret the data or write the report.

Individual Versus Group Test Administration

Particularly in the assessment of cognitive abilities (intelligence, aptitude, and achievement), individual testing is time-consuming and costly. The time to administer an intelligence test alone may require upwards of 2 hours per test-taker, and additional time subsequently will be needed for scoring, interpreting, and report writing. In addition, individual testing requires a highly trained psychologist examiner, whose practice and training in testing are necessary for "a competent administration that produces a reliable result" (Hood & Johnson, 2002, p. 106). Given the amount of time involved, individual tests typically are used only for specific concerns about how well an individual is learning, such as when help is sought in developing strategies to improve learning performance (Wodrich, 1997).

Individual tests have the following advantages:

1. Items tend to be more varied (e.g., paper/pencil, puzzles, blocks, pictures, mazes, words presented orally, or even items presented totally in a "language-free" manner using pantomime and nonverbal gestures), rather than being restricted to written items on a test booklet that require considerable reading comprehension skills.
2. The results of individually administered tests are more likely to be integrated with other assessment data and the sociocultural context of

a person's life because the focus is on the individual's performance, and the examining psychologist is responsible for integrating all of the assessment data.

Group tests of intelligence and achievement, in contrast, are considerably more cost-efficient in terms of the time and expense involved. Group tests typically are paper/pencil tests in a multiple-choice or true/false answer format. Psychologists may or may not be present for group test administration, as the instructions for the test items usually are contained in a printed test book and another professional, such as a teacher, may substitute as a test proctor.

Because the group(s) taking the test can be large (e.g., all the third, sixth, ninth, and twelfth graders in an entire school system; all volunteer recruits being inducted into the armed services; all high school students seeking college admission), the results typically are machine-scored by a computer or an electronic scanner. In addition, the construction of group norms is made considerably easier when the standardization sample is composed of 10,000 to 20,000 individuals per age or grade, rather than 100 to 200 individuals per age or grade, which is more customary in standardization samples of individual intelligence tests (Robertson, 2003). Group tests are used frequently to assess how well *groups* of individuals are learning content based on specific classroom instruction (Wodrich, 1997).

Disadvantages of group tests are that they require a relatively high degree of reading proficiency and verbal comprehension in standard English and may not be appropriate for children who come from culturally or linguistically different backgrounds, have learning disabilities in reading and verbal comprehension, or have neurological processing difficulties. Further, the integration of group test results with other assessment data typically would occur only if an individual's performance on a group test subsequently generated a referral for a follow-up individual psychological or educational assessment.

Computer-Assisted Administration

The use of computers has had a major impact on psychological assessment and testing, and an increasing number of intelligence tests, achievement tests, and personality tests have both computer-based versions and the traditional paper/pencil version (McCullough & Miller, 2003). Depending on the specific measure, computers can be used in test administration, scoring, and interpretation. The discussion here considers only computer-assisted administration. Computer-assisted interpretation is discussed separately later in the chapter (under "Test Interpretation").

Computer-assisted administration can be as simple as the computer presenting a test item on a video screen in a manner similar to the traditional written test booklet, or it can be sophisticated in adapting which items are presented, based on test-takers' previous responses (Hogan, 2003). Clients taking IQ tests, projective tests, or other personality inventories can enter their responses more quickly on a keyboard than on an answer sheet (Bootzin and Acolcella, 1988). Further, the presentation of single items at a time on a video monitor seems to avoid creating a sense of discouragement or distraction that test-takers may have felt when looking the daunting list of questions in the old-style examination booklets.

Advances in computer programming now permit *adaptive testing*: The computer selects the appropriate sequence and type of item to be presented in response to answers given to key questions early in the test. Computers are able to adapt the presentation of items through complex mathematical models that have been developed to assess the pattern of responses, which takes into account that some answers marked correct are derived from guessing rather than having actual knowledge of the content. Computer-adapted testing "can improve motivation, reduce testing time, and administer fewer items per examinee, all without sacrificing measurement accuracy" (McCullough and Miller 2003, p. 631).

Use of Psychological Assistants in Test Administration and Scoring

Large testing centers and/or individual psychologists who specialize primarily in diagnostic assessment may call on assistants to administer and score one or more tests with clients. Assistants typically have substantial training in psychology but are not doctoral level, licensed psychologists.

Katz (1985) described the advantages of using psychological assistants as:

- a more efficient use of time;
- another source of observation about clients' functioning during the evaluation;
- a source of opinions about the client; and
- a source of collegial support and who, in the cases of clients exhibiting violent or threatening behaviors, can provide a measure of additional physical security during the evaluation process.

A disadvantage of using assistants to administer tests is that it eliminates the observational data available to examining psychologists when they administer tests to clients directly. Sometimes knowing *how* a test-taker produced a response is just as important as knowing *what* the response was.

The main point to remember here is that doctoral-level, licensed, supervising psychologists, not psychological assistants, have the legal and professional responsibility for interpreting the results of test scores along with the findings from nontest data into a comprehensive assessment report. This should include explicit recommendations and suggestions for case planning decisions.

Test Scoring

The manner in which responses are scored is a potential source of unreliability in testing (Hogan, 2003). Pragmatically, scoring can be done by hand (e.g., using a stencil or a transparency overlay) or electronically (e.g., a scanner or a computer). Machine-scoring is one means of reducing potential errors in recording scores. Computers also offer the advantage of storing test scores, although this poses ethical concerns about the security of test results.

Psychometric theories and statistics provide the conceptual and pragmatic foundation by which psychologists can derive meaning from test scores and make inferences about what test results may reveal about individuals' functioning in the real world (Sapp, 2002). Traditionally, the numeric scores generated by a test fall into one of four types of scales, also referred to as *levels of measurement* (Hogan, 2003; Kline, 2000):

- *Nominal scales* assign numbers based on the name or classification of the variables being measured (e.g., male = 0, female = 1). The numbers are used for coding purposes only and do not signify quantification—more or less of something.
- *Ordinal scales* assign numbers to represent both classification and rank in a hierarchy (e.g., a restaurant critic's listing of the best places to eat in town; a late night TV host's listing of humorous "top 10" absurdities; a school's ranking of individuals in terms of academic proficiency within a given class year). Ordinal scales do not specify the amount of difference between the rankings.

- *Interval scales* assign numbers to represent classification, rank, and equal values between the rankings. Intervals of equal magnitude represent the same amount of difference along the range of the scale. Interval scales, however, lack a true zero point (e.g., when Sherman, the boy weather anchor in Frostbite Falls, Minnesota, says that "December temperatures will average a daytime high of –5° and a nighttime low of –25°," the scale points on a Fahrenheit thermometer all represent equal intervals but the temperatures that fall below "zero degrees" on the scale do not represent the absolute absence of heat).
- *Ratio scales* assign numbers to represent classification, ranks, and equal magnitude between scale intervals, and they have a true zero point, too (e.g., in the physical and natural sciences, measures of an object's height and weight are based on scales that have a true, or absolute, zero point that really refers to the absence of the trait being measured).

These levels of measurement indicate the relationship of the numbers to each other within the scale and also define the type of mathematic and algebraic operations that can be done with those numbers. For example, addition and subtraction can be done with interval scales, but multiplication and division cannot, as interval scales lack a true zero point (Hogan, 2003). Most psychological tests use ordinal or interval levels of measurement.

In what likely will come as a distinct surprise to many referring professionals, severe attacks have been mounted against these conventional psychometric theories and statistics as not being scientific at all. Mitchell (cited in Kline, 2000) has argued that the claim that these conventional psychometric measurements are scientific is "essentially delusional" (p. 635). Conventional theories of psychological and educational test scores include the "classic theory" referred to earlier—that an *obtained score* will encompass both a hypothetical *true score* and non-specific *error scores*. Although additional theories of test scoring have been developed, the classic theory remains the most widely used conceptual model for understanding the meaning of scores in test construction (Sapp, 2002).

The critics point out that almost all of the time, test developers simply have assumed, without empirical demonstration, that the trait they are attempting to measure has a "quantification structure"—that is, whether the trait shows the capacity to vary in terms of having greater or lesser amounts, which is the basis for all subsequent mathematic operations. The critics argue that the algebraic operations involved in transforming raw test scores into standardized scores might be simply an artifact of the scale being used, not an actual characteristic of the underlying trait being measured.

A further problem is that the interval scales used in most psychological and educational tests do not make clear what is being measured. For example, it is hypothetically possible to receive a zero score on an intelligence test or an achievement test, but no psychologist would ever claim that a zero score represents that the individual has zero intelligence. Thus, these critics argue that the measurement of human attributes and abilities will not advance until ratio scales are developed similar to those used in the natural sciences (Kline, 2000).

Why should referring professionals care about scores, scales, and seemingly arcane debates about the levels of measurement? As Hogan (2003) so pithily put it: "We do need to worry about the nature of our scales in order to make meaningful statements about our measurements, or, conversely, to avoid saying stupid things about them" (p. 74). Referring professionals often are awed, if not actually cowed, by the quantitative scores reported by psychologists—or are "number phobic," as Sapp (2002) suggests. Rather than accepting scores unquestioningly as incontrovertibly true and objective, it is helpful to see them as they are regarded in psychology—useful indicators that are by no means perfect. Even critics of conventional test-scoring methods concede that, despite their limitations, they should not be abandoned, "especially, since there [is], as yet, no replacement " (Kline, 2000, p. 636).

Perhaps of more practical help to referring professionals, Table 3.2 provides definitions of the various terms used in reporting scores.

Test and Assessment Data Interpretation

"The rubber meets the road" as psychologists complete the scoring of all the tests administered and begin the process of interpreting the test data and nontest data (e.g., interviews, observations, histories, review of records) prior to writing their reports. This section provides discussion of some general approaches to interpretation and also pays special attention to the uses and controversies regarding computer-assisted interpretation of psychological tests.

TABLE 3.2	Definitions of Scoring Terms
SCORING TERMS	**DEFINITIONS**
Observed Score	Also known as *obtained score* or *raw score*, refers to an individual's actual score on a test. Usually, this is the number answered correctly.
Derived Score	A score derived from a frequency distribution that shows where individuals are in comparison to a normative group.
Cutoff Score (or "cut-score")	A score in either a norm-referenced or criterion-referenced test that is used to separate one level of responses from another, such as "pass/fail," "at-risk/not-at-risk," "proficient/not proficient," etc.
Equivalent Score (i.e., age or grade equivalents)	A derived score that compares a person's score in terms of whether it is typical of the scores in a comparison group at various age or grade levels.
Critical Item	An item on a test that is flagged for special attention, irrespective of whether it contributes to the total score of the test. Critical items often are reported in objective personality tests and standardized behavior rating scales. For example, marking items such as "cruel to animals" or "secretly sets fires" as "True" or "Frequently Occurring" typically will be flagged for the examiner's attention, whether the item does or does not contribute to a total test score indicating problems with aggression and antisocial behaviors.

General Approaches to Interpretation and Integration

Because there are many different approaches to interpretation, the following steps should be regarded as a general outline only. Individual psychologists are likely to show considerable variation regarding how these steps are accomplished, depending on the instruments used and the nature of the evaluation.

1. Interpretation of assessment findings rests squarely on psychologists' professional competence. As noted in chapter 2, the ethical principles and practice standards of psychology require that examining psychologists use only those tests in which they have specific education and training (Hersen, 2004). With the use of computer-assisted interpretation of test findings, this has become an even larger concern, as the

interpretation may be accessed and used by those lacking the required professional competence.

2. Before beginning the process of test interpretation, psychologists often have to determine whether individuals answered a sufficient number of responses for the test results to be considered reliable and valid. Test manuals typically provide instructions on the minimum number of responses necessary for the test to be considered a reliable and valid administration. The scoring for some instruments (e.g., MMPI-2) actually provides this information routinely in the form of "validity scales," which are inspected before interpretation of the clinical scales measuring psychopathology.

3. If a test administration has been determined to be reliable and valid, psychologists will convert raw scores into scaled scores and consult a series of tables included in the norm-referenced test manual, to interpret an individual's performance on the test in relation to the norms derived from the test's standardization sample. These tables provide comparisons both on broad indices generated by the test (e.g., IQ scores in an intelligence test, or global measures of pathology in a personality inventory) and on narrow subtests (e.g., verbal and nonverbal reasoning subtests in a measure of intelligence, or deviance subtests scores in a measure of personality disturbance).

4. In interpreting measures of intellectual abilities, several authorities (Glutting, Watkins, & Youngstrom, 2003; Kaufman & Litchenberger, 2003) advocate the use of a hierarchical or top-down model of interpretation. That is, they begin by examining the global indices first, then proceed to examine individual subtest scores, and finally to examine responses to individual test items.

5. Katz (1985) advocates a similar approach when interpreting and integrating intelligence and personality test results. He suggests beginning with the global, most objective measure that has been obtained, and then proceeding to examine subtests and other measures to identify patterns and similar findings across different measures.

6. As psychologists integrate test results with nontest data, they continue to look for patterns that may have emerged and begin to develop hypotheses and predictions about the meaning of the data. Psychologists typically go back and forth across their dataset looking for information that either confirms or disconfirms their hypotheses and predictions.

7. The final step in interpretation is to develop a conceptual formulation that explains the test finding, including accounting for any

discrepancies or contradictions that have emerged from all the data. Psychologists may also indicate additional assessment information that should be gathered to rule in or rule out various diagnostic hypotheses or possibilities. This conceptual formulation subsequently becomes the basis upon which psychologists offer recommendations for case planning and treatment planning decisions facing the referring consumer (Katz, 1985; Maruish, 1994).

Computer-based interpretation.

Referring professionals have to be familiar with the advantages, limitations, and controversies regarding computer-based interpretation of psychological test results, particularly because the reports they receive about their clients increasingly will include diagnostic and intervention statements generated by computer software programs. Widely used tests, such as the *Minnesota Multiphasic Personality Inventory-Second Edition* (MMPI-2), the *Behavior Assessment System for Children* (BASC) and the *Achenbach System of Empirically Based Assessments* (ASEBA)—behavior rating systems using parent, teacher, and youth self-report for rating the presence of both problem and prosocial behaviors in children and adolescents—can be computer-scored and interpreted (Achenbach & McConaughy, 2003; McCullough & Miller, 2003; Thorpe, Kamphaus, & Reynolds, 2003).

In computer-based interpretation, the raw data scores entered are either input manually or are scanned into a computer and/or are sent to a computer testing interpretation service. An extensive narrative report subsequently is generated, based on interpretations derived from *actuarial data* (aggregate data obtained from very large groups that focuses on the calculation of risk, which are based on numerous multivariate statistics and algorithms [McCullough & Miller, 2003]). The narrative report typically contains a variety of information such as the degree to which the individual being tested matches clinical profiles drawn from the aggregate group; clinical hypotheses about the client, based on research into certain score patterns that were seen in the aggregate group; and recommended interventions, based on outcome research studies regarding practice effectiveness with certain diagnostic groups.

Computer-based interpretation has several advantages, according to McCullough and Miller (2003):

1. It enables efficient use of psychologists' and clients' time, including the fact that clients may receive the results of the tests back much

more quickly than when psychologists do all of their own scoring and interpretation by hand;

2. It provides a consistent interpretative framework across clients; and
3. The computer can analyze and integrate a tremendous volume of information in making diagnostic, interpretive, and prescriptive statements, more so than can be done by any individual psychologist working without the aid of a computer.

Computer-assisted interpretation may be particularly important in forensic evaluations, as to counter claims that interpretations formulated by individual psychologists are biased.

Disadvantages are (McCullough & Miller, 2003):

1. Interpretation may be restricted to the test findings only, excluding the unique history of each respondent and all of the individual and environmental factors that may influence performance on tests (Bootzin & Acocella, 1988; Eyde et al., 1993); and
2. Validity studies about computer-based interpretations may be hard to find in the professional literature and/or remain unpublished because the interpretative framework developers may treat them as proprietary or the studies may be lacking altogether. The test-users' responsibility is "to determine both the strengths and weaknesses of interpretative test services and the appropriateness of reports for each application" (Eyde et al., 1993, p. 44). It is *never* appropriate for psychologists to substitute a computer-generated narrative for a comprehensive assessment report (McCullough & Miller, 2003).

Case Planning Considerations

Referring consumers should consider the following general guidelines when making case planning decisions that rely on psychologists' assessment findings, conclusions, and recommendations:

1. Case planning recommendations that are based on *multiple assessment sources, multiple assessment methods, and multiple settings in which the evaluation was conducted* provide a stronger basis for decision making with clients than assessments that rely only on a single method, single source, or single setting, whether it be a psychological test, a clinical interview, a behavior rating scale, or a client observation in a single setting (e.g., the psychologist's office).

2. Recommendations should be based on psychological assessment procedures and tests that are *used for the purpose for which they were designed*. Consumers should be wary of psychologists who claim special or unique diagnostic expertise in interpreting test results in ways other than what the test developers intended (Wodrich, 1997). For example, using cognitive achievement test results to diagnose personality disorder would be considered an improper (and unethical) use of test findings (Eyde et al., 1993).

3. All psychological tests contain measurement error. Quantitative scores should not be treated not as infallible measurements of underlying traits but, rather, as *probabilistic estimates* that a person's true abilities fall within a band of variation around the obtained score. The more reliable the scale, the narrower the band of variation will be (i.e., the smaller the error variation will be).

4. Given the potential impact of psychological assessments on individuals' lives, case planning decisions should be based, as much as possible, on reliable tests. Table 3.3 provides a practical rule that practitioners may wish to consider when evaluating the adequacy of a test's reliability, most often with reference to internal consistency. [Note: Reliability coefficients range from −1.0 to 0 to +1.0, and are usually reported as decimals or percentages (the decimal multiplied by 100). Higher positive numbers indicate greater internal consistency (Sapp, 2002).]

TABLE 3.3   Rules of Thumb for Desired Internal Consistency Reliabilities

INTENDED USE	DESIRED RELIABILITY
Decision making (e.g., classification, diagnosis, program placement)	.90 or higher
Screening	.80 or higher
Research	.70 or higher

Based on *Psychological Testing: A Practical Introduction*, by T. Hogan, 2003, New York: John Wiley & Sons; *Psychometric Theory*, 2nd edition, by J. C. Nunnally, 1978, New York: McGraw-Hill; and *Psychological and Educational Test Scores*, by M. Sapp, 2002, Springfield, IL: Charles C Thomas, Publisher.

As the uses of tests increase the potential to impact individuals' lives, so do expectations about the reliability of measures used to assess them. When the purpose is formative or experimental, such as often is the case in initial research efforts, a reliability of .70 may be deemed adequate. In the case of internal consistency estimates of reliability, this would suggest that about 70% of an individual's score on a test was attributed to "true score" variance and 30% was attributable to error. This is a relatively high degree of error and, while appropriate for some purposes, clearly is not desirable for the type of decision making that goes on in most treatment planning (Kayser & Lyon, 2000).

The bottom line is that the more important the case planning decision is in terms of impact on individuals' lives, the higher the reliability of individual tests has to be. In addition, the greater the impact the case planning decision has on the client's life, the greater is the requirement for the test to be *one of several sources* rather than the sole source involved in the assessment (Hogan, 2003).

5. Projective measures should not be stand-alone measures for classifying clients' functioning as abnormal or as evidence of psychopathology (Kline, 2000; Wodrich, 1997). Further, projective tests are difficult to interpret in the absence of understanding clients' intellectual abilities, particularly when these tests are used with children (Kayser, Silver, & Lyon, 2001). This suggests that assessments that utilize projective measures also include an appraisal of clients' intellectual abilities, to provide a context for understanding how test-takers are responding to the presentation of ambiguous stimuli.

6. There is a trade-off between the reliability and the length of a test (Kline, 2000). Shorter tests are often preferred in assessment practice because, as noted previously, psychological testing is time- and labor-intensive. Shorter psychological tests traditionally have been held to be less reliable than longer tests. Note, however, that newer methods of test scoring have suggested that, in some cases, shorter tests can be as reliable as longer tests (Sandoval, 1998). In the case of intelligence tests, a number of brief intelligence tests have been developed that have proven to be reliable and valid measures of cognitive abilities (Kaufman & Lichtenberger, 2002).

Referring professionals should be particularly wary of psychologists who offer recommendations based only on the *administration of selected subtests* (i.e., administering one or two subtests on verbal and nonverbal reasoning), and treat subtest results as if they are the reliable and valid equivalent to the findings that would be derived from completing the full test administration. Unfortunately, this is an assessment strategy advocated by some psychologists who work in the managed care industry (Werthman, 1995).

7. Finally, there is an important interaction between the empirical structure of tests or assessment instruments and the skill and competency of the evaluating psychologist. Carson (cited in Wolber & Carne, 1993) notes that psychologists who have great familiarity, practice experience, and expertise with certain assessment instruments are capable of assessment performances that far exceed the standards for the instruments themselves.

Additional Resources

A number of resources offer further information about psychological assessments and tests. The following list is divided into specialized resources that psychologists themselves likely would use, and those that might be of more general interest to referring professionals, though interested consumers may wish to consult the specialized resources directly.

1. Specialized resources on tests include comprehensive lists and reviews of published and unpublished tests, such as the current editions of books or online resources such as *Tests in Print*, *Mental Measurement Yearbook*, *Directory of Unpublished Experimental Mental Measures*, *ETS Test Collection*, and *Test Critiques* (Hogan, 2003). These resources are available in most university and large public libraries and can be found through test locator services on websites such as Educational Resources Information Center/Clearing House on Assessment and Evaluation (ERIC) at http://ericae.net; Buros Institute of Mental Measurement at University of Lincoln-Nebraska (www.unl.edu/buros/); or Educational Testing Service (http://www.ets.org).

   Also, there are numerous professional journals in which psychologists and researchers report the results of test development and reliability and validation studies. In addition, hundreds of books are devoted to single topics or tests, such as assessment of intelligence, personality, vocational interests, academic achievement, assessment of minority clients, and so forth.

2. General interest and/or nontechnical resources on psychological testing written primarily for nonpsychologists include *Psychological Testing: A Practical Introduction* (Hogan, 2003); *Psychological and Educational Test Scores: What are They?* (Sapp, 2002); and *Children's Psychological Testing: A Guide for Nonpsychologists* (Wodrich, 1997; Wodrich & Kush, 1990).

3. One manual written specifically for training psychologists in the use of tests also may be of great interest to referring professionals: *Responsible Test Use: Case Studies for Assessing Human Behavior* (Eyde et al., 1993) was developed by the Joint Committee on Testing Practices, formed by the American Counseling Association, American Psychological Association, American Speech-Language-Hearing Association, and National Association of School Psychologists. It presents a wide variety of case scenarios involving the uses and misuses of psychological testing, highlighting the general factors and specific elements involved in appropriate use of tests.

4. Two books specifically addressing the use of psychological assessments in treatment planning, research, and psychotherapy/mental health interventions are *The Use of Psychological Testing for Treatment Planning and Outcome Assessment* (Maruish, 1994), and *Psychological Assessment in Clinical Practice: A Pragmatic Guide* (Hersen, 2004).

Conclusion

This chapter has introduced the major concepts and methods involved in developing and using psychological and educational assessments and tests. Considerable attention has been devoted to the measurement of mental abilities, to illustrate some of the broader assumptions involved in psychological testing. Many similar debates surrounding constructs, evidence, testing strategies, and pragmatic applications can also be found in efforts to measure other human traits and behavior. Nearly all of the major constructs that are the focus of psychological assessments and testing (e.g., personality, psychopathology, cognition, emotions, and behavior) typically are characterized by fierce debates within psychology about how they should be conceptualized and measured, similar to the debates examined in this chapter about intelligence. Consumers, therefore, should keep in mind that these constructs (and their measures) are not intrinsically true or uncontrovertibly objective simply because numeric scores are attached to them.

The chapter also initiated a discussion of psychological assessment and testing of people from diverse cultures. This topic is continued in the next chapter.

Chapter 4

Psychological Evaluations of Multicultural Clients and Clients With Special Needs

Chapter Outline

*Psychological tests are
measures of behavior, and
to the extent that culture
affects behavior,
its influence is going to
be detected by tests.
Results from psychological
and educational diagnoses
made as result of
such testing data should
be treated with caution.*

(Hood & Johnson, 2002, p, 344)

T his chapter contin-
ues the topic intro-
duced in chapter 3 regard-

O V E R V I E W

ing psychological evaluations of clients from culturally and linguistically
diverse backgrounds. Although considerable attention is devoted here to
the psychological evaluation of those from racial and ethnic minority
groups, the chapter examines additional dimensions of multiculturalism,
such as age, gender, socioeconomic status, sexual orientation, and disabilities. A related topic—assessment of persons with special needs, such as
those with mental retardation, physical disabilities and impairments, and
those whose age and health status often requires specialized assessment
approaches—also is explored. The ethical principles and practice guidelines developed in psychology regarding culturally competent assessment
and intervention services are reviewed. A culturally competent practice
model of psychological evaluations is presented.

Demographic Profile of Multicultural and Special Needs Populations

Most helping professionals no doubt are aware of the increasing diversification both in society-at-large and in their client caseload. Demographic
trends noted in the 2000 census indicate that the United States is becoming increasingly more racially and ethnically diverse—with 67% of the
population identifying as White, 13% as African American, 13% as
Hispanic, 4.5% as Asian/Pacific Islander, 1.5% as American Indian or
Alaskan Native, and 7% as some other race (which includes individuals
belonging to multiple racial groups) (APA, 2002b).

Children of color are the most rapidly growing age group in the country, and by 2020 this group is expected to constitute 40% of the population under 19 years old (Friedman, 2001). One-seventh of all U.S. school-
aged children speak a language other than English at home (Sandoval,
Frisby, Geisinger, Scheuneman, & Grenier, 1998):

> Of these children, as many as 5.5 million, come to school without English-speaking skills. About 75% of these speak Spanish, and many others speak Vietnamese, Hmong, Cantonese, Cambodian, or Korean. (p. 3)

Another important demographic trend is the aging of the population, in the United States and throughout world. "In the United States, one person in seven [currently] is over 65, and by the year 2025, this figure will be one in five" (Hood & Johnson, 2002, p. 363). At present, more than 35 million persons are age 65 and older (Seligman, 2004).

Furthermore, the percentage of the population with disabilities is on the rise. According to Whiston (2000), nearly one-fifth of the population in the United States ages 15 years and older has some sort of physical disability. These include 2 million Americans with significant visual impairments, 15 to 16 million with reduced or impaired hearing, 150,000 with spinal cord injuries, and 5 million with epilepsy (Seligman, 2004).

The cultural diversification in society-at-large often does not match the cultural diversification in the helping professions, particularly in regard to race and ethnicity. Thus, when multicultural and special-needs clients are referred for psychological evaluations, they likely will be evaluated by psychologists who differ from them in one or more of the following cultural characteristics: race/ethnicity, gender, age, social class, sexual orientation, language, ability, and religion (APA, 2002b). Whether and how psychologists consider the impact of culture on clients' functioning greatly influences how the evaluation is conducted, the results that are reported, how they are interpreted, and the recommendations and services that subsequently may be provided.

Definition of Key Multicultural Terms

Before tackling the thorny complexities involved in psychological evaluations of multicultural and special-needs clients, we must define some of the key terms used in this chapter. Definitions are provided in three categories: general cultural concepts, specific cultural characteristics, and assessment-specific cultural concepts or issues. These definitions have been drawn from the psychology and professional literature, including the APA's (2002b) *Guidelines On Multicultural Education, Training, Research, Practice, and Organizational Change for Psychologists.*

General Cultural Concepts

Three important general concepts relevant for psychologists and referring professionals to consider in their work are as follows.

Culture

Culture refers to the shared way of life of any social group (Gopaul-McNicol & Armour-Thomas, 2002). In psychology there is no universally accepted definition of culture (Frisby, 1998). The concept generally refers to a "complex whole," encompassing the beliefs, values, customs, norms, religious and spiritual practices, childrearing and socialization patterns, languages, social institutions, and pattern of structured relationships within social groups. Culture implies a worldview that is both socially constructed and transmitted across generations in a fluid, dynamic, and continuous manner.

All persons are assumed to be cultural beings, sharing attributes in common with other members within the same culture, as well as having unique individual attributes that differ from others in the same culture (APA, 2002b). Societies and nations have many different types of culture configurations, ranging from those that are communal in nature to those that are more individualistic in nature.

Diversity

Diversity refers to the *multiplicities of individuals' social identities* that include: age, gender, sexual orientation, ability/disability status, socioeconomic status, race/ethnicity, language, education, religious and spiritual beliefs, work roles, family roles, and other cultural dimensions. In its broadest sense, the term *multiculturalism* has been used interchangeably with diversity to suggest the *multiple identities between and within people*. Multiculturalism also has been used more narrowly in psychology to refer specifically to the interactions between racial/ethnic groups in the United States (APA, 2002b).

Acculturation

Acculturation refers to changes in the original cultural pattern of groups that have continuous, direct contact with one another (Dana, 1993). Acculturation typically brings stress to all members of cultures in contact with one another (not just to members of the "culturally different" or "minority" cultural group). The term connotes a continuum of cultural pluralism or cultural integration, including (Dana, 1993):

assimilation—loss or relinquishment of the original culture;
biculturalism—integration of the retained original culture and acquisition of the dominant culture);
traditionalism—adherence to the original culture);
marginalization—original culture not retained and the dominant culture not accepted.

Stresses and strains can be experienced at any of the levels but seem to be more likely when individuals lose touch with their original culture or become marginalized by failing to achieve a coherent, cohesive, cultural identity.

Specific Cultural Characteristics

Within the context of these broad definitions, culture-specific terms are used to classify distinct groups of people, in terms of characteristics such as *race, ethnicity, gender, social class, sexual orientation,* and so forth. Psychologists often have used these terms loosely to describe and conceptualize human differences (Gopaul-McNicol and Armour-Thomas (2002). To use them with more precision, these terms are defined as follows:

- *Ethnicity:* the group mores and practices of one's culture of origin that provide a sense of belonging and identity (APA, 2002b).
- *Race:* a socially constructed phenomenon more than a biologically based one. Biologically, there is a very large similarity in the genetic make-up among people (on the order of 85%), with only 6% of the variation accounted for by differences *between races* (Samuda, 1998). Thus, there is no such thing as a pure race: "It is the way in which genes cluster and organize ... that differentiate people" (p. 56). As a socially constructed phenomenon, race is the category to which others assign individuals, based on their physical characteristics (e.g., skin color, type of hair) and the resulting generalizations and stereotypes about individuals in those categories (APA, 2002b).
- *Racial identity:* that portion of a person's worldview that is "shaped by societal attributions of value" ascribed to ethnic groups (i.e., based on the physical characteristic associated with perceived racial differences) (Dana, 1993, p. 117).

- *Social class:* also referred to as *socioeconomic status* (SES), a socially constructed term referring to a measure of prestige within a social group, usually based upon years of schooling completed, level of income, and occupation, either in a person's family-of-origin or through the person's individual attainment (Valencia & Suzuki, 2001).
- *Sexual orientation:* individuals' relationships with partners of the opposite sex, same sex, or both sexes involving sexual intimacy and affection (Berger & Kelly, 1995). Sexual orientation is a concept distinct from that of *gender identity* (a person's identification of himself or herself as male or female) and *gender roles* (a set of learned behavior regarding what generally is expected of males and females in society) (Comstock, 2005).
- *Disabilities:* some physical or cognitive impairment, usually long-lasting, which impacts individuals' functioning in settings such as home, school, and work. As a cultural characteristic, the term signifies one point on the ability/disability continuum. Given the longer lifespan of people in today's society, individuals are increasingly likely to experience a physical or cognitive impairment at some point during their lifetime (Ivey & Ivey, 2003). According to these authors, those of us who currently do not have any physical or cognitive impairment or limitation in functioning might think of ourselves, at best, as "temporarily abled!"

  Psychologists often are involved in making formal appraisals of disabilities, such as evaluating children's learning disabilities and other educational disabilities for placement in special education classrooms or evaluating whether adults' physical or mental disabilities render them unable to work and hence make them eligible for benefits under the Social Security Act (Gettinger & Koscik, 2001; Melton et al., 1997).

Assessment-Specific Cultural Concepts

When clients from multicultural backgrounds and/or those having special needs are seen for psychological evaluations, several additional assessment issues must be considered:

Accommodation

Accommodation is the "reasonable" modification or adaptation of psychological test materials and procedures in the assessment of individuals with disabilities, to ensure that the tests accurately measure what they purport to measure, such as a person's abilities, not simply the disability (unless the disability directly relates to the skills the test is designed to measure) (Hood & Johnson, 2002). Reasonable accommodation is mandated by several federal laws, such as the *Rehabilitation Act* of 1973, the *Americans with Disabilities Act* of 1990 (ADA), and the *Individuals with Disabilities Education Act* of 1997 (IDEA, reauthorized in 2004), and may take many forms, such as

- being tested in an accessible location;
- being given extra time on a test;
- having testing materials in large-type print or Braille (for visually impaired);
- receiving testing instructions on a prerecorded audiotape with amplified sound or in sign language rather than orally by the examiner (for hearing impaired);
- using adaptive devices as an alternative to paper/pencil responses or traditional computer keyboard (e.g., voice input, joystick, pneumatic controls, head pointers, simplified keyboards, Braille keyboards, etc.);
- having other accommodations designed or tailored to meet the individual's specific needs.

Bias

Bias refers to the *systematic* (or *nonrandom) error* that psychological tests may have, particularly those that measure intelligence and personality variables in multicultural clients, leading to (among other things) an underestimation of their cognitive abilities and/or an overestimation of the extent of emotional or behavioral disturbances. According to Reynolds and Kaiser (2003), the criticisms that standardized psychological tests are biased have centered on several areas of concern, such as

- inappropriate content of items on a test, in which some cultural groups have had an opportunity to learn but others have not;
- inappropriate standardization samples, which lack representation of people of color according to their proportion in the U.S. population;
- examiner and language bias (e.g., psychologists evaluating clients from racially and/or linguistically different backgrounds without recognizing those cultural differences);

- inequitable social consequences of test results, which further disadvantage racial and ethnic minority clients through labeling, self-fulfilling prophecies regarding ability to learn, and being programmed into less-challenging educational curricula or poorer quality schools;
- tests measuring different constructs in majority and non-majority populations (e.g., standardized intelligence tests were alleged to really be a measure of individuals' adhering to Caucasian, middle-class values rather than of their general ability to reason and solve problems); and
- test results differentially predicting a variety of outcomes, such as academic achievement, with greater accuracy for the dominant cultural group than for minority groups.

Cultural Loading

Cultural loading is the notion that the content of all tasks on psychological tests, whether verbal or nonverbal, is learned within a cultural context (Valencia & Suzuki, 2001). Cultural loading becomes particularly problematic when the cultural content of test items and the cultural background of the person being evaluated are not congruent. The greater the mismatch or incongruence, the more likely the test will be alleged to be culturally biased.

Equivalence

Equivalence is the degree to which the scores from translated or adapted versions of a standardized test can be compared (van de Vijver, 2003). As noted in chapter 3, a core tenet of psychological tests as "standardized instruments" is that all those taking the test have received uniform administration. Reasonable accommodation involving modification of materials or method of administration directly contradicts this principle: "When testing professionals make changes in either testing materials or in test administration, they are appreciably changing the nature of an examination" (Geisinger, 1998, p. 29).

Test users must determine whether specially accommodated versions of test are equivalent to the general forms of the examination. Further, cross-cultural equivalence of standardized tests cannot be assumed but must be demonstrated empirically through appropriate statistical techniques used in reliability, validity, and norming studies (Frisby, 1998).

Past and Present Controversies about Multicultural Assessment

The following summary is a brief history of the controversies surrounding the use of psychological tests to assess multicultural clients.

Origin of Intelligence Tests

Although the term "mental tests" was used as early as 1890, the origin of modern psychological tests can be dated to 1905, when Alfred Binet (a psychologist) and Theophile Simon (a physician) responded to the concern of French government officials about how to educate children with mental retardation in Paris public schools (Tulsky et al., 2003). They designed a brief intelligence test to determine which children could not benefit from instruction in a general classroom (Reynolds & Kaiser, 2003). Binet's concept of intelligence recognized the importance of individual learning styles, the affective component in learning, and the importance of assessing mental abilities using simple, everyday problems, unrelated to classroom instruction (Guthrie, 1976).

Binet viewed his test as being a reliable measure of *individual differences* in mental ability but cautioned about its limitation as a measure of *group differences* in intelligence, because the groups would have to have approximately the same environments and educational opportunities for the test scores to be considered valid. The Binet-Simon test was the first test to report scores in terms of *mental ages*—reflecting a hierarchical arrangement of cognitive tasks of increasing difficulty, corresponding to the expected chronological ages at which these abilities presumably were mastered.

Hereditary Views of Intelligence

Of the numerous translations of the Binet-Simon test, the test developed by Lawrence Terman at Stanford University in 1916 became the standard (the *Stanford-Binet Intelligence Scale*) (Terman, 1922). Terman's concept of intelligence was narrower than Binet's, focusing primarily on verbal and quantitative abilities. Terman introduced the concept of *intelligence quotient* (IQ) in which mental age was divided by chronological age, then multiplied by 100 to yield a single score as a measure of general intelligence. His views on group differences in mental abilities were race-based, emphasizing the role of heredity in intelligence.

> [Mental retardation] represents the level of intelligence which is very, very common among Spanish-Indians and Mexican families of the Southwest and also among the negoes [sic]. Their dullness seems to be racial. (Terman, quoted in Guthrie, 1976, p. 51)

Terman's work helped to provide the "scientific evidence" for the mental superiority of the white race, a position that predominated among psychologists well into the 1930s (Samuda, 1998). As noted by Valencia and Suzuki (2001), however, the standardization samples of the 1916, 1937, and 1960 versions of the Stanford-Binet included only white children, and not until 1972 "nearly six decades after the original Stanford-Binet intelligence test was developed, that minority children were included in the standardization sample" (p. 6).

The view of Terman and others on the hereditary basis of innate intelligence did not go completely unchallenged, however. Studies by Horace Mann Bond (an African American psychologist), George Sanchez (a Hispanic psychologist), and a small group of others (including some Caucasian psychologists) began to point out the cultural bias in existing testing instruments and practices (Guthrie, 1976). Sanchez emphasized the importance of language as an important variable in the assessment of intelligence.

Studies of Group Differences in Intelligence

During World War I, psychological testing of intelligence became widespread. The intelligence tests developed for the U.S. Army introduced *Form Alpha*, primarily a verbal test for English-speakers who were literate, and *Form Beta*, primarily a nonverbal test for non-English-speakers/limited-English speakers and those who were illiterate. These two forms are the forerunners of the *verbal* and *performance* subtests on later intelligence scales, such as the Wechsler instruments.

Numerous psychology studies of group differences of intelligence emerging from this era revealed that the mean score of African Americans was one standard deviation below the score of whites. The findings were interpreted as evidence that one race was genetically superior to another race in terms of their innate intelligence. As noted earlier, this interpretation rested upon an unequivocal belief that mental traits in people are inherited and fixed, are not altered by environmental forces, and remain unchanged over the course of a person's development (Samuda, 1998).

Environmental Factors and Intelligence

A contrasting interpretation arising in the 1960s was that *environmental factors* accounted for the major difference in test scores (Samuda, 1998). Proponents argued that rich, stimulating environments provide more opportunities and reinforcement for learning than environments characterized by poverty, poor nutrition, social deprivation, inadequate schooling, and lack of educational opportunities. These negative environmental forces were seen as decreasing the opportunities and motivation of racial and ethnic minority individuals to learn. Thus, differences in motivation and opportunity, not innate differences in intelligence, were considered to have the greatest influence on minority clients' lower performance on standardized measures of intellectual ability and academic performance.

This interpretation subsequently has been criticized as ethnocentric, but because the dominant, privileged culture was assumed to be the norm or standard for comparison, all other cultures by default were assumed to be deficient or defective in some manner (Sue, 1980). Also, the interpretation conveniently omitted attention to the low expectations that educators, school officials, and others in positions of power may have had regarding the cognitive abilities and potentials of individuals from disadvantaged groups. As a result, members of racial and ethnic minority groups continued to be victimized through negative labeling and the low demand for educational competency.

Criticism of Standardized Tests

In the 1960s, attention began to be directed to the testing instruments themselves as sources of bias (Dana, 1993). Psychological assessment instruments that had been widely used for decades (primarily, the original versions of the Stanford-Binet, the Wechsler child and adult intelligence scales, and the MMPI) came under severe criticism because their standardization samples did not include people of color. As a result, people of color had been consistently and falsely pathologized—with deficits in intelligence and elevated scores of pathology compared to whites— because the norms upon which these tests were based were applied incorrectly to members of different cultural groups (Samuda, 1998).

The criticism of standardized objective testing as biased instruments spread to other widely used instruments, such as the *Scholastic Aptitude Test* (SAT), used as part of the criteria for determining admission to college. The SAT was criticized for denying ethnic and racial minority individuals opportunities equal to whites to advance in society.

Legal Challenges to the Use of Intelligence Tests

Major court challenges to the use of standardized intelligence tests to determine school placement for minority children were launched in the 1970s in California and Illinois. The suits alleged that "improper assessment with IQ tests led to over-representation in classes for the educable mentally retarded, handicapped, of linguistically different minority children" (Wodrich & Kush, 1990, p. 204).

In the California suit the court found that IQ tests such as the *Wechsler Intelligence Scale for Children-Revised* (WISC-R) were biased against minority children, and issued a ban against its use along with other intelligence tests by California school systems (*Larry P. et al. v Wilson Riles et al.*, 1974–1979). In the Chicago suit the court ruled just the opposite, the intelligence tests were not biased against black children, and thus their use was permitted by school systems [*Parents in Action on Special Education (PASE) v Hannon*, J., 1980)]. As a result, the Association of Black Psychologists and other groups called for a moratorium on psychological testing of minority-group children. The call for a moratorium was controversial itself because it left decisions about the educational placement of children with mental retardation to the subjective judgments of teachers and school officials (Sharma, 1986). Further, the exclusive focus on testing bias in the court decisions did not address the failure of these school systems to develop effective educational programs for these populations of students (Gopual-McNicol & Armour-Thomas, 2002).

Restandardization of Tests

As a result of these criticisms, the profession of psychology enacted rigorous empirical standards ensuring representativeness of the normative sample in constructing new psychological tests. (These standards are discussed in chapter 3.) For example, the MMPI, the Wechsler intelligence scales, and the Stanford-Binet all were restandardized subsequently to include the representation of people of color. The success of those revisions, however, continues to be a subject of debate (Dana, 1993, 2000; Roberts & DeBlassie, 1983; Samuda, 1998). For example, using census-based standardization samples (i.e., race/ethnicity groupings included in strict proportion to their distribution in the U.S. population) actually yields low numbers of people (Valencia & Suzuki, 2001).

In one instance, a census-based standardization sample totaling 1,700 people ranging in age from 2 to 20 years, would yield approximately 1,100 Caucasians, 280 African Americans, 200 Hispanics, 50 Asians, and 20 American Indians. As a result, a number of test developers are moving to "over-sampling procedures" to increase the chances of attaining a normal distribution of scores for each race/ethnic group. Using small numbers of people of color in census-based standardization samples makes it difficult to include representation of gifted and talented minority individuals whose scores are more likely to fall in the upper range of the distribution (one to two standard deviations above the mean).

Investigations of Bias in Tests

The allegations of test bias in standardized tests, particularly in standardized intelligence and achievement tests used in assessing minority clients, became the subject of multiple investigations and intense debate within psychology in the 1970s and 1980s. This debate also was intertwined with a revival of the controversies surrounding the contribution of *nature* (the notion that intelligence is based largely on hereditary endowment) versus *nurture* (the notion that intelligence is based on the quality of the social environment and the opportunity to learn). [This debate is reviewed separately below.]

As summarized by Reynolds and Kaiser (2003), taken as a group, the studies of test bias have supported the conclusion that bias in content validity, construct validity, and predictive (criterion-related) validity of measures of intelligence is rare, has no discernable pattern, and that differences in test scores across racial categories are real and not an artifact of test bias. According to Frisby (1998):

> Comprehensive reviews of standardized cognitive ability tests have indicated that well-developed instruments are not biased when properly used with native-born English-speaking groups such as African Americans. (p. 65)

Several minority investigators strongly dispute the broad sweep of that conclusion. In a detailed critique of studies of intelligence tests supporting the "no bias" conclusion, Valencia and Suzuki (2001) note that

- most of these studies have concentrated primarily on the Wechsler intelligence scales (particularly the original WISC and its successor, WISC-R), to the exclusion of most other standardized instruments;

- most of the comparisons between racial groups have been between African Americans and Caucasians, and other minority groups have been studied far less frequently;
- mean score differences in IQ between racial groups are much less than a standard deviation when the samples are matched on socioeconomic status (SES), and would likely be even lower with more refined matching; and
- while acknowledging that the bulk of studies on standardized intelligence tests shows them as unbiased, a sufficiently large number of studies yield mixed findings (showing some type of testing bias); this indicates that the "no bias conclusion" cannot be accepted as categorically or conclusively correct.

Alternative Forms of Assessing Cultural Influences on Intelligence

Between the 1940s and the late 1970s several attempts were made to develop alternative means of assessing intelligence, either independent of cultural influences or moving in the opposite direction, with explicit attention to culture. Representative of the first approach is the *Culture-Free Intelligence Test*, subsequently retitled the *Culture Fair Test of Intelligence* (Cattell, 1940, 1959). An example of the second approach is Mercer's (1979) *System of Multicultural Pluralistic Assessment* (SOMPA), designed to compare individuals within their own sociocultural background.

Subsequently these instruments were criticized on a number of grounds (Dana, 1993; Gopaul-McNicol & Armour-Thomas, 2002; Roberts & DeBlassie, 1983; Samuda, 1998):

- the impossibility of isolating tests of general ability from the effects of culture;
- the confusion of culture with the conditions of the social environment;
- the difficulty in separating local norms for the various ethnic/racial groups;
- the difficulty with the heavy reliance of some tests on verbal instructions in English, which presented difficulties for test-takers with limited English proficiency; and

- the amount of time needed to administer instruments such as SOMPA, as well as the amount of time needed to train examiners.

Problems with Projective Personality Tests

Problems have arisen, too, with the use of projective measures such as sentence-completion tests, story/picture cards, and inkblot tests with multicultural clients, leading to what Dana (1993) has called an "interpretive fiasco" (p. 147). The problems include lack of culturally relevant stimuli, lack of representative sampling in constructing norms, and failure to distinguish cultural-specific ways of responding to ambiguous stimuli from psychopathology. There has been a marked lack of attention to issues of race and ethnicity in the major works on and scoring systems developed for the *Rorschach*, based, in part, on the assumption that the nature of ambiguous stimuli of the inkblot cards precludes cultural bias (Gray-Little and Kaplan, 1998).

Some older projective measures, such as the *Thematic Apperception Test* (TAT), have developed adaptations for different racial and ethnic groups, but the low response rates to both the original and the adapted versions have continued to be a concern. More recently, projective measures have been developed specifically for blacks (*Themes Concerning Blacks*) and Hispanics (*Tell-Me-A-Story*) (TEMAS) that have shown some promise as appropriate for individuals with those backgrounds who live in urban settings. The comfort and acceptance of multicultural clients in the testing situation, the level of their education and degree of acculturation, and the examiners' skill in building rapport seem to influence heavily the quantity and quality of responses to projective testing.

Problems with Objective Personality Tests

Similarly, standardized objective personality inventories, such as the *MMPI*, the *MMPI-2* and newer instruments such as the *Millon Clinical Multiaxial Inventory* (MCMI), have been criticized as culturally biased. As reviewed by Gray-Little and Kaplan (1998), a number of studies indicated that African Americans frequently scored higher than whites on the *MMPI* and *MMPI-2* scales measuring schizophrenia and hypomania, resulting in overdiagnosing severe psychopathology in blacks. In contrast, other investigators (Hood & Johnson, 2002) have concluded that these standardized personality inventories can be used appropriately with African Americans). It is important to note that the majority of these studies involve black–white comparisons, with few studies of other racial groups.

Nature Versus Nurture Debate

As noted earlier, the race-based position on the hereditary nature of intelligence was widely held during the first half of the 20th century. In the later part of the 20th century, it was revived by Arthur Jensen (1969, 1980), Lloyd Dunn (1987, 1988), and more recently by Richard Herrnstein and Charles Murray's (1994) controversial book, *The Bell Curve: Intelligence and Class Structure in American Life*.

In the view of these authors, differences in intelligence scores between racial groups reflect real differences between racial groups, in which Caucasians are seen as the intellectually superior group compared to African Americans and Hispanics. Jensen (1980) dismissed criticism that standardized tests are biased (because they consistently have shown differences in intelligence between racial groups) as an "egalitarian fallacy"—a naive belief that all human population groups have identical mental traits and abilities. To other investigators, these views are nothing short of racist. In their view, unequal scores on intelligence tests do not reflect differences in mental abilities of different racial groups but, rather, the reality that the groups hold unequal positions in society (Gopaul-McNicol & Armour-Thomas, 2002; Samuda, 1998; Valencia & Suzuki, 2001).

Psychological Testing in Special Education

Another significant development was the passage of landmark special education legislation, the *Education for All Handicapped Children's Act* of 1975—amended in 1990, 1997, and 2002, and now known as the *Individuals with Disabilities Education Act* (IDEA, 2004), which mandates a comprehensive assessment as a requirement to determine eligibility for special education services. This places school psychologists in a lead role in identifying students' educational difficulties such as learning disabilities, mental retardation, speech and language disabilities, and significant emotional or behavioral problems (Riccio & Hughes, 2001). Despite the requirements of these special education laws that children be assessed with nonbiased instruments and that testing be conducted in their native language or other mode of communication, the overrepresentation of racial and ethnic minority group children in special education programs remains a serious concern (Sandoval & Irvin, 2003).

Allegations of Gender Bias

Although most of the heated discussion and debate about cultural bias has been directed to the allegations of testing bias against racial and ethnic minority clients, additional concerns have been raised about gender bias within psychology (Hood & Johnson, 2002). The gender-bias studies have emphasized measures of aptitude, personality, and vocational interest. In general, intelligence tests do not show significant differences between men and women. On specific aptitude tests, however, women tend to score higher on verbal abilities, and men higher on quantitative reasoning. This finding has sparked the same type of controversy and debate discussed earlier regarding the evaluation of racial and ethnic minorities—whether these test results are the product of inherent differences between men and women or a result of unequal opportunities to learn and stereotypic attitudes on the part of parents and teachers regarding the math and science skills of females. Gender bias also was noted in some vocational-interest inventories, such as wording that used only masculine pronouns and portrayed stereotypical occupations for each gender. Test developers subsequently have eliminated most of these items.

Apart from concerns about the instruments themselves, a more germane consideration is how tests are used. This becomes a major issue when evaluating psychologists have unrecognized attitudes of sexism and patriarchy. Consider the following egregious example: In the 1970s and 1980s a nationally known child-protection training and research center published a widely used handbook (Schmidt, 1978) that included a chapter on the psychological evaluation of child-maltreatment cases (Bond, 1978). In one case, teenage parents (the father was age 19, and the mother was age 16) had a 6-month-old daughter who was hospitalized for multiple bruises and fractures. The father claimed that the injuries were inadvertent, a result of his playing too roughly with his daughter. Both parents reported that they argued frequently, particularly about the wife's lack of interest in sex and her inability to organize the household.

A male psychologist saw the 16-year-old mother for individual psychological testing, which included a clinical interview, an intelligence test, a personality test, and a projective test. Results from the evaluation revealed that the mother was in the low–average range of intelligence. Projective testing (the Rorschach) indicated that mother's personality was passive and overly compliant. Her submissive behavior with her husband was seen as evidence of a dependent personality disorder. Based on the psychologist's report, the child-abuse team recommended that the daughter remain in out-of-home placement, that the parents be seen in marital therapy, and that *the mother be seen for individual therapy to resolve her sexual difficulties* [italics added].

Seen in the light of present-day feminist thinking regarding the pervasiveness of sexism and patriarchy in society, this case example reveals clear gender bias by the male examiner, who conducted no separate testing of the father, did not evaluate the father's potential for physical violence toward mother or child, did not address the 3-year age difference between the teen parents or question whether the pregnancy and marriage truly were consensual, and apparently accepted without question the teen father's assertion that the cause of the marital difficulties was the wife's lack of interest in sex.

Controversies Surrounding Annual Educational Testing

More recently, criticisms alleging bias also have been made against annual, mandated "high-stakes" educational testing, such as that required by the federal government's *No Child Left Behind Act* (2001), as well as by many states. These policies require local school districts to measure elementary and secondary education students' proficiencies in reading, math, writing, and science (Heubert, 2000). Particularly when single test scores are used to evaluate students' proficiencies, this approach may have harmful effects on racial and ethnic minority students, who either may be retained in a grade or be placed in lower-performing tracks.

Assessment of Intelligence and Personality in Multicultural Clients

While the above history highlights significant problems in the development, use, and interpretation of results from psychological tests with minority clients, substantial efforts within the profession of psychology to develop nonbiased means of evaluating intelligence, achievement, and personality must be acknowledged.

The case scenario illustrates some of the major variables that potentially must be considered in the psychological evaluations of multicultural clients. As discussed below, these variables include *client characteristics*, *assessment instruments*, *evaluator characteristics*, and the *context* or *setting* of the evaluation. All of these variables may interact with each other.

Case Scenario 4.1

An Anglo American psychologist, Dr. Gerald Johnson, is meeting for the first time with a new patient, Denise, age 35, an enrolled member of the Lakota tribe who recently was admitted to an inpatient psychiatric hospital because of apparent psychotic symptoms. The referral for psychological assessment was made jointly by the inpatient social worker and the attending psychiatrist, who requested help in arriving at an accurate diagnosis regarding Denise's symptoms, which seem to include both disturbances in thinking and disturbances in mood.

The patient reported a history of alcoholism, although she stated that she has been sober for the past 3 months. Denise grew up on a Lakota reservation in the northern, rural part of the state. For the past 17 years, however, she has lived in an urban area, and only recently reestablished regular contact with other tribal members.

Dr. Johnson decided to administer a standardized structured personality–psychopathology inventory designed to differentially diagnose symptoms of mood disorder, thought disorder, and alcoholism. He began the interview by asking Denise if she speaks Lakota.

After a lengthy hesitation, she replied, speaking slowly: "I know...some words."

Dr. Johnson then began the clinical assessment: "Now I'm going to ask you some questions that may seem a little bit strange. If you don't want to answer some of them, that's okay. We'll just skip them and move on."

The first introductory question on the standardized instrument is designed to gather some basic demographic information: "What was the highest grade you've achieved?"

After a delay of several seconds, Denise replied slowly: "I graduated...from...high school."

As Dr. Johnson recorded this answer on the form, Denise waited patiently. Just before he was able to ask another question, she added: "I went... to....community college."

Dr. Johnson frowned and began erasing the first answer. After the new information was recorded, Denise added: "I transferred...to...art school...in the city."

Puzzled at the changing information, Dr. Johnson attempted to clarify the information: "How far did you get in college?"

After another lengthy pause, Denise replied: "I went...through...my junior year."

Looking somewhat surprised, Dr. Johnson erased the previously recorded response yet again. Glancing at his watch, he worried that he would not be able to complete the examination of Denise during the time originally allotted.

Consideration of each variable generates a variety of useful *cultural hypotheses* that may be clinically relevant in understanding clients' current functioning and in developing appropriate treatment plans. Failing to consider these hypotheses likely will result in misdiagnosis as well as the delivery of culturally inappropriate and potentially harmful services.

Client Variables

Among the relevant client characteristics are Denise's race and ethnicity, extent of acculturation into (or integration with) the dominant culture, gender, social class, and education, as well as her current mental status and recent health and medication history. These variables would have to be considered in determining whether, among other issues, her slow, delayed manner of providing information

- is a culturally mediated communication style (e.g., telling a story in an unfolding manner of a journey taken rather than stating only the factual end-point in her educational attainment, as might be more customary with a Western European/Anglo American linear thinker);
- is a manifestation of her anxiety at being with an unfamiliar male in a position of power;
- is an expressive/receptive language problem;
- indicates the presence of active psychotic symptoms that are interfering with her current mental status orientation to person, place, or time;
- is a possible indication of the effects of medication; or
- is the lingering effect of recent intoxication.

Other relevant client variables might include Denise's test-taking abilities in general, and specific previous experience or exposure to psychological testing, test anxiety, and general level of self-esteem. Ascertaining which of these variables are relevant for this client would provide useful direction to the treatment planning process.

Instrument Variables

Consideration of relevant instrument characteristics address the following question: To what extent is the standardized clinical instrument chosen by the psychologist a unbiased instrument, appropriate for use with American

Indian clients? As noted earlier, standardized instruments may have a variety of bias problems including item selection, content bias, scoring norms, administration, and interpretation. Thus, the basic question is whether this instrument has been empirically validated with members of one or more Indian tribal groups. In this particular case, Dr. Johnson would want to know whether the standardization sample included members of the Lakota tribe.

In addition, given the specific referral question the psychological assessment is attempting to answer, it is of paramount importance to know whether the instrument differentiates shared cultural or religious beliefs among American Indian peoples from psychotic delusions or thought disorders. Some standardized instruments pose difficulties for certain American Indian clients who are not used to the subtleties in probe questions and/or who have cultural differences in time perception (Dana, 1993). Modification in administration may be required before this instrument could be considered an appropriate, nonbiased choice. These limitations suggest the importance of Dr. Johnson not relying on results from a single instrument to determine Denise's mental health diagnosis.

Interviewer Variables

> Knowing the culture in which clients must live, survive, and find a place is as essential as knowing their test scores…. In the final analysis, the assessor is more crucial to the assessment process than the instruments, especially the psychological tests. (Sharma, 1986, p. 114)

Relevant interviewer variables in the vignette include Dr. Johnson's own cultural background. Many professional helpers who come from the dominant Anglo American culture in society lack awareness of themselves as racial and ethnic beings, and thus may be insensitive to the influence of cultural variables in others (Cooper & Lesser, 2002).

It is unclear whether Dr. Johnson has knowledge of Denise's tribal culture or whether he perceives himself as grounded in a cultural worldview and racial/ethnic heritage of his own. Possible cultural insensitivity might be inferred from his perfunctory attempt at building rapport; his expectation that asking objective questions will be answered using the same Western European linear thinking and communication style that he uses customarily; his unfamiliarity with the storytelling approach Denise is using to communicate her information; Dr. Johnson's apparently preconceived negative expectations about her level of education (e.g., seemingly surprised that she had completed 3 years of college); and failure to adjust his timeframe for completing the clinical instrument and other assessment tasks to the client's conceptualization of time and tasks.

Context Variables

Relevant context or setting variables include the testing situation itself, and both short- and longer-term organizational and institutional factors in the inpatient unit that may affect a client's performance. The testing situation can be problematic for culturally diverse clients, who may lack familiarity with test-taking skills, such as the need to work rapidly and steadily (Roberts & DeBlassie, 1983). Short-term organizational factors are those present at the time of the client's admission to the psychiatric unit (i.e., the amount of staff, work load, and degree of patient acuity).

In the case scenario the evaluation seems rushed. This suggests that contextual factors at the time of the evaluation may account in part for Denise's slow response style. Tests administered to persons of color by unfamiliar Anglo American examiners typically produce responses of caution, vagueness, and restricted storytelling (Dana, 1993). Longer-term institutional factors also may be relevant here, including the extent to which the inpatient hospital demonstrates a commitment to providing culturally competent services to its multicultural patients, such as by hiring and training a culturally diverse staff.

Assessment of Clients with Special Needs

Psychological evaluations are widely used with a diverse array of clients who have special needs. These include individuals with physical impairments, disabilities, and handicaps resulting from injury or disease; cognitive delays or mental retardation; memory loss, cognitive confusion, or dementia, or whose age status requires specialized assessment procedures. Space considerations permit only a brief discussion of these topics.

Before proceeding, two important points should be made.

1. Individuals with special needs are multidimensional human beings and should be assessed as such, using an array of measures that capture their strengths and capacities, help to identify areas of distress or dysfunction, and are sensitive to the cultural dimensions of health beliefs and practices.

2. Psychologists working in these areas require special training and competencies over and above the general ones listed in chapter 2.

Physical Impairments, Disabilities, and Handicaps

Psychologists working in health clinics, hospitals, and rehabilitation centers are familiar with the World Health Organization (WHO) distinctions among impairment, disability, and handicap (Heinemann, 2000).

- *Impairment*: the loss or abnormal functioning of some integral component of the body, whether from physical or psychological origins.
- *Disability* (or *disablement*): effects of the impairment on an individual's performance and behavior in daily life, which have both intrapersonal and environmental components.
- *Handicap*: effects of the impairment on the fulfillment of social roles, such as employment or school performance.

Psychologists may work with a vast range of health conditions—spinal cord injuries, traumatic brain injuries, brain tumors, limb amputation, chronic pain, vision and hearing losses, neuromuscular and musculoskeletal disorders, multiple sclerosis, burn injuries, and so on (Frank & Elliot, 2000; Hooper & Baglio, 2001). Psychological evaluations may be used narrowly, to assess the severity of the impairment in terms of an individual's ability to perform activities in daily living, and more broadly, to assess his or her perceptions of the quality of life (which includes identifying social support, emotional well-being, energy level, degree of pain, spiritual beliefs, and so forth).

Evaluation measures may include

- clinical interviews;
- behavioral observations;
- regular or adapted versions of standardized tests of intelligence, aptitude, and achievement;
- neuropsychological tests;
- objective measures of personality (discussed in chapter 3).

Individuals with chronic health conditions might be assessed for co-occurring depression or substance abuse, which could slow their recovery or adjustment to their disability. In addition, assessments might try to identify instructional strategies or vocational assistance that may improve patients' performance in school or work settings. Psychologists also may be involved in patient and parent/family education to maximize individuals' abilities and potentials and to assess patients' pain management and adherence to prescribed rehabilitation protocols and medications (Brown & Macias, 2001).

Cognitive Delays and Mental Retardation

Mental retardation is not assessed on the basis of intelligence testing alone but includes an evaluation of *adaptive behavior*—individuals' competence to meet the natural and social demands of their environment (Hood & Johnson, 2002). The American Association of Mental Retardation (AAMR) has defined mental retardation as

> substantial limitation in present functioning...characterized by significantly sub-average intellectual functioning, existing concurrently with related limitations in two or more adaptive skill areas: communication, self-care, home living, social skills, community use, self-direction, health and safety, functional academics, leisure and work [that is] manifested before age 18 years. (AAMR, 1992, p. 5)

Sub-average intelligence in defined as two standard deviations below the mean on an individually administered intelligence test (Burns, 2003). On the widely used Wechsler intelligence scales, this would mean a Full Scale IQ below 70. Recall the discussion from Chapter 2 regarding the "normal curve" distribution of abilities, and the presence of random measurement error inherent in all psychological tests. Interpretation of any IQ score takes into account the statistical probability that an individual's *true score* falls within a band of scores above or below the obtained score.

The definition in the fourth edition of the American Psychiatric Association's *Diagnostic and Statistical Manual of Mental Disorders* (DSM-IV-TR) (American Psychiatric Association, 2000) separates mental retardation into four categories, based on severity of intellectual impairment (as measured by IQ):

mild retardation	=	50–55 to 70
moderate retardation	=	35–40 to 50–55
severe retardation	=	20–25 to 35–40
profound retardation	=	below 20 or 25

Suspected mild or moderate mental retardation can be appropriately diagnosed using standardized intelligence tests such as the *Wechsler Preschool and Primary Scale of Intelligence* (WPPSI), the *Wechsler Intelligence Scale for Children, Fourth Edition (WISC-IV)*, the *Differential Abilities Scales* (DAS), and the *Bayley Scales of Infant Development, Second Edition*. But few instruments are available for assessing individuals with severe mental retardation (Burns, 2003). Sandler and Hatt (2004) note that evaluators may have to distinguish between mental retardation and severe speech and language deficits, and might employ nonverbal measures of intelligence and measures of nonverbal intelligence such as the *Comprehensive Test of Nonverbal Intelligence* (CTONI), the *Universal Nonverbal Intelligence Test* (UNIT), or the *Leiter International Performance Scale*.

In addition, these authors recommend the use of a second measure of intelligence, based on newer theories of intelligence that incorporate multiple abilities and information-processing strategies, to reduce the risk of bias when evaluating clients from culturally or linguistically diverse populations. This might include the nonverbal measures mentioned above, as well as the *Differential Abilities Scales* (DAS).

A number of norm-referenced measures of adaptive behavior are available, such as the *Vineland Adaptive Behavior Scales*, which enlist parents and teachers as informants to rate adaptive skills in the home, school, and community. Adaptive behaviors encompass conceptual, social, and practical skills. Sandler and Hatt (2004) caution, however, that "cultural variables should be taken into account when evaluating adaptive behavior, as the value placed on independent functioning is sometimes culturally influenced" (p. 329). Those authors further suggest that a variety of additional measures be used to assess adaptive behaviors, including clinical interviews; structured observations in the home, school, or other natural settings; social skills training; and direct testing of adaptive behaviors.

Mental health problems such as anxiety, depression, and conduct disorders can co-occur in individuals with mental retardation. Psychologists may employ clinical interviews with parents and caregivers, as well as special rating scales developed for clients with mental retardation. Other assessment procedures used with moderate to severely retarded individuals include conducting a functional behavioral assessment to identify what stimulates and maintains problematic behaviors, such as biting and head banging (Burns, 2003). Psychological evaluations can also contribute information by identifying sources of support currently available for individuals with mental retardation, as well as evaluating the impact of additional supports on clients' functioning.

Assessment of Older Adults

The elderly population can be divided roughly into two subgroups—the "younger old" (ages 60 to 79) and the "older old" (age 80 and up)—each having different health profiles and treatment needs (Lichtenberg & MacNeill, 2000). Some studies suggested that younger-old clients had more severe co-occurring health problems than the older-old clients, including elevated rates of depression and alcohol use. In contrast, older-old clients seem to comprise a group that maintained good health throughout their 60s and 70s but whose current health problems are attributable to the frailties of advanced age.

Psychologists may be involved in

- assessing the ability of elderly clients from either group to recover from illness, injury, or stroke;
- assessing the onset of memory loss, cognitive confusion, dementia, and Alzheimer's;
- assessing preexisting psychological disorders prior to the onset of illness or injury;
- assessing depression and drug/alcohol use related to declining health and functioning.

Assessment measures may include the *Mini-Mental State Examination*, the *Clinical Assessment Scales for the Elderly*, the *Wechsler Memory Scale, Third Edition*, and other assessment measures that can be filled out by clients or a knowledgeable relative or caregiver (Hood & Johnson, 2002; Lichtenberg & MacNeill, 2000).

Ethical Consideration and Practice Guidelines in Multicultural Assessment

Now we turn to an examination of the ethical considerations and practice guidelines for psychologists who work with multicultural clients, defined here as those from racial and ethnic minority groups, and with gay, lesbian, and bisexual clients. Korman (as quoted in Gopaul-McNicol & Armour-Thomas, 2002, p. 25) states unequivocally that

> the provision of professional [psychological] services to persons of culturally diverse backgrounds by persons not competent in understanding and providing professional services to such groups shall be considered unethical.

Dana (2000) uses the term *cultural malpractice* to refer to bias in providing psychological services when scientific methodology and statistics are used to make comparisons about diverse social groups exclusively from a Euro-American perspective. Building upon these broad ethical considerations are specific practice guidelines for working with racially and ethnically diverse clients, and with gay, lesbian, and bisexual clients.

Racially and Ethnically Diverse Clients

In 1992 APA developed its first set of practice guidelines for psychologists working with ethnic, linguistic, and culturally diverse populations (APA, 1992a). This was a relatively brief document, setting forth nine general principles primarily involving practice issues. In 2002 APA developed a new set of six guidelines in a considerably longer document, addressing not only clinical practice issues but also the implications of race and ethnicity in the education and training of psychologists, psychological research, and organizational change (APA, 2002b).

The difference between these sets of practice guidelines is striking. Whereas the 1992 guidelines are largely client-focused, the 2002 guidelines address more explicitly the problematic history of psychology in working with multicultural clients from a traditional Western, Eurocentric perspective. Psychologists now are encouraged to place themselves in the story—recognizing themselves as cultural beings, acknowledging the possibility of cultural bias in their work, committing themselves to lifelong learning about individuals and groups that are culturally different from themselves, and dedicating themselves to seeking organizational and societal change in the service of the ideals of equity and social justice. The 2002 practice guidelines are summarized below (APA, 2002b). [The full text of these guidelines is available on the APA website: www.apa.org]

1. Psychologists' self-understanding should include the recognition that they are cultural beings, whose attitudes and beliefs may negatively influence their perceptions of and interactions with individuals who are ethnically and racially different from themselves.
2. Psychologists should increase their multicultural sensitivity, knowledge, and understanding of individuals who are ethnically and racially different from themselves.
3. Psychologists should be exposed to the constructs of multiculturalism and diversity in their professional education and training.

4. Psychologists should conduct research among persons from ethnic, linguistic, and racial minority backgrounds in a culture-centered and ethical manner.
5. Psychologists should use culturally appropriate skills in their practice.
6. Psychologists should be advocates for developing culturally informed organizational policies and practices.
7. Psychologists should consider whether adverse social, environmental, and political factors have had an impact on clients when assessing problems and designing interventions.
8. Psychologists should work to eliminate biases, prejudices, and discriminatory practices.
9. Psychologists working with culturally diverse populations should document in their reports culturally and sociopolitical relevant factors that appear to be affecting clients' functioning.

Gay, Lesbian, and Bisexual Clients

The APA developed a separate set of practice guidelines for working with lesbian, gay, and bisexual clients (APA, 2002c). [The full text can be obtained from the APA website: www.apa.org] Though addressing psychotherapy practice specifically, the guidelines seem to have a broader application to other practice areas as well because they conceptualize psychological assessments as part of the treatment planning process.

1. Psychologists' *attitudes and knowledge* about lesbian, gay, and bisexual issues may be relevant to assessment and treatment. Whether their view of homosexuality or bisexuality is accurate or prejudicial may affect the client's presentation in treatment and the therapeutic process. First, psychologists must recognize that homosexuality and bisexuality are not indicative of mental illness. When indicated, psychologists should seek consultation or make appropriate referrals, being aware that social stigmatization (prejudice, discrimination, and violence) poses risks to the mental health and well-being of lesbian, gay, and bisexual clients.
2. Psychologists should be knowledgeable about and respect lesbian, gay, and bisexual *relationships*, which may include relationships with partners, children, and parents, and members of an individual's family of origin. For example, lesbian, gay, and bisexual parents may face unique obstacles and challenges in childrearing. The families of lesbian, gay, and bisexual people may include those who are not legally

or biologically related. A person's homosexual or bisexual orientation may have an impact on his or her family-of-origin and the relationship with that family of origin.

Psychologists should recognize the unique life issues or challenges facing lesbian, gay, and bisexual members of racial and ethnic minorities, which are often related to multiple and often conflicting cultural norms, values, and beliefs. Psychologists also should understand the challenges facing bisexual individuals; the special problems and risks for lesbian, gay, and bisexual youth; the generational differences and challenges of lesbian, gay, and bisexual older adults; and the challenges of lesbian, gay, and bisexual individuals who have physical, sensory, and/or cognitive/emotional disabilities.

3. Psychologists' *professional education and training* should include content on lesbian, gay, and bisexual issues. Psychologists should expand their knowledge and understanding of homosexuality and bisexuality through continuing education, training, supervision, and consultation. Psychologists should be familiar with relevant mental health, educational, and community resources for lesbian, gay, and bisexual people.

These guidelines build upon the 1975 APA statement that homosexuality per se is not a psychological impairment or a mental health disorder (Bohman, 1996). The guidelines note that "an extensive body of literature has emerged that identifies few significant differences between heterosexual, homosexual, and bisexual people on a wide range of psychological functioning" (APA, 2002c, p. 3). But "societal and judicial ambivalence" is significant in parenting cases (Melton et al., 1997, p. 490), such as disputes over enlisting gay and lesbian individuals as adoptive or foster parents; disputes between former gay/lesbian domestic partners pertaining to the custody or visitation of children; and disputes between gay/lesbian individuals and former heterosexual partners or spouses.

Dyer's (1999) review of the research on the impact of gay and lesbian parents' sexual orientation on their children indicates that

- parents' homosexual relationships alone do not harm children;
- children raised by lesbian mothers generally have positive psychological outcomes when the grown children are evaluated in young adulthood;
- lesbian and heterosexual women do not differ in overall mental health or approach to childrearing;
- the majority of children raised by gay fathers and lesbian mothers describe themselves as heterosexual; there is no evidence of

elevated rates of homosexuality among the children of gay and lesbian parents;

- no significant differences have been found in children's relationships with peers between those having heterosexual parents and those having homosexual parents;
- gay men are no more likely than heterosexual men to perpetrate sexual abuse of children; and
- as a whole, the evidence thus far suggests that gay and lesbian parents provide a supportive, enabling home environment for children's psychosocial growth comparable to that of heterosexual parents.

Models of Culturally Competent Psychological Assessments

The following discussion section presents a culturally competent approach to psychological assessments as synthesized from several noted authorities (Gopaul-McNicol & Armour-Thomas, 2002; Canino & Spurlock, 1994; Dana, 1993, 2000; Samuda, 1998; Sharma, 1986; Valencia & Suzuki, 2001). While some models in the literature emphasize the testing instruments themselves, the approach described here is broader in scope—considering the interactions among client variables, assessor variables, instrument variables, and context variables. In addition are suggested contributions that referring professionals can make in providing culturally relevant collateral information to examining psychologists. A number of the points below are discussed at greater length in later chapters— chapter 7 on writing referral questions; chapter 8 on client preparation; chapter 9 on evaluating the structure and quality of psychologists' reports; and chapter 11 on interdisciplinary collaboration.

Preliminary Considerations

Given the problematic history and controversies regarding the use of psychological tests and assessment procedures with culturally different clients, reviewed earlier, evaluating psychologists must consider the following when evaluating clients from multicultural backgrounds:

1. The extent to which clients' behavior may be shaped by culture, by the social groups to which they belong, and by cultural stereotypes and stigmatizations that others hold about them.

2. The extent to which tests and assessment protocols used in the evaluation are recognized as being, to a greater or lesser extent, *culturally loaded*—embedded with culture-based experiences, knowledge, values, and concepts. As noted earlier, cultural loading has been a particular concern in tests of achievement and ability. The discussion below on *assessing cognitive potential* is one means of going beyond standardized testing to examine individuals' functioning in the context of their own culture.
3. The extent to which psychological evaluation practices and methods are not based on unrecognized ethnocentrism, sexism, heterosexism, ageism, or "able-bodyism."
4. The extent to which psychologists recognize that psychological tests and interpretation of test scores can result in differential treatment that can disadvantage members of certain cultural group (women; people of color; gay, lesbian, bisexual, and transgendered people; individuals with disabilities).

The above points raise broader issues than bias in individual psychological and educational tests and measures, in terms of the test items or construction of standardization samples. Psychologists must have a fundamental concern with *fairness*—which is more than the absence of bias (Bracken & Naglieri, 2003). Ultimately, fairness has to do with how the test is used.

A Culturally Competent Evaluation

Given these broader issues, the following is a synopsis of what a culturally competent psychological evaluation might look like.

Purpose of the Evaluation

Psychological assessments should aim to discover ways to help clients achieve their potential, while deemphasizing classification and labeling (Canino & Spurlock, 1994; Sharma, 1986).

Client Preparation

Psychologists should attempt to increase clients' interest and motivation in the assessment process by taking time to build rapport and explain the purpose of the evaluation. Multicultural clients who are unfamiliar with psychological evaluations may fear the testing situation. They may cope with their anxiety in a variety of ways, such as showing lack of interest or motivation in completing tests or by rushing through them, answering items in an impulsive or random fashion (Sharma, 1986).

Evaluator's Cultural Awareness

Psychologists should demonstrate self-awareness of how their own cultural background (ethnicity/race, social class, gender, sexual orientation, age, language, ability/disability, etc.) influences the assessment process. They should attend to how oppression, discrimination, and prejudice have affected not only the clients they are evaluating but also themselves as professionals and/or as members of social groups (privileged or unprivileged) in the society (APA, 2002b; Gopaul-McNicol & Armour-Thomas, 2002).

Further, psychologists should recognize the limits of their skills, training, and expertise in conducting assessments with multicultural clients. They should obtain appropriate training, practice experience, supervision, and consultation in working with multicultural clients. This may involve the use of *cultural guides* (learning from individuals from cultural backgrounds similar to those of the client being evaluated) as well as, when necessary, deferring to the expertise of professionals who have more knowledge of and experience with clients from different cultural groups.

Information from Collateral Contacts

Psychologists should augment their assessment findings by drawing upon collateral information that referring professionals typically can provide, such as

- culturally contextualized observations of clients' behavior or performance at home, classroom, or work;
- clinical interviews that gather social history information about clients' socialization patterns, prior experiences of oppression and discrimination from the dominant culture, childrearing practices, family members' experiences of displacement, loss of homeland, and immigration; and
- clients' and family members' health beliefs and healing practices.

Determining Clients' Cultural Orientation

Before selecting their cognitive or personality assessment instruments, psychologists should determine clients' overall cultural orientation, which includes obtaining information about clients' *cultural identity and degree of acculturation* (extent of cultural integration achieved between clients' culture-of-origin and the dominant culture within the larger society) and their *linguistic abilities* (Dana, 1993, 2000). Samuda (1998) listed a number of relevant instruments, including:

- *Intercultural Relations Survey*: assesses the intercultural relationships between managers/supervisors and workers;
- *Language Background Questionnaire for the Bilingual Child*: assesses the language skills of preschool and school-aged children;
- *Majority-Minority Relations Survey*: assesses the acculturation attitudes of Hispanics and Asian Americans who are newly arrived or multigenerational immigrants, permanent residents, naturalized citizens, or U.S. citizens;
- *Suinn-Lew Asian Self-Identify Acculturation Scale*: assesses acculturation and biculturalism in Asian ethnic groups, including Chinese, Japanese, and Korean;
- *Themes Concerning Blacks*: elicits both positive and negative themes from African Americans using projective story cards; and
- *Williams Awareness Sentence Completion*: assesses feelings of conflict that African Americans may have about their own race, as well as prejudicial or positive attitudes that whites have toward blacks, using the projective technique of sentence completion.

For further information on these measures, including their psychometric properties and where to obtain them, consult Samuda (1998).

The rationale for this approach is that knowing the extent of acculturation would help to determine the suitability of using (or modifying) standardized tests with multicultural clients and the appropriateness of using DSM-IV diagnostic categories and formulations. Knowing something about clients' cultural identity also helps in designing cultural-specific interventions.

Similarly, Gopaul-McNicol and Armour-Thomas (2002) propose that psychologists conduct an *ecological assessment*, through informal observation of clients in the contexts in which they typically function (home, school, community) as well as other instruments, such as surveys or clinical interviews, to assess individuals' performance in non-standardized settings. This component would include assessing and examining the cultural dimensions in a personality assessment.

Ecological assessments provide an excellent opportunity to collaborate with referring professionals from other disciplines who may have more extensive contact with clients than typically is available to examining psychologists.

Assessment Strategies

Psychologists should employ a flexible assessment strategy, using formal and informal assessment approaches and multiple assessment measures (qualitative and quantitative) to provide a comprehensive approach toward understanding the psychological functioning of clients from diverse cultural backgrounds (Dana, 2000; Gopaul-McNicol & Armour-Thomas, 2002). Culturally competent assessment strategies include conducting the assessment in clients' primary or preferred language. Evaluators must be competent in understanding clients' verbal and nonverbal communications. If psychologists lack these competencies, they should refer clients to professionals who are competent in the clients' language and psychological assessment processes or an appropriately trained interpreter who understands the principles of psychological assessment and the ethical principles of client confidentiality.

Family members should not be enlisted as translators, because the conflicting roles of family member and translator present a variety of problems. They tend to minimize problems to avoid embarrassing a family member or the family unit. Also, family members may be unfamiliar with terms or concepts used by assessment professionals.

Psychometric Assessment of Cognitive Abilities

As noted by Gopaul-McNicol and Armour-Thomas (2002), administering standardized measures of psychological functioning (cognitive abilities/intelligence, academic achievement, adaptation, socioemotional functioning, etc.), enables the psychologist to identify an individual's *current level* of performance. Clients' strengths and weaknesses in specific domains of interest are assessed under standardized conditions of test administration, scoring, and interpretation.

For bilingual clients, intelligence tests should be administered in both languages "on the assumption that the ability repertoire in the separate languages would seldom overlap" (Sharma, 1986, p. 122). In addition, dual-language learners are not included in the standardization samples of most intelligence tests; hence, some authorities argue that comparing their scores to those from a monolingual English-speaking norm-referenced group is not a valid comparison (Ochoa, 2003). As an alternative, nonverbal comprehensive tests of intelligence have been developed for culturally and linguistically different clients (Bracken & Naglieri, 2003; Ochoa, 2003).

Most contemporary authorities strongly advise against the use of translated intelligence tests, unless the translation has been independently standardized, normed, and validated (Geisinger, 1998; Ochoa, 2003). In this regard, a cross-cultural analysis of adapted and translated versions of the WISC-III used in several countries in North America, North and Central Europe, and East Asia concluded that the WISC-III "is a remarkably robust measure of intelligence with cross-cultural relevance" (Georgas, Weiss, van de Vijver, & Saklofske, 2003, p. 311).

In addition to norm-referenced tests, in which an individual's score is compared to others, criterion-referenced tests should be used, in which an individual's score is compared to some established criterion or performance standard (Samuda, 1998). Other alternative assessment strategies might include compiling a portfolio of work products to assess academic achievement or skill proficiency (Gopaul-McNicol & Armour-Thomas, 2002).

Psychometric "Cognitive Potential" Assessment

After the standardized testing has been completed, the psychologist can use a series of diagnostic probes and alternative testing strategies to identify client *potentials or emerging skills* that standardized testing may obscure. For example, in assessing cognitive functioning of children, a number of alternative dynamic assessment strategies can include (Gopaul-McNicol & Armour-Thomas, 2002; Samuda, 1998; Sharma, 1986):

- allowing clients to work at their own pace to complete test items, rather than penalizing them for working too slowly in standardized timed tests;
- asking clients to use vocabulary words in context (e.g., using the word in a sentence) rather than asking clients to define the meanings of words presented in isolation, as is done with many standardized measures of intelligence and verbal reasoning skills;
- allowing clients to use paper/pencil methods of problem solving and computation after completion of the standardized administration of arithmetic items;
- after the standardized administration of nonverbal reasoning items has been completed, using a *test-teach-retest* approach to explain the purpose of the test, teach the specific skills or abilities being evaluated, then retest the client on items failed in the standardized assessment procedure.

Assessment of Other Intelligences

Roberts and DeBlassie (1983) observed that "intelligence is not a single, universal dimension, but is made up of many components, most of which are not measured on IQ tests" (p. 841). As suggested by Gopaul-McNicol and Armour-Thomas (2002), the evaluating psychologist could employ Gardner's (1983, 1993) theory of multiple intelligences to inquire about clients' kinesthetic, musical, spatial, and interpersonal competencies that may not be assessed adequately on standardized measures of intellectual functioning, which tend to heavily weight verbal reasoning over other cognitive abilities. This information would be gathered from clients themselves, as well as from parents, other family members, teachers, coaches, and other knowledgeable informants.

Assessment of Personality

Results from objective measures of personality must be interpreted conservatively in light of the elevated results that African Americans and Hispanics obtain on some personality inventories, such as the MMPI and the MCMI. Gray-Little and Kaplan (1998) observe that the behavioral implications of these higher elevations generally are unknown for either normal or clinical African American or Hispanic samples, and that studies of other cultural groups are few.

Projective measures generally have much lower reliability than objective measures. Some psychologists avoid them altogether, and others choose to include them as part of the assessment of personality on the assumption that the ambiguous stimuli of measures such as the *Rorschach* are not culturally loaded to any great extent. Clearly, however, when they are used, evaluating psychologists must have considerable skill in building rapport with clients, as well as advanced assessment skills to integrate the projective findings with data gathered from other sources.

Interpretation, Diagnosis and Treatment Recommendations

Test interpretation should be based on the results of multiple instruments and protocols rather than a single score or only a few scores (Sharma, 1986). When assessing multicultural clients, psychologists must understand the limits of their assessment instruments and procedures. Psychologists should state the reliability and validity of their assessment tests and procedures with culturally and linguistically different groups.

Differential diagnosis for intellectual functioning, educational achievement, visual-motor assessment, and personality assessment must take into account cultural factors (Gopaul-McNicol & Armour-Thomas, 2002). The recommendation section should address implications of the assessment findings to the client's functioning in the home, school/work, and community, and suggest culture-specific interventions.

Reporting Results

When psychologists disseminate their findings in oral and written reports:

- Evaluators should document their familiarity with clients' culture and/or prior experience with other clients with a similar background, addressing explicitly any intra- or cross-cultural factors that may be relevant in understanding assessment results and recommendations.
- The behavioral observation section of the report should document the preparation and rapport-building activities that were undertaken to increase clients' interest and motivation and to decrease test anxiety. The success or nonsuccess of these activities should be noted as part of the assessment context in which evaluators describe how clients "presented" during the evaluation (their response to the evaluation session, their cooperation or motivation).
- Psychologists' reports should document the impact of cultural and sociopolitical factors (e.g., oppression, discrimination) on clients' functioning.
- The reliability and validity of assessment tests and procedures with culturally and linguistically different groups should be described clearly, as should any limits or qualifications on evaluators' conclusions and recommendations. The use of adapted or translated measures should be clearly identified.
- In the section where the results of psychological tests are reported, "the report should be qualitative. . . .describing the [client's] strengths and weaknesses in the constructs measured by each subtest" (Gopaul-McNicol & Armour-Thomas, 2002, p. 123), rather than presenting the numeric scores alone, without any accompanying narrative regarding their meaning. Canino and Spurlock (1994) suggest that evaluators begin with a discussion of clients' strengths before moving to a discussion of their deficits and impairments.

Case Planning Considerations

Returning to the case scenario presented earlier in the chapter, what would the social worker and the referring psychiatrist (or any professional from another discipline) do differently if they had been informed consumers about psychological assessments? The following ideas are offered to help professional consumers of psychological services select evaluators who are sensitive to cultural issues:

1. Discover ahead of time information about the psychologist's experience and expertise in evaluating clients from specific cultural backgrounds. As noted in chapter 2, having an evaluating psychologist's curriculum vitae or resume on file is one means of ascertaining the evaluator's work experience with culturally diverse populations or communities. Ask the psychologist directly about his or her experiences with clients from various cultural groups. A tactful way of doing this is to ask the evaluating psychologist if he or she can suggest helpful literature or resources regarding how to work effectively with this population of diverse clients. Some confidence can be gained if evaluators respond by sharing their own prior education or training in multicultural client assessment or by pointing out relevant resources or literature. In situations where evaluators have had little or no previous contact with clients from a specific cultural background, referring professionals should ask what steps the psychologists plan to take to educate themselves about the client's cultural background.
2. Ask knowledgeable people or community leaders from the client's culture or racial/ethnic social group whom they consider to be competent psychological evaluators. Develop working relationships with psychologists whom other multicultural clients have found to be helpful. Develop a referral list of bicultural and/or bilingual psychologists who have specific types of assessment expertise. Develop referral lists of psychologists who have expertise in working with lesbian, gay, bisexual, and transgendered populations.
3. Ask clients for information about any previous experiences they have had with educational or psychological evaluations and testing procedures. Find out what they think was helpful or unhelpful in previous evaluations, and ask clients' permission to convey that information to current evaluators.
4. In making the referral for psychological evaluations, convey to psychologists how clients' cultural background may influence their

perception of the assessment procedures. Make sure that the psychologist knows the client's primary or preferred language. If the psychologist is not fluent in the client's own language, ask the psychologist what steps will be taken to ensure that the evaluation is completed in a culturally competent manner.

5. Upon completion of the evaluation, ask the client for feedback on the evaluation, including the psychologists' cultural sensitivity. Likewise, ask the psychologist for feedback on the assessment sessions with the client, whether any cultural barriers to an accurate assessment were present, and, if so, how these were addressed during the evaluation.

6. Model for the evaluating psychologist respect for cultural pluralism. Share with the evaluator your own efforts to develop cultural competence with clients from diverse backgrounds. Approach the evaluation as an opportunity for interdisciplinary collaboration regarding how best to meet multicultural clients' needs. (Further discussion of interdisciplinary collaboration can be found in the Postscript to this book.)

7. Examine the psychologist's reports for evidence of whether the evaluator adapted or modified any assessment procedure to take into account the client's unique cultural or linguistic characteristics. Ascertain whether the client was evaluated only under standardized testing conditions or whether other assessment strategies were employed. Determine whether the evaluator was flexible in accommodating the client's schedule (and sense of time) or whether all evaluation procedures were completed in one setting during a single time period. Examine the report to determine if it noted the client's test-taking skills and response to structured timed tasks.

8. When a client's cognitive abilities are the subject of the evaluation, examine the report to determine if the evaluator assessed other forms of intelligence not typically captured in standardized intelligence tests. Determine whether the evaluator assessed clients' cognitive ability and also gave an estimate of their cognitive potential. Examine the report for the evaluator's consideration of the role that culture plays in shaping learning styles and problem-solving abilities. In addition, examine whether clients' literacy proficiency in their primary and/or secondary language(s) was taken into consideration in the assessment of their intellectual abilities.

9. When a client's personality functioning is the subject of the evaluation, examine the report to determine if the evaluator took into consideration the client's degree of acculturation/cultural identity; migration or refugee history; norms for acceptable behavior from the client's

own social group; the client's level of support from extended family members, community, work or school; and whether the evaluator differentially diagnosed mental health disorders or emotional-behavioral problems from culturally specific responses to oppression and discrimination. As Gopaul-McNicol and Armour-Thomas (2002) noted, care must be taken to differentiate disruptive disorders and defiant behaviors from the angry, aggressive behaviors that may erupt when clients feel they are being discriminated against, disrespected, or oppressed. Determine whether multiple measures were used in the assessment of personality functioning.

10. Look to see if the evaluator's opinions, conclusions, and intervention recommendations take into account the client's cultural characteristics and are congruent with the client's cultural norms, beliefs, or practices.

11. Make a regular habit of providing feedback to the evaluating psychologist about how the psychological assessment information impacted your case planning decisions. In building a collaborative working alliance with psychological evaluators, provide feedback on the clinical usefulness of the evaluation in revealing clients' strengths and potential, as well as areas of weakness and impairments. Within that context, provide feedback to the psychologist on his or her effort to address relevant cultural factors in the evaluation report. Having an established working relationship with the psychologist will make it much easier to directly raise and resolve problems in this area. If the evaluation be done in a culturally sensitive manner, the psychologist will appreciate the positive feedback.

Additional Resources

The following are resources on culturally appropriate psychological instruments and information about national organizations involved in advocacy, practice, training, or research with various ethnic and racial groups in the health and human service area.

Instruments

Dana (1993, 2000) has suggested that psychologists employ culturally universal assessment instruments (*etic*) as well as culturally specific instruments (*emic*) when evaluating multicultural clients, particularly when they have experienced oppression, discrimination, prejudice, acculturation stress, and other problems of living. For a further description of these types of instruments, interested readers may consult Samuda's (1998) compendium of psychological tests for minority adolescents and adults, which examines in greater detail achievement and aptitude tests, sensory-motor tests, and neurological tests. As noted earlier, this compendium contains a number of measures of cultural identity for different ethnic/racial groups, measures of acculturation stress, and measures designed to tap individuals' knowledge and attitudes about different cultural groups.

In addition, the Educational Resources Information Center (ERIC), a government clearinghouse, has a wide variety of information about culturally appropriate instruments and tests, as well as information on working with diverse clients in school settings and multicultural counseling and the training of culturally sensitive professionals (website: www.ed.gov/databases/ERIC; phone: 1-800-LET-ERIC). Valencia and Suzuki (2001) also have provided a detailed examination of the cultural diversity in the standardization samples of the major tests of intelligence, achievement, and aptitude currently used with children.

Organizations

Various private and governmental organizations are dedicated to research, training, and practice with specific cultural groups. A partial listing follows.

- *Association of Black Psychologists* (ABPsi) is a professional advocacy organization devoted to improving the quality of psychological services to African American clients. www.abpsi.org Association of Black Psychologists, PO Box 55999, Washington DC, 20040-5999. Phone: 202-722-0808
- *National Alliance for Hispanic Health* is an organization aimed at improving health-care outcomes and services to Hispanic Americans. It has extensive information on issues related to vaccination, immunization, and maternal and child health. It has two health-related telephone hotlines where confidential information and referral services are available from bilingual counselors: *Su Familia* (National Hispanic Family Health Hotline): 1-866-783-2645; and *La Linea Nacional Prenatal Hispana* (National Hispanic Prenatal Helpline): 1-800-504-7081. A nationwide database of prenatal care and related services for Hispanic parents is available

through the latter number. Website: www.hispanichealth.org. National Alliance for Hispanic Health, 1501-16th Street, NW, Washington DC 20036; Phone: 202-387-5000.

- *National Center for American Indian and Alaska Native Mental Health Research* (NCAIANMHR), one of several components of the American Indian and Alaska Native Programs at the University of Colorado Health Sciences Center, has an extensive list of publications, resources, and web links on mental health and substance-abuse problems with American Indians and Alaskan Native populations. Website: www.uchsc.edu/ai/ncaianmhr. National Center for American Indian and Alaska Native Mental Health Research, Nighthorse Campbell Native Health Building, PO Box 6508, Mail Stop F800. Aurora, CO, 80045-0508; Phone: 303-724-1414.
- *National Coalition of Hispanic Health and Human Services Organizations* (COSSMHO) is an organization consisting of 700 agencies and individuals advocating for the health, mental health, substance abuse, and psychosocial well-being of the Hispanic population in the United States. Website: http://latino.sscnet.ucla.edu. COSSMHO, 1030 15th Street, N., Suite 1053, Washington, DC, 20005; Phone: None listed).
- *National Indian Child Welfare Association* has a variety of information on research, training, and practice with American Indian children in the child welfare system. Website: www.nicwa.org. National Indian Child Welfare Association, 5100 SW Macadam Avenue, Suite 300, Portland, OR, 97239; Phone: 503-222-4007.
- *National Research Center on Asian American Mental Health* focuses on research, policy, service delivery, and training to Asian Pacific Americans. Website: www.nrcaamh.ucdavis.edu. National Research Center on Asian American Mental Health, Dept. of Psychology, University of California, One Shields Center, Davis, CA, 95616-8686; Phone: 530-752-1400.

Conclusion

This chapter has provided a broad look at the history and contemporary practice issues regarding the psychological assessments of multicultural people. Cultural competence is examined as an ethical issue for psychological evaluators, whose practice should be guided by national practice standards regarding the delivery of psychological services to racially/

ethnically and linguistically different clients, and to lesbian, gay, bisexual, and transgendered clients. The chapter also presents a culturally competent model of psychological assessments. Case planning must consider the opportunities for referring professionals to work in partnership with multicultural clients and evaluating psychologists in the assessment process.

A final word about the topic of racial and ethnic *group differences in intelligence*: At the present time, the debate about these differences continues in the profession of psychology, albeit in a more muted form than in the 1970s and 1980s. In the end, William Tucker's observation (quoted in Valencia and Suzuki, 2001) is the most appropriate.

> For well over a hundred years, some of the finest scientific researchers with the best academic credentials have investigated racial differences in intelligence … [which] has produced little of scientific value…. Judicious use of our scientific resources would seem inconsistent with the pursuit of a goal that is probably scientifically chimerical and certainly lends itself to socially pernicious ends. (p. 183)

Chapter 5

Assessment of Parent–Child Interactions

Observation is theory-laden.
We see what we expect to see
and may miss what
we do not expect to see.
Unless you take
special precautions,
you may miss what
is there to be seen and
see things that aren't there.

(Gambrill, 1997, p. 387)

O bservation of par-
ent–child interac-
tions is an assessment

technique frequently employed by psychologists and referring professionals alike in a wide variety of practice and research settings. Traditionally,
these observations have been assumed to yield important information
about the nature of the relationship between parents and their children and
about parents' abilities as appropriate caregivers. Parent–child observations have played a central role in certain types of high-stakes psychological evaluations, such as those concerning suspected child maltreatment,
disputes between divorcing parents about shared parenting time or
changes of custody, and termination of parental rights. Recently, this
widely used assessment tool has been challenged, and some critics have
argued that including it in the psychological assessment process has little
justification.

This chapter examines the underlying theoretical assumptions and
threats to the reliability and validity of parent–child observational data.
Reviewing the supporting and contravening evidence illuminates the challenges that referring professionals face in drawing conclusions from parent–child observations in their case planning decisions. Included in this
chapter is a discussion of the special ethical issues involved in observation, such as obtaining clients' informed consent. The case planning
guidelines and cautions offer advice on how to use parent–child observations appropriately when formulating treatment interventions or making
recommendations about the care and custody of children.

Rationale, Types of Observational Data, and Methods of Collection

Parent–child observations are used widely in mental health, child welfare, early childhood interventions, maternal–child health, and special
education, for clinical as well as forensic purposes. In addition, parent–
child observations have been used in clinical research when assessing the

Case Scenario 5.1

Mr. and Mrs. Bailey and their 7-year-old daughter Bridget participated in a "parent–child interactional," as one component of a comprehensive, court-ordered psychological evaluation. Bridget had been in foster care for the past 3 months because of physical abuse by her parents. Her teacher reported suspected abuse after observing bruises on her arms and legs, apparently from an earlier spanking by her father. The purpose of the observational procedure was to assess the strength of the child's attachment to her biological parents and the quality of their parenting.

Dr. Yolanda Hale, the clinical psychologist evaluator, arranged for an observation period, lasting 60 minutes, using the one-way observation facility at the social services department. Structured interactions (playing a game, making a snack, reading a book) and spontaneous, unstructured interactions between the parents and the child were observed.

Following the observation period, Dr. Hale conducted a one-hour clinical interview with the parents to assess their feelings about and perceptions toward their daughter. In addition, each parent independently filled out a standardized attitudinal measure about typical sources of stress related to childrearing.

While the parents were completing this survey, Dr. Hale conducted an individual play interview with Bridget in the playroom at the social service office. During this session, Bridget developed a play story with a dollhouse and puppet family that indicated an enduring attachment to her parents and her fantasies about being reunited with them.

Dr. Hale also sought out alternative sources of information. She reviewed the case notes of the Baileys' ongoing child protection worker, which contained rich behavioral descriptions of the interactions between Bridget and her parents during the supervised visits. Dr. Hale contacted the caseworker directly to discuss these observations. She also contacted the foster parents to obtain their observations regarding Bridget's before-and-after visits with her parents.

In her report to the court, Dr. Hale was able to contrast the observations obtained through the one-way mirror at the social services office, in which the Baileys appeared to be overwhelmed and immobilized when Bridget became clingy, demanding, and bossy, with those provided by the ongoing caseworker and foster parents. The latter observations provided examples showing that the parents were able to implement suggestions about more effective management techniques. On the parenting survey measures, both parents scored high on the presence of environmental stressors during the past 12 months.

(continued)

> Based on all these sources of information (e.g., multiple observations obtained from different sources in different settings, review of case history information, clinical interview with parents, play interview with Bridget, and results of the parental attitudinal measure), Dr. Hale drew the following conclusions:
>
> 1. Environmental stressors were a significant contributor to a single incident of physical abuse.
> 2. Corporal punishment was not the Baileys' usual form of discipline.
> 3. The parents' difficulty in managing Bridget when observed through the one-way mirror reflected, in part, the parents' high anxiety about being observed and the fear of making a mistake.
> 4. With sufficient supports in place, the Baileys had the capacity for more positive, safe, and effective parenting of Bridget.
>
> Dr. Hale's findings supported the caseworker's permanency planning recommendations: to work towards reunification. The court accepted these recommendations and ordered the parents to work with the caseworker to mitigate the environmental stresses currently impacting the family. In addition, Mr. Bailey was ordered to attend an anger-management class, and both parents were ordered to attend a series of parenting classes. Finally, the court ordered that Bridget receive individual child psychotherapy to deal with her feelings about the abuse as part of the plan of eventually being returned home.

quality of attachment and emotional availability between adult caregivers and children, including infant–mother interactions. Observational data can be obtained in a variety of ways, such as through home visits, classroom visits, observations in waiting rooms, and the use of specialized, controlled settings involving one-way mirrors and audio- and videotaping. Observational data may be used as the primary or sole source of information in a psychological assessment, but (more commonly) they are integrated with other sources of information, including clinical interviews and the results of psychological tests.

Rationale and Underlying Assumptions

What assumptions do evaluators generally make in gathering observational data on parent–child interactions? The answers to this question include the following points:

1. Evaluators assume that there may be significant *discrepancies* between parents' global report about their children's behavior obtained

in interviews, and children's behaviors subsequently observed by others in the home, school, or clinic settings (Patterson, 1977). Parents may "underestimate the rates of deviant child behavior in general and … overestimate improvement in those behaviors" (p. 310). Indeed, as Lindaman, Booth, and Chambers (2000) observed:

> Many patterns of interaction are outside the awareness of either partner and hence direct questioning is of little use. Seeing how the problems emerge in the interaction gives added insight into how they occur and how they can be changed. (p. 375)

2. Evaluators assume that the specific behaviors parents and children exhibit toward each other are expressions or *manifestations of their relationship* (Roggman, Boyce, & Newland, 2000). Observations of such interactions recognize "the bi-directional and reciprocal influence that parents and children have on each other" (Smith, 2000, p. 342). For example, Bridget's clingy and bossy interactions with her parents and their ineffective management style (as seen in the social services observation room) are assumed to be in response to each other.

3. Clinical and forensic evaluators frequently assume that the behaviors observed in one setting on one occasion are *manifestations of stable patterns* that generalize to *unobserved* patterns of behavior in other contexts on many different occasions (Haynes-Semen & Baumgarten, 1994). According to this view, Bridget's behavior in the controlled observation setting would be assumed to be representative of her typical interactions with her parents in the home, and the behavior displayed by her parents in the observation setting likewise would be assumed to be characteristic of their usual style of childrearing.

   In the case scenario, Dr. Hale was careful to test these assumptions—an essential step that some evaluators unwisely omit because of the additional time involved. Dr. Hale gathered a substantial amount of data beyond her own observations to confirm or disconfirm the impressions she had formed initially about the strength of the attachment between Bridget and her parents and their ability to raise her safely and appropriately.

4. Evaluators assume that it is possible to *directly observe and differentiate healthy from problematic interactions* between parents and children. For example, in the case of child custody disputes, there is a heavy reliance on observational data to ascertain which parent is the more adequate caregiver for the child (Bricklin, 1995). Likewise, in child protection evaluations, observational data are used to assess

whether children have been physically or sexually abused or neglected by parents (Haynes-Semen & Baumgarten, 1994).

Goals of Observation

According to Mahoney, Spiker, and Boyce (1996), the general goals in assessing parent–child interactions are to determine whether parents

- are able to provide optimal conditions for their child's development,
- use assistance or support, or
- place their child at risk for developmental or behavioral problems.

Sattler (1998) suggests that observing parent–child interactions is useful when assessing whether parents

- can relax and be comfortable with their child;
- can demonstrate acceptance of and affection for the child;
- can show sensitivity to their child's needs, wants, and desires;
- can take the child's perspective;
- can balance keeping children safe and protected from harm while also allowing them freedom to explore their environment, within the limits of the child's age and abilities; and
- can help the child to acquire new skills.

Types of Observational Data

Evaluators draw on several types of observational data in assessing parent–child interactions: those occurring in naturalistic settings, those occurring in analogue settings, and those having features of both.

Naturalistic Observations

In *naturalistic observations* behaviors are observed and recorded in the day-to-day environment, such as home, school, neighborhood, or work (Merrell, 1994). Naturalistic observations aim to capture information about the observed behavior in the context in which it typically occurs. The time and place selected allow observations of the relevant behaviors and events of interest, including antecedents and consequences of the behaviors. In addition, observations in the natural environment may allow data to be collected on multiple occasions over a longer time, so as to gather a larger sample of behavior. Gambrill (1997) recommended that data be gathered between 2 and 5 days or until the behavior has been observed a minimum of 10 to 15 times, to establish a consistent pattern before treatment or intervention services begin.

Observations in the natural environment have the greatest potential for *external validity*, which means that the results obtained from the observations may generalize to behavior observed in other settings. But naturalistic observations may also be subject to considerable interference from unexpected interruptions and distractions.

Most psychologists cannot realistically gather firsthand naturalistic observational data because the vast majority of their evaluation procedures are done in a time-limited manner in an office setting. As noted later in the chapter, however, referring professionals from other disciplines may have more contact with parents and children in their natural environments, such as the home or school. Sharing these data with psychologists helps them to compare the types of behaviors they observe during their own interactions with parents and children and the types of behaviors clients reliably are reported to display on multiple occasions in other settings.

Analogue Observations

Analogue observations occur in highly structured, controlled settings designed to simulate or approximate the conditions of the natural environment while controlling for extraneous or distracting stimuli (Merrell, 1994). An example of an analogue situation is role-playing during an interview in which clients are directed to reenact or simulate what they do in real life (Gambrill, 1997). Also, parent–child interactions can be observed behind a one-way mirror, in a standardized manner, such as a sequence of parent-initiated activity, child-initiated activity, and unstructured free play (Bricklin, 1995; Haynes-Semen & Baumgarten, 1994; Herrenkohl, Herrenkohl, Toedter, & Yanushefski, 1984; Lindaman et al., 2000; Smith, 2000).

Often, analogue observations are collected on one occasion during time-limited sessions as brief as 10 to 30 minutes or extending several hours. Because extraneous variables can be controlled, analogue observations tend to have a high degree of *internal validity*—meaning that the behaviors observed can be explained, with reasonable probability, as a function of the parent–child relationship and not some other factors. Table 5.1 summarizes the advantages of analogue observations described in the professional literature.

TABLE 5.1	Advantages of Observing Parent–Child Interactions in Analogue Settings

ADVANTAGES	DESCRIPTION
Evaluator control	Evaluators rather than parents control the task selection and the behavioral dimensions being observed.
Multiple observers	There can be more than one observer, either in "real time" behind a one-way mirror or in "asynchronous time," such as observers' watching a videotape of an earlier recorded interview. Videotaping also allows multiple occasions of watching the same parent–child interaction, either by a single observer or by an entire team.
Standardizing interactions between parents and children	A standardized protocol is designed to elicit a range of behaviors, including those deemed clinically relevant by the observer (e.g., presenting a task to elicit noncompliant behavior in a child being evaluated for suspected emotional and behavioral problems), within a relatively short time, enabling greater efficiency in gathering observational data.
Reliable rating instrument	Agreement among observers can be ascertained readily if they are using the same rating instrument. A number of authorities hold that structured analogue observations conducted in a standardized manner have far greater potential than nonstandardized naturalistic observations for capturing accurately the types of behaviors that typically occur between parents and children.
Basis for comparison	The set of structured tasks allows comparisons among parent–child behaviors at different points in time, as well as between different parent–child dyads.

Adapted from *The Custody Evaluation Handbook: Research-Based Solutions and Applications*, by B. Bricklin, 1995, New York: Brunner/Mazel; "Assessing Parent–Child Interactions With the Marshak Interaction Method (MIM)," by S. Lindaman, P. Booth, & C. Chambers, in *Play Diagnosis and Assessment*, edited by K. Gilitin-Weiner, A. Sandgrund, and C. Schaefer, 2000, New York: John Wiley & Sons; and "Parent-Child Interaction Play Assessment," by D. Smith, in *Play Diagnosis and Assessment*.

Mixed Observational Data

The *mixed observational data* form—having elements of both naturalistic and analogue forms—is frequently used (and perhaps misused) by mental health and social service professionals in formulating conclusions and recommendations about the quality and strength of parent–child interactions. These are observations of parent–child interactions in an agency's or evaluator's waiting room. The setting itself is controlled, at least in part, and artificial (hence, the similarity to analogue observations), yet the observations are naturalistic—in that they are made in the context of where the behaviors occur. Child therapists typically begin their observations in the waiting room, observing the manner in which children relate to their parents, how much ease or difficulty is encountered when children are asked to separate, and children's interactions with parents upon their return to the waiting room.

Observing what happens in the waiting room is a *sample of convenience*, which may or may not be representative of how parents and children interact in less stressful settings. These waiting-room interactions, in the absence of observational data from other sources, do *not* constitute an adequate basis for making judgments about the quality of parenting.

Collection Methods

The three different methods of collecting observational data are as follows.

1. In the most common method in clinical practice, observers do not use a formal assessment tool for making judgments about the quality of parent–child interactions or relationships but, rather, rely on "their own intuition, which reflects both their own personal experiences and their beliefs about parent–child interaction that have been informed by the professional literature" (Mahoney, Spiker, & Boyce, 1996, p. 32).

   Problems arising from this approach include the fact that *the target behaviors being observed are not specified in advance*. Instead, observers often end up making global judgments about overarching constructs, such as the "quality of attachment" between children and adult caregivers, rather than obtaining information about the presence or absence of specific behaviors or interactions.

2. Observers may employ some type of formal interaction assessment instrument but use it as a general guide rather than a standardized measure in evaluating parent–child interactions. A good example of this approach can be found in Jerome Sattler's (1998) text, *Clinical and Forensic Interviewing of Children and Families: Guidelines for Mental Health, Education, Pediatric, and Child Maltreatment Fields*. Sattler's criteria for observing parent–child interactions (pp. 164–173) include attention to three different child developmental levels (infant, toddler, and school-age child) and six major areas of family functioning (problem-solving style, communication patterns, roles and structures,

affective responses, control mechanisms, values and norms). These criteria, drawn primarily from the clinical literature, are subsequently organized into a "family rating checklist" as a guide for clinical thinking rather than a formal evaluation tool. Although this represents considerable advancement over relying on clinical intuition alone, the reliability and validity of such tools are not directly ascertained.

3. The third collection method is "an established and validated protocol for evaluating parent–child interactions" (Mahoney et al., 1996, p. 32). Typically, this requires that (a) the behaviors of interest be operationally defined, (b) coding procedures be developed to reliably record individual and interactive behaviors, (c) raters be sufficiently trained in the use of the coding procedures, (d) the observation and coding of behavior is done in an unobtrusive manner, and (e) the observation is done at a time and in a context in which the behaviors of interest are likely to occur.

The coding procedures for many of these observation protocols include *event recording* (frequency counts), *interval recording* (ascertaining whether the behaviors of interest occurred during short time intervals), and *time sampling* (ascertaining whether the behaviors of interest occurred over a longer time). A number of protocols employ a *global rating* approach, such as 3-, 5-, or 7-point Likert-type scales to rate behaviors on polar opposite dimensions (i.e., rejecting versus accepting parental behavior) (Field, 1991; Herrenkohl et al., 1984). Others use *semantic differential scaling*, in which categories of behaviors are rated along a developmental continuum from negative to positive (Lindaman et al., 2000; Smith, 2000).

Theoretical Assumptions and Frameworks about Observational Data

As the chapter opening quotation from Gambrill (1997) noted, observational data are theory-laden. For example, radical behavioral psychology holds that direct observation is the only empirically sound method of assessment because it involves quantifying overt, observable behavior (Merrell, 1994). As such, analysis of parent–child interactions aims at understanding the *function* of the observed behavior rather than attributing the behaviors to enduring personality traits or characteristics.

In contrast, observation methods framed within psychoanalytic theory assume that it is possible to see far deeper than immediate overt behaviors. According to Haynes-Semen and Baumgarten (1994), "Observing the child with each parent not only provides information about the child's experiences but also gives access to the parent's own childhood experiences" (p. 19). Within this theoretical perspective, the "threads of continuity in psychic function between the infant and the adult are astonishingly clear" (Steele, quoted in Haynes-Semen & Baumgarten, 1994, p. 19).

The difference between these two contrasting theoretical views of observational data is the distinction between *description* and *inference* (Gambrill, 1997). Behavioral theory emphasizes descriptions of the behavior actually occurring, whereas in psychoanalytic theory, inferences about the meaning and the origins of the behaviors receive far greater prominence. Most advocates of observational data seek to *minimize the degree of inference* involved in making judgments about the nature of the behavior.

Observational methods and theory frameworks have mutually influenced each other. For example, the psychological constructs of "attachment" and "emotional availability" originally arose out of observations of infants' and young children's interactions with their primary adult caregivers (Bowlby, 1969). As these theoretical conceptualizations emerged, additional observations in controlled research settings were undertaken to refine and extend the concept (Ainsworth, Blehar, Waters, & Wall, 1978). Now psychologists and other professionals use these constructs in a variety of nonresearch clinical settings when making evaluative judgments on the quality of the parent–child relationship or the adequacy of parental caregiving abilities.

A brief review of the major theoretical constructs used in interpreting parent–child interactions follows. A common element in these conceptualizations is the importance of *reciprocal interactions* between specific parental attributes or behaviors (responsiveness, playfulness, etc.) and specific child attributes or behaviors (signaling, exploring, etc.).

Developmental Perspective

Parent–child observations should be based on a *developmental framework* (Sattler, 1998; Smith, 2000); the observation must take into account the developmental needs and stages of individual children (i.e., infant, toddler, school-aged child, adolescent). In addition to this traditional emphasis on the child's development, the observational data should include attention to each adult family member's own stage of individual development

(Harper-Dorton & Herbert, 1999), the development stage of their evolution as parents (Benedek, 1970), as well as the developmental stage of the family system (Carter & McGoldrick, 1988; Solomon, 1973). As discussed in chapter 4, evaluators, too, must have knowledge of *diverse patterns of childrearing* among multicultural families (Sattler, 1998) and the impact that poverty and low socioeconomic status may have on parent–child interactions (Herrenkohl et al., 1984).

Attachment

As reviewed by Biringen (2000), attachment theory holds that infants develop secure attachment relationships with a primary adult caregiver (most often the mother) when the parent accurately and consistently deciphers the infant's signals and communications and responds to them promptly. This conceptualization is based on a "distress" model of interaction. As an infant signals distress (from hunger, cold, wet, need for stimulation for comfort), the caregiver's nurturing responses reduce the distress, leading to the infant's sense of contentment and gratification.

As this cycle repeats itself over time, an infant (ideally) begins to learn that the outer world can be relied upon consistently to meet her or his needs. Gradually, that predictable external world becomes internalized within the child as a "working model" or beginning cognitive schema, resulting in an enduring affectional bond between child and parent. Although its specific manifestations vary across cultures, attachment is a universal phenomenon having four main functions (Davies, 1999):

1. providing a sense of security,
2. regulating affect and arousal,
3. promoting an expression of feelings, and
4. serving as a basis for exploration.

Based on the research of Ainsworth (1982) and Main and Hesse (1990), several different clusters of infant attachment behaviors have been classified and are summarized in Table 5.2. These classifications are based on assessing the child's reactions to brief separations from caregivers in a controlled setting.

Emotional Availability

A related construct of "emotional availability" has subsequently been developed, taking into account more precisely the idea that "emotion is

TABLE 5.2	Classification of Attachment
TYPE	**DESCRIPTION OF ATTACHMENT BEHAVIORS**
Securely attached	Infants are able to cope with brief separations from a primary caregiver because they are confident of the parent's responsiveness. As a result, they are able explore their environment with security.
Insecurely attached	(three subtypes, described below)
• avoidant attached	Infants show little distress when separated from their mothers—playing independently and ignoring her upon her return.
• anxious or ambivalently attached	Infants show great distress at separation from parents, followed by few exploration activities. Upon the mother's return, the anxiously attached infant resists being comforted and appears to demonstrate ambivalence about the predictability and availability of the caregiver.
• disorganized or disoriented	Infants may show contradictory behavior—signaling both approach and avoidance behaviors toward the primary caregiver.

Adapted from "Attachment: Retrospect and Prospect," by M. Ainsworth, in *The Place of Attachment in Human Behavior*, edited by C. M. Parker & J. Stevenson-Hilded, 1982, New York: Basic Books; "Parents' Unresolved Traumatic Experiences are Related to Infant Disorganized Attachment Status: Is Frightened and/or Frightening Parental Behavior the Linking Mechanism?" by M. Main & E. Hesse, in *Attachment in the Preschool Years: Theory, Research, and Intervention* (pp. 161–184), edited by M. T. Greenberg, D. Cicchetti, and E. M. Cummings, 1990, Chicago: University of Chicago Press.

likely to be a sensitive barometer of the relationship between a parent and a child" (Biringen, 2000, p. 104). In this view, emotional availability refers to the extent to which children and parents express emotion and are responsive to the emotions of the other.

In contrast to the attachment construct, which is geared more toward the child, "emotional availability" is conceptualized as having both parent and child dimensions. On the parental side, the attributes of *sensitivity, structuring, nonintrusiveness*, and *nonhostility* are seen as key facets of emotional availability and include both parental signaling and parental understanding of the child's signaling. On the child side, the dimensions are the *child's responsiveness*—age- and context-appropriate ability to explore on his or her own, and "to respond to the parent in an affectively available way" (p. 107) and the *child's ability to engage and involve the parent* by making eye contact, asking questions, telling, showing, or demonstrating something to a parent in a comfortable and positive manner.

As applied to actual practice, these theoretical constructs direct the observer's attention to the parents' abilities to interact appropriately with their child's current developmental status and the parents' ability to provide appropriate limits and discipline within the context of an enduring affectional bond with the child.

Controversies About the Reliability and Validity of Parent–Child Observations

Despite their wide use, considerable controversy has raged about the use of parent–child interactions. At the center of this controversy is a debate over whether these observations can be regarded as objective.

From a behaviorist perspective, Merrell (1994) asserts that "direct behavioral observation is the most empirically sound of the direct measurement techniques…[and] is one of the most direct and objective tools available" (p. 44) in the assessment of children's emotional and behavioral problems. In contrast, Gambrill (1997), writing from a social constructivist framework, states that observations are not neutral but, rather, are laden with theory and value-based lenses. Further, Bricklin (1995), in summarizing previous custody evaluation research studies on parent–child interactions, concludes that "[unstandardized] observations, whether conducted in the home or the professionals' office, were equally tainted as sources of information" (p. 58).

In addition to potential bias from theoretical frameworks, a number of threats to reliability and validity must be taken into account—whether observations of parent–child interactions take place in a controlled analogue setting using a standardized protocol or instrument or are done in naturalistic settings. "The accuracy, validity, and reliability of behavioral observational data are often not adequately established" (Merrell, 1994, p. 57). Table 5.3 summarizes the threats to reliability and validity. Each threat is then discussed at greater length.

Threats to Reliability

Threats to reliability are briefly described in the following.

Observer Drift

Changes over time in the observer's use of the behavioral coding system are referred to as *observer drift* (Wicks-Nelson & Israel, 1997). To avoid

TABLE 5.3	Threats to the Reliability and Validity of Parent–Child Observational Data

THREATS TO RELIABILITY	THREATS TO VALIDITY
Observer drift	Situational specificity of behavior
Observer effects and evaluation context	Failure to use social contrast data
Length of observation	Instrumentation
Physical location of the observation	Content validity threats
Reactivity to being observed	Construct validity threats
Observer bias	Criterion validity threats

Adapted from "Clinical Assessment of Parent-Child Interaction: Are Professionals Ready to Implement This Practice?" by G. Mahoney, D. Spiker, & G. Boyce, 1996, *Topics In Early Childhood Special Education, 16*, 26–50; *Social Work Practice: A Critical Thinker's Guide*, by E. Gambrill, 1997, New York: Oxford University Press; *Assessment of Behavioral, Social, and Emotional Problems: Direct and Objective Methods for Use with Children and Adolescents*, by K. Merrell, 1994, New York: Longman; and "Naturalistic Observation in Clinical Assessment," by G. Patterson, 1977, *Journal of Abnormal Child Psychology, 5*, 309–322.

observer drift, Mahoney and colleagues (1996) recommend a minimum of 40 hours for observer training, consisting of the following steps:

1. Review the criteria for each of the items on the rating scale.
2. Have multiple observers rate a sample videotaped observation simultaneously.
3. Rate tapes independently until an acceptable level of agreement is obtained, such as .80 for global ratings, and .90 for time or event sampling.

Even then, observers commonly depart gradually from the original definitions of the behavior and begin to use the rating or coding system in idiosyncratic ways (Merrell, 1994). Patterson (1977) suggests that the limit of "observer endurance" is 5 minutes, particularly when coding complex sequences of interaction, which require the complete attention of observers. Roggman and colleagues (2000) note that "the simpler the coding scheme, the greater the likelihood that observations will remain reliable throughout the data collection period" (p. 319). Periodic retraining of observers and/or reliability checks between observers, therefore, is essential in maintaining the accuracy of parent–child interactions.

Observer drift may be a particular problem for clinicians who work independently or without supervision (Merrell, 1994). Enlisting a colleague or videotaping observational situations and then scoring the observation multiple times as a self-check are possible remedies for observer drift for independent practitioners. For example, Dr. Hale could have recruited a second observer to watch from behind a one-way mirror so each person could rate parent–child interactions independently, then compute their overall rate of agreement. These ratings could then be compared to a second set of ratings a few days later, after each had watched a videotaped replay of Bridget's interactions with her parents. Finally, the rate of agreement between them could be compared to the rate of agreement obtained when both observers were initially trained in using a parent–child interaction measure to determine if they were maintaining a predetermined level of reliability needed for making accurate measurements.

Observer Effects and Context

Many forensic and clinical observational protocols used to assess parent–child interactions (e.g., custody evaluations, child maltreatment evaluations, special education assessments) require parents to be directive with their child, such as initiating a parent-led activity (e.g., reading a book, fixing a snack, solving a puzzle, building a tower of blocks). "When asked to perform specific tasks … parents invariably direct their children to perform specific activities more frequently than in observations that merely require them to play with their child" (Mahoney et al., 1996, p. 33). This, in turn, could result in the parent being rated higher on "directedness" (either positively or negatively) than would be the case in a low-task, low-demand situation.

Further, observing a parent responding to an upset child will yield different ratings than observing a parent interacting with a child who is calm. "Generally, observations conducted in stressful contexts result in a picture of the parents' childrearing style that has little, if any, resemblance to how parents typically interact with their children" (p. 34).

In the case scenario, Mr. and Mrs. Bailey clearly felt threatened by the observations in the social services observation room because a great deal was riding on the outcome (i.e., whether Bridget would be returned home). Thus, the specificity or vagueness of the evaluator's instructions to the parents regarding what they are supposed to do during the observation period may further increase parents' apprehension about the observation process. This may result in atypical behavior from parents and child.

Length of Observation

According to Mahoney and colleagues (1996), assessments of parent–child interactions are typically based on observations lasting between 10 and 30 minutes. It is questionable whether that amount of time is adequate to obtain an accurate sample of parent–child behaviors, particularly of clinically significant but infrequently occurring behaviors. For example, Mr. Bailey may be in control of his temper most of the time but when under great stress intermittently loses control and becomes physically abusive. A brief observation period is not likely to capture this type of behavior.

Conversely, when observations in some settings are much longer—an hour or more—and parents and children are required to remain in sustained contact with each other, the contact may exceed the typical duration of their interactions at home or other natural settings. As the interactions required in analogue observations exceed this customary limit, parents and children "are likely to engage in atypical patterns of behavior" (p. 34). In the case scenario, it would be useful to determine how much time, on average, both parents typically spend *together* with Bridget at home, to gauge whether the 1-hour period Dr. Hale had allotted for observation exceeded the amount of time they normally sustained contact with each other.

Physical Location

Whether observations take place in the home, at a clinic or practitioner's office, or in some specialized setting such as social services screening room or an infant-studies laboratory, the physical setting is likely to have a significant effect on the behaviors observed. Although standardized settings have the advantage of controlling extraneous variables and potential sources of distraction, they tend to present an artificial and contrived location in which families are expected to interact.

Even observations done in a natural setting, such as the home of the parent(s) and children, are not immune to this drawback, especially because observers typically require all family members to stay in the same area of the house or apartment so they can be observed continuously for the required time (Merrell, 1994). In the case example, the requirement that family members stay in proximity may have prevented observers from seeing Mr. and Mrs. Bailey using effective distancing or disengaging maneuvers to reduce tension or avoid conflict with Bridget, such as going to another room.

Reactivity

Reactivity refers to individuals' awareness of being observed and the impact of such awareness on the behaviors they subsequently display. Reactivity has been the subject of considerable debate in the clinical and research literature. Many authorities caution that reactivity is a major problem in obtaining reliable observational data (Mahoney et al., 1996; Merrell, 1994; Wicks-Nelson & Israel, 1997). "With uncanny perceptiveness, children seem to understand and react to the presence of a 'stranger' in the observational setting" (Merrell, 1994, p. 59). Likewise, "The child knows what he or she is doing is a 'performance' and will 'perform' with whoever is available" (Bricklin, 1995, p. 60).

Children and parents alike may become self-conscious during the observation and, therefore, behave differently. Observers' presence in the home "often induced anxiety or triggered abnormally considerate and tolerant behaviors in families" (McDermott, Tseng, Char, & Fukunaga, 1978, p. 108). Parents and children may each try to be "on their best behavior" or perform according to what they perceive are the observers' expectations.

In infant–mother studies, when mothers were aware of being video-taped, they stayed closer to their infants, offered and demonstrated toys more frequently, engaged in interactional games more often, vocalized more frequently, and engaged their infants in more productive play than when the observers were in the room (Field, 1991). Mothers reportedly were less nervous with the video camera than with live observers. But the effects of being observed are not always in the direction of social desirability (Patterson, 1977). "Normal" parents apparently can make their children behave in desirable or undesirable ways, but "deviant parents could make their children only look bad, not good" (p. 316).

Other authors seem less concerned and think reactive effects may be temporary. "Over time, clients may become used to the observer's presence and their behavior may return to its natural pattern and rates"

(Gambrill, 1997, p. 387). In the case scenario it would have been helpful if Dr. Hale had allowed a warm-up period for Bridget and her parents to become accustomed to the presence of the observer, the one-way screen, recording devices, and instruments, before rating parent–child observations during this period (Herrenkohl et al., 1984; Roggman et al., 2000).

Observer Bias

Observer awareness of the family status (clinical or normal) or treatment status (baseline or intervention) may affect the observer's global judgments of what is going on, although ratings of specific behaviors seem to be unaffected (Patterson, 1977). Also, inter-rater reliability may be affected when the rater has had prior contact with the parent, as would be the case in most clinical settings. "Many observers find it difficult to separate their prior knowledge of the parent from the judgments they make about the observed behavior" (Mahoney et al., 1996, p. 35). Even when observers have no prior knowledge about a parent, "they still form personal opinions about the parents' style of interaction that are based on their personal views regarding what is 'good' or 'bad'" (p. 36).

In effect, observers' reactions toward parents are never completely unbiased. The more established the relationship between clinicians and parents becomes, the greater is the likelihood that clinicians' judgments about the observed interactions will be influenced, positively or negatively.

Referring again to our case scenario, Dr. Hale certainly was aware that Bridget had been removed from the parents' care because of physical abuse. Although this knowledge may have influenced her judgment about the quality of parenting, she took considerable steps during the controlled observation setting to incorporate the observations from other sources in an effort to increase the reliability of the observational data.

Threats to Validity

Several potential threats to validity of observational data of parent–child interactions are as follows.

Situational Specificity of Behavior

The importance of the context in which observations occur has been discussed as a potential threat to reliability. A related issue is that of *situational specificity* of behavior, which can threaten the validity of the observation. Children's and parents' behaviors in one setting may or may not reflect their performance in other settings (Merrell, 1994). Unless data are gathered about what behavior actually occurs (not just assumed or inferred) in multiple settings, there is no way to verify whether the behavior observed in one context generalizes to other contexts. Determining enduring patterns of behavior requires that observations be conducted on multiple occasions, from multiple contexts or settings, using a standardized rating instrument, and (ideally) using highly trained multiple observers.

Especially when observations are made in analogue settings, evaluators must make "validity appraisals" by asking children and parents whether the interactions observed in the controlled setting are representative of those occurring elsewhere. In the case scenario, Dr. Hale did make a careful comparison between the analogue observational data she obtained at the social services office with observational data obtained by the ongoing caseworker and foster parents.

Failure to Use Social Contrast Data

Behavioral observation must include social contrast data—the observer must randomly select "two or three nonreferred subjects in the same setting and alternate the observation between the referred subject and the social comparison subjects on a rotating basis" (Merrell, 1994, p. 59). Social contrast data are particularly important when attempting to assess the *severity* of the problem behaviors, because a determination can be made directly as to whether the interactions of the children and parents being evaluated differ markedly from the behaviors of parent–child peers in the same setting. Unfortunately, this is rarely done in clinical practice. No doubt, part of the problem is in the difficulty of recruiting sufficient numbers of nonreferred children and parents and arranging a suitable context for them to be observed, along with the specific child and parents being evaluated.

The issue becomes even more complex if family members are observed in multiple settings, as each requires social comparison data. Evaluators may have to be particularly creative and flexible in obtaining social contrast data. For example, if Bridget and her parents were observed as they sat in the social services waiting room with similarly referred parents and children, Bridget's family would be unlikely to provide sufficient contrast to be able to judge whether their relationships are severely impaired. But if they were observed at a school or community event (e.g., back-to-school night) with numerous interactions between nonreferred children and parents, this situation would be far more valuable in drawing conclusions about the quality of their interactions.

Where setting up social contrast observations involving both referred and non-referred children and parents is not feasible, evaluators can obtain some information through interviewing. For example, Dr. Hale might have asked the Baileys a series of questions such as, "How does Bridget compare to other same-aged girls (say, those in her class at school) in complying with adults' directives?" If the Baileys had given permission for Dr. Hale to contact Bridget's teacher, similar social contrast data could be obtained. Another way of obtaining social contrast data might be to have the child complete a standardized self-report behavioral rating scale in which the child's individual results are compared to those derived from a normative group.

Instrumentation

Using inappropriate recording techniques to rate parent–child behaviors may affect the validity of the results (Merrell, 1994). For example, attempting to observe a low-frequency but clinically meaningful behavior, such as a suicidal attempt, with an interval-rating instrument designed to capture high-frequency behaviors could result in the infrequently occurring but potentially life-threatening behaviors not being recorded at all. Obviously, such a mismatch between observed behavior and the rating system used could result in invalid conclusions about the seriousness of the behavior. The selection of rating instruments should be congruent with the length of time of the observation.

Content Validity Threats

As noted in chapter 3, content validity refers to whether the items on a scale are representative of the items contained within some defined domain or content universe. "Most of the research scales that are currently being used to assess parent–child interaction have not been developed to reflect a predefined domain of parenting effectiveness" (Mahoney et al., 1996, p. 37). In these authors' view, most scales are a "conglomerate of traits and constructs" derived from the clinical and research literature.

Although the stated purpose of many of these observation scales is to differentiate the qualities of effective and ineffective or harmful parenting, the scales do not identify "the outcome that parents should be effective at accomplishing, or even acknowledging that different types of parenting traits may lead to differential child outcomes" (Mahoney et al., 1996, p. 37). Thus, the items on the parent–child observation scales do not distinguish between parenting behaviors that have little or no bearing on children's developmental outcomes and those that have a probable or causal relationship. According to these authors, many of the parenting characteristics appearing on these scales have little empirical support despite the "intuitive logic" that the items are related to parental effectiveness.

Construct Validity Threats

Construct validity addresses the question of whether the ratings or scores derived from the assessment procedure actually measure the dimensions of behavior they purport to measure. In this case, the question is whether time-limited observations of parent–child interactions (ranging from 10 minutes to several hours), usually obtained on one occasion only, in settings likely characterized by some defensiveness and reactivity by parents and children, provide a true reflection of the general types of interactions between parents and children in their natural environments?

One way that psychology answers this question is to determine the strength of association between a recently developed instrument, such as a new intelligence test, and an existing one, such as the Wechsler Scales, whose reliability and validity have been established already. In summarizing their own research in correlating three different maternal–child interaction scales on the same set of observations, Mahoney and colleagues (1996) noted that there seemed to be "little commonality in how different scales measure similarly named and defined constructs" (p. 40). They questioned whether any of the parent–child interaction scales they reviewed actually assesses the constructs that these scales claim to measure.

Criterion Validity Threats

Parents' ratings on these interactional scales may have little or no relationship between either their child's current developmental functioning (concurrent validity) or the child's development at future points in time (predictive validity). Mahoney and colleagues (1996) conducted a study of the criterion validity of three parent–child observational scales, examining how items measuring the constructs of maternal responsiveness, directiveness, and affect were related to children's current developmental level and the quality of their play and interaction with their mothers at the time of the initial observations and 12 months later.

The results indicated that variables measuring maternal interaction had low-level correlations to concurrent child development measures and only slightly higher correlations to their developmental functioning a year later. These investigators cautioned that "the amount of variability in children's functioning that can be measured through existing measures of parent–child interaction may be clinically insignificant" (p. 41).

Other studies have suggested that some parent–child observational scales do show evidence of either concurrent or predictive validity. For example, a study of the *Behavior Coding Scale* indicated that parents' rating of problem children's behaviors correlated .69 with children who scored high on observed deviant behaviors (aggression or conduct problems), which seems to adequately demonstrate concurrent validity (Patterson, 1977). Also, significant differences were found in the observed behavior of aggressive boys in their pre- and posttreatment scores, which seem to demonstrate predictive validity. Other research-based scales for observing parent–child interaction reported some evidence for *discriminate validity*—the ability to detect differences among groups known to differ on the characteristics or variables in question, such as compliance (Eyberg & Robinson, 1983; Field, 1991; Forehand & McMahon, 1981; Herrenkohl et al., 1984; Patterson, 1977).

A major threat to interpreting parent–child observational systems is the lack of normative data regarding how parents interact with their children (Mahoney et al., 1996; Smith, 2000).

> There are no standard behavioral items or markers about parents' interactive behavior for which we even have descriptive data about their form or frequency of occurrence, and certainly nothing comparable to the normative data available for children's cognitive, motor, or language development. (Mahoney et al., 1996, p. 42)

Further, existing measures of parent–child interactions do not seem to direct adequate attention to distinguishing between individual differences in parent–child interactions and cultural patterns of childrearing (Roggman et al., 2000). The "norms" for these instruments typically are not derived statistically but, rather, are generic statements derived from the clinical literature, such as, "The parent provides clear structure appropriate to the child's developmental level" and, "The child accepts adult structure."

Obviously, a great deal of subjective judgment or inference by evaluators is involved in ascertaining whether a given child–parent dyad meets or falls short of these norms. In addition, the norms are phrased as universal statements, taking no account of cultural differences in childrearing or in parent–child relationships, which may be problematic when evaluating clients from diverse multicultural backgrounds. For instance, childrearing practices in some cultural groups emphasize early autonomy and exploration in their children, whereas in other cultures childrearing may foster a longer period of nurturing and dependency. Parents from these different cultural groups are likely to be rated quite differently on items in which the "normative guideline" is for parents to encourage independence in their children.

Ethical Issues

As noted in chapter 2, psychologists are bound by a professional code of ethics, which requires that "parents…[be] informed of the purposes for which they are being observed and/or assessed" (Mahoney et al., 1996, p. 34). Ideally, this process should be collaborative, so clients and evaluating professionals decide together who will observe, what will be observed, when to observe, where to observe, and how long to observe, as well as how to minimize observer intrusiveness and how to record the data being collected accurately and efficiently (Gambrill, 1997).

In many practice settings, the observational process is threatening to parents, particularly if major decisions or outcomes are at stake, such as whether a child will be admitted to a special education or a mental health treatment program, undergo a change of custody or visitation, or whether an allegation of suspected parental physical abuse, neglect, or sexual abuse will be sustained as a result of the evaluation.

According to Mahoney and colleagues (1996), some professionals attempt to allay parents' anxiety by making the child the focus of the informed consent instructions, using statements such as, "We would like to observe how you and your child spend time together," rather than more direct statements such as, "We are observing your childrearing skills"— which tends to put parents on the defensive. Clients who are court-ordered to participate in a parent–child interaction deserve candor, too, but it remains unclear whether diversionary or "soften-the-blow" tactics meet the ethical requirements for full disclosure.

Bricklin (1995) asserts that "parents know there is a very strong probability that they are being observed when they are anywhere near the mental health professional's office" (p. 58), but that does not lessen the professional's ethical obligation to ensure that parents, and secondarily children, clearly understand the purposes of the observation. This issue is considered further in chapter 8, which examines ways to prepare clients for the evaluation process.

Case Planning Considerations

Observational data remain an important component of parent and child assessments, but referring professionals and evaluating psychologists alike must understand their limitations, as observations can alter family members' life trajectories dramatically—for better or worse (Mahoney et al., 1996). Incorporating observational data into effective case planning decisions requires that psychologists, social workers, and other helping professionals follow these guidelines regarding parent–child interactions:

1. Observational data in and of itself cannot be considered entirely objective and unbiased, notwithstanding the claims of behavioral theory. Theoretical lenses shape what is seen by constructing the setting in which parent–child interactions take place, the tasks and materials that children and parents are instructed to use during the observation sessions, the methods used to code behaviors, and how much inference is involved in deriving meaning from the observational data. Thus, referring professionals should expect psychological evaluators and other clinicians to distinguish clearly between *descriptions* of observed behavior and *inferences* about the meaning or origin of the behavior. This is especially critical when the observational data are used for forensic purposes.

2. Recall from chapter 3 that one of the basic assumptions underlying psychological tests is the notion that human traits are enduring and stable across time, place, and space. Referring professionals should also note an important corollary to that assumption: that human behavior frequently is *role-* and *context-specific* to different situations. Thus, behavior occurring in one setting does not necessarily mean that behavior will generalize to other settings and contexts. At best, structured observations in time-limited periods should be regarded as but one sample of behavior rather than a determination (in the absence of other data) that the observed interactions constitute enduring patterns of behaviors.

3. Data on parent–child interactions and relationships should be gathered using a variety of assessment methods, sources, and settings. For example, clinical interviews with parents and children can incorporate *ethnographic questions* about a typical day or week in the family, what activities adults and children often do together and where these activities usually occur, and how the family members typically interact when problems or conflicts arise (Jordan & Franklin, 1995).

Ethnographic questions are designed to elicit rich descriptions of clients' experiences in the everyday contexts of their lives, as opposed to traditional forms of mental health interviewing, which usually probe for information on clients' feelings, thoughts, desires, and so forth.

In addition, a daily log of parent–child activities and a self-rating scale on how satisfactory or unsatisfactory those activities were to each partner in the dyad or family unit could be obtained as part of baseline information. Further, the observational rating scales in the multi-assessment systems such as the *Child Behavior Check List* (CBCL) or the *Behavior Assessment Scale for Children* (BASC)— even though these scales are limited to the child's behavior—can be used to some extent as a means of cross-checking the types of behavioral problems in the family (Achenbach & McConaughy, 2003; Reynolds & Kamphaus, 2003).

4. To be considered reliable and valid, observations of parent–child interactions must be made, at a minimum, on *multiple occasions*, in *multiple settings*, by *multiple observers*, using the *same operational definition of behavior*—whether observations are made in a natural setting or an analogue setting. As with other types of assessments, it is best to *triangulate the data* on parent–child interactions from multiple sources, settings, and occasions (Merrell, 1994). Where possible, use of the same coding system of recording by the different observers would help to determine inter-observer and cross-setting reliability, as well as permit an interdisciplinary opportunity to collaborate in working with children and parents.

5. Parents and children should be *fully informed* about the purposes of the observation. In addition, observations are best undertaken when initial rapport has been established between evaluators and parents. A warm-up period should precede the behavior ratings. Evaluators' reports of parent–child interactions should clearly describe what steps the evaluators took in preparing the children and family for the observation process.

6. Evaluators should acknowledge that anxiety about being observed and/or unfamiliarity with the assessment process can interfere markedly with task performance. Thus, parents may perform worse, or less than their typical abilities, when they are observed and/or asked to perform tasks, even those that appear routine, under stressful circumstances. Situational anxiety should be clearly differentiated from enduring traits or recurring patterns of functional or dysfunctional behaviors.

7. Observations can be contaminated both by client factors (social desirability, malingering, etc.) and by evaluator factors (confirmatory bias, observer drift, etc.). In particular, parent–child interactionals that are based solely on the judgment of a single clinician may be influenced by the evaluator's previous information about the family (interviews, review of records, etc.), as well as preconceived notions about the quality of the parent–child relationship. Referring professionals should read observers' reports carefully for any evidence that evaluators gathered additional information about parents and children, as Dr. Hale did in the case scenario.

8. Where observations are obtained in a controlled analogue setting, raters who are not familiar with the family should be used to reduce observer bias. This is particularly crucial when observational data are used for forensic purposes.

9. Rating "norms" regarding parent–child interactions must pay attention to variation in childrearing and parent–child relationships among diverse cultural groups. Referring to the case scenario, Dr. Hale, who grew up in an African American family headed by her mother and grandmother, should be familiar with the general cultural characteristics of traditional Irish families such as the Baileys, in which the father, as family patriarch, frequently takes the role of stern disciplinarian.

10. Referring professionals should treat cautiously any conclusions about parent–child observations that are derived solely from analogue settings conducted on a one-time basis.

Additional Resources

The parent–child observation protocols or rating instruments annotated below are representative of the types currently available in a variety of practice situations, such as child custody disputes, child sexual abuse investigations, mental health treatment planning, early childhood intervention, and treatment of aggressive, conduct-disordered adolescents. These observational systems vary greatly in terms of the theoretical constructs guiding the observation—whether analogue or naturalistic observations were used; the relative complexity or simplicity of their methods for gathering and coding observation data; whether parent–child pairs or the entire family were observed separately; and whether the reliability and validity of the observation results had been ascertained.

Bricklin, B. (1995). *The Custody Evaluation Handbook: Research-based Solutions and Applications.* New York: Brunner/Mazel.

Bricklin (1995) developed a parent–child observation protocol to observe parent–child interactions that can be used in either an office setting or during a home visit as a component of custody evaluations. Observations take place in two sets of conditions, spontaneous and structured. The spontaneous observations rated may be in the waiting room before introductions or during a home visit in the living room and may include playing a game of the parents' choice and playing a game of the child's choice. The other set involves observing parents' capacity for teaching competency skills of both simple and complex tasks, which includes evaluating the parent's ability to be a valuable source of information to children and to facilitate cooperative problem solving. Parents are rated according to the following categories:

• ability to *meaningfully* communicate a sense of warmth, love, and acceptance [italics in original];
• ability to communicate clearly;
• ability to teach and to be a role model for competent problem solving;
• ability to understand and acknowledge the child's point of view and feelings;
• ability to accurately gauge the child's emergent needs and/or ability to set appropriate limits;
• ability to engender independence and a sense of self-sufficiency on the child's part.

One noteworthy feature of Bricklin's approach to parent–child observation is his insistence that both parents be present, rather than to observe each child separately with each caregiver. This allows direct observations of the quality of the child's relationship with each parent in the same context.

Haynes-Semen, C., & Baumgarten, D. (1994). *Children Speak for Themselves: Using the Kempe Interactional Assessment to Evaluate Allegations of Parent–Child Sexual Abuse.* New York: Brunner/Mazel.

This is a psychoanalytic forensic parent–child interaction observation protocol used to evaluate parents who are suspected of sexually abusing their children. Observations are conducted in a comfortable room furnished with couches and chairs for the adults and small chairs, tables, and play materials for the children. The interactions are videotaped through a one-way mirror. The protocol consists of

> standard sessions [including] a time when parents are alone, reunion of the children with their parents, unstructured play among the family prior to the clinical interview of the parents, the child's presence and play during the clinical interview, a snack shared by parents and children, and separation of parents and children. When the parents are divorced, a transition between the noncustodial and custodial parent may also be videotaped. (p. 21)

Subsequently the parent–child sessions and play interviews with children are transcribed. All verbal statements are recorded, and the evaluator in addition notes physical behaviors, eye contact (or avoidance), spatial relationships, proximities and touching, affect (particularly any discordant affect between parents and children), activities with people and objects, content of drawings, willingness to engage each other and things fully, and lack of action or response.

The transcripts and video recordings of the observations, sessions, and interviews are reviewed by an interdisciplinary team of psychologists, social workers, psychiatrists, nurses, and attorneys. The protocol information is then integrated with data collected from other sources, such as police reports and information supplied by social service caseworkers. Although the authors portray the Kempe Protocol as a "design for a complete and objective process," no reliability and validity data are presented to support this claim. The instrument relies heavily on clinical inference. For example, observers are instructed to "imagine" that what they observe is a repetition of a recurring pattern between child and parent and to project the likely benefit or harm of that interaction accordingly.

Marschak, M. (1960). "A Method for Evaluating Parent–Child Interaction under Controlled Conditions," *Journal of Genetic Psychology*, *97*, 3–32.

The *Marschak Interaction Method* (MIM) was developed by Marianne Marschak (1960) to assess various components of the identification process in children. Subsequently, the MIM has been revised as a primary means of assessing parent–child inter-actions prior to beginning treatment (Lindaman et al., 2000). Although it is used primarily in treatment planning, the MIM also has been used for social services forensic evaluations, chemical dependency evaluations, Head Start evaluations of children and their mothers, and martial therapy. It also has been used with pop-ulations from different cultural backgrounds and/or nationalities, as well as with a variety of clinic populations, such as children with autism and schizophrenia, and HIV-infected mothers and their newborns.

The MIM consists of a series of tasks designed to elicit a range of behaviors from the parent–child dyad. Parents are assessed according to whether they can

- structure the environment and set appropriate expectations and limits,
- engage a child in interaction while being attuned to the child's emotional state and reactions,
- respond in a nurturing way to a child's needs, and
- provide a child an appropriate challenge (i.e., tasks that encour-age children's development and independence).

Children are assessed according to whether they can

- accept structure from adults,
- engage with adults,
- accept nurturing care from the adults, and
- respond to appropriate challenge.

A rating form is used to code the verbal and nonverbal behaviors of children and parents, as well as to generate hypotheses of what may be occurring and to mark particularly noteworthy transac-tions for later use in giving feedback to the family. Information from the MIM then is integrated with data obtained from other sources such as clinical interviews, developmental screening inventories, paper and pencil questionnaires and self-report inven-tories, standardized tests, and projective drawings and tests.

A MIM session takes 30 to 45 minutes, and children usually are evaluated with each parent on separate days. The session typ-ically takes place in a clinic or an office equipped with a one-way mirror and videotaping equipment. The evaluator prepares a list

of tasks ahead of time and places each task in a numbered enve-
lope, along with the corresponding materials, next to where the
parent is seated. The tasks consist of a variety of developmentally
appropriate activities in some combination of parent-led and
child-led activities. After the tasks have been completed, the
evaluator returns to the room and asks the child and the parent
whether what they did during the session was similar to how they
interact at home and to identify their favorite and least liked
activities.

Goldberg, S. (1977). "Social Competence in Infancy: A Model of
Parent– Infant Interaction." *Merrill-Palmer Quarterly, 23,* 163–178.

> Goldberg developed the theoretical construct of *mutual compe-
> tence* to describe the development of effective communication
> between parent and infant (Bernstein, Campbell, and Akers,
> 2001). Mutual competence is defined as any interchange between
> parents and children in which the parties feel secure, valued, suc-
> cessful, and happy. Observations are recorded on a 2 × 3 mutual
> competence grid. Observers record two types of behaviors—those
> that represent mutual competence between parents and children,
> and those that indicate a concern about either the parent or the
> child. In the third column the observers record their ideas about
> ways to strengthen the parent–child relationship, which can be
> used for brainstorming in team meetings, clinical supervision, and
> work with parents. Observations occur in home visits with at-risk
> children and their families and during clinic visits.

Smith, D. (2000). "Parent–Child Interaction Play Assessment." In K.
Giltin-Weiner, A. Sandgrund, and C. Schaefer (Eds.), *Play Diagnosis
and Assessment* (2nd ed.), pp. 340–370. New York: John Wiley &
Sons.

> The *Parent–Child Interaction Play Assessment* (P–CIPA) is a
> diagnostic tool used in mental health settings to assess the
> strengths and weaknesses of the parent–child relationship and to
> suggest ways to make the change (Smith, 2000). P–CIPA sessions
> are typically conducted in a specialized observation room having
> a one-way mirror and videotape equipment. This system requires
> only one observer, which may make it more feasible to use in
> many practice settings.

Children and parents are observed during two 15-minute periods of interaction—one structured and one unstructured. In the unstructured period the parent and the child are instructed to pretend that they are at home having some uninterrupted free time and to do what they usually do during those times. In the structured period parents are asked to have their child do three tasks: clean up toys in the room, follow a command or perform an activity, and demonstrate self-care behaviors (e.g., take off shoes and socks independently). Following this, the evaluator makes a "validity appraisal" by asking the child and the parent how representative they thought the interactions and behaviors were during the unstructured and structured periods compared to what occurs at home.

During the unstructured play session, 13 categories of behavior are scored, and during the structured portion, eight categories are scored. Half of the unstructured categories are ratings of the parent's behavior, and the other half of the ratings are of the child's behavior. Five of the structured categories focus on parent's behaviors, and three on the child's responses.

Categories of parent behavior are affect, intrusiveness, praise, attention, developmental sensitivity, responsiveness to child's interactions, and involvement. Categories of child behavior are compliance, willfulness, and aggressiveness. Ratings are on a 9-point continuum of behavior (semantic differential scale) representing a low to high progression of behaviors (e.g., "1 = Parent ignored all of child's behaviors" to "9 = Parent paid attention to all of child's desirable behaviors, ignored all negative ones").

Patterson, G. (1977). "Naturalistic Observation in Clinical Assessment." *Journal of Abnormal Child Psychology, 5,* 309–322.

The *Behavior Coding System* was created as part of the program of research on aggressive and antisocial behavior in preadolescent boys conducted at the Oregon Social Learning Center. Two noteworthy features of this observation system are that the data are derived from observations taken in the home rather than a controlled analogue setting and that the interactions among *all family members*, not just the parent–child dyad, are coded. Family members are observed at a consistent time, in late afternoon just before dinner.

A time sampling procedure is used in collecting data. Two observers observe each family member for two 5-minute periods each day, over a 2-week period, resulting in 60 to 100 minutes of observation per family member. Twenty-eight family interactions are recorded, organized into six behavioral categories according to whether the interactions are verbal, nonverbal, or both.

Verbal behaviors coded include commands, command negative, cry, humiliate, laugh, negativism, whine, yell, and talk. Nonverbal behaviors coded include destructiveness, high-rate, ignore, physical negative, attention, normative, no response, receive, and touch. Behaviors that could be either verbal or nonverbal also are coded: approval, compliance, disapproval, dependency, noncompliance, play, tease, work, and self-stimulation. Behaviors are rated according to whether they are "first order" (behaviors of chief interest, such as compliance, aggressiveness, teasing) or "second order" (all other types of behaviors).

Conclusion

This chapter has reviewed the advantages and disadvantages of measures of parent–child observations. Advantages are that they permit observational data to be collected in a standardized manner; more child and parent variables can be tracked; the observations may yield more precise estimates of prosocial and dysfunctional behaviors and interaction sequences; and where more than one rater is employed, the inter-rater reliability of the instruments can be directly ascertained.

These measures also seem to have serious flaws. Referring professionals should keep in mind that most of these scales were developed for the purpose of measuring *severity* of disturbance or dysfunction in the parent–child relationship. Yet, the lack of empirically derived norms means that the interactions of one parent–child dyad cannot be compared against a representative comparison group. *The psychometric properties of these scales are best suited for comparing a given parent–child dyad to itself at different points in time.*

Other drawbacks to observational data are the need for extensive observer training; the possibility that as the complexity of observational categories increases, the accuracy of the observations may decline correspondingly; the brief time when behaviors actually are observed; the expense and time-consuming nature, making observations difficult to implement on a large scale; and overestimation of agreement between raters if chance agreements (random error) is not taken into account.

A final caution in using observational rating systems of parents and children is to ascertain the system's sensitivity to cultural differences.

> Developmental and behavioral norms and professional practice are based on the majority culture and may be diametrically opposed to those of a minority culture…. Cultural differences must be considered when talking to parents about their children…. Acting honestly with a heightened awareness of the differences will help the child. By displaying a willingness to learn and desire not to offend, families and [professionals] will build a partnership for the child. (Nilsen, 1997, p. 130)

Chapter 6

Substance Abuse Assessment and Treatment Planning

Karen Mooney[1] and John Kayser

[1] Karen Mooney, LCSW, CAC III, is a licensed clinical social worker and a certified addictions counselor. As a child welfare caseworker, she established the first addiction evaluation and referral program that was part of a county department of human services in Colorado. Subsequently she was employed as a program manager for an alcohol and drug managed service organization jointly owned by several community substance abuse treatment centers in the Denver area. Currently she is Coordinator of Women's Treatment, Colorado Department of Human Services, Alcohol and Drug Addiction Division.

*Self-report is an
essential component of
the assessment process in that
it represents the client's
present willingness to report
what he or she perceives
to be going on.
This self-perception is where
the change process begins—
with the client's...willingness
to disclose information.*

(Wanberg, 2000, p. 4)

This chapter intro-
duces referring pro-
fessionals to drug and

| OVERVIEW |

alcohol assessments. Although some psychologists have specialized training in this area, substance abuse evaluations are done more commonly by
bachelor- or master-level clinicians who are state certified or licensed as
drug and alcohol counselors. Many clients with drug and alcohol problems also have co-occurring mental health problems or disorders, such as
major depression, ADHD, anxiety, panic attacks or phobias, or conduct or
personality disorders, that may necessitate concurrent psychological or
mental health evaluations. The challenge for referring professionals is to
learn how to incorporate substance abuse assessments *and* psychological
assessments into effective treatment planning.

Although professionals encounter people with drug and alcohol
problems in a wide variety of practice settings, this chapter is directed
primarily to drug and alcohol evaluations of addicted or impaired parents
who are receiving child protection services, because these parents are at
greater risk for having their children removed from their custodial care.
Substance abuse assessment, in conjunction with other assessments, can
help referring professionals develop a comprehensive view of the needs
of the entire family system that takes into account children's needs for
safety and security as well as parents' potential to benefit from substance
abuse treatment.

The chapter begins by defining some of the key terms used in substance abuse assessments and summarizes the prevalence rates of *alcohol
and other drug* (AOD) use in the United States. A brief history of the substance abuse treatment field is provided as background information. The
chapter then examines some of the conflicts and controversies that have
arisen when substance abuse professionals and child welfare professionals have been jointly involved with the same clients, such as whether substance-abusing parents are entitled to confidentiality in the evaluation
process, whether evaluations of parental substance abuse should be clinical or forensic in nature, and whether parental self-reports of AOD use can
be reliable and valid.

Phases of drug and alcohol evaluations and commonly used measures of assessment are reviewed. The qualifications of drug and alcohol evaluators are examined briefly. In addition, a sample substance abuse evaluation report is presented and critiqued in detail. The case planning discussion examines the ways in which referring professionals can draw on the findings and recommendations from substance abuse evaluations and psychological assessments as they formulate effective treatment interventions.

Definitions of Key Terms

Professionals have to become familiar with the *DSM-IV-TR* definitions regarding different types of substance misuse, distinguishing between *substance-induced disorders* and *substance-use disorders* (American Psychiatric Association, 2000). This distinction points to the bidirectional relationship between behavioral disorders and substance abuse; either "may be the cause or the consequence" of the other (Adesso, Cisler, Larus, & Hayes, 2004, p. 148). Many substance-abuse professionals are critical of the DSM-IV system of classifications, however, as being simplistic and arbitrary. In their view, substance use is conceptualized more accurately as existing on a continuum from nonuse to dependence (Brems, 2000):

1. *Substance-induced disorders* "are those in which the presenting symptoms are phenomenologically similar to those of a behavioral disorder but are attributable to the use of substance" (Adesso et al., 2004, p. 149). Presenting symptoms include intoxication, withdrawal, and a variety of other mental health-type symptoms such as dementia, delirium, amnesia, psychosis, mood disorders, anxiety disorders, sexual dysfunction, and sleep disorders, which are induced by using substances.

2. *Substance-use disorders* refer to symptoms instigated by the use of *psychoactive substances*—those that alter a person's thought processes or mood by affecting the central nervous system. In addition to alcohol, psychoactive substances include amphetamines, caffeine, cannabis, nicotine, cocaine, PCP (phencyclidine), inhalants, hallucinogens, opiates, and sedatives (Brems, 2000; Hood & Johnson, 2002).

   Caffeine, though having known health-risks, generally is not included in the list of substances leading to either substance abuse or dependence (Adesso et al., 2004). Some authorities, however, particularly those working with adolescents, include nicotine in the class of psychoactive substances leading to substance-use disorders because preadolescent use of cigarettes has been found to be associated with the use of marijuana in early adolescence; this, in turn, can become a gateway drug to the use of other illicit substances (Brems, 2000; Winters, Newcomb, & Fahnhorst, 2004). Given the addicting properties of nicotine and the undisputed links between smoking and cancer, it should be seen as a dangerous drug in its own right, not only as a gateway to illicit drug use.

3. As defined by the *DSM-IV-TR* (American Psychiatric Association, 2000), substance-use disorders are broken down further into two subtypes: substance abuse and substance dependence.

   a. *Substance abuse* is the maladaptive use of substance(s) that leads to recurrent and significant impairments in an individual's functioning at home, school, or work, and that lasts more than 12 months. At least four of the following symptoms must be present (Winters, Newcomb, & Fahnhorst, 2004):

      - failing to fulfill expected role obligations;
      - placing oneself in physically hazardous situations (such as driving while intoxicated);
      - having legal problems; and
      - having negative social consequences or interpersonal difficulties related to substance use.

      According to Adesso et al. (2004), substance *abuse* "is viewed as a less pervasive problem than substance *dependence*.... The criteria for substance abuse focus on the harmful consequences of repeated use and exclude tolerance, withdrawal, and a pattern of compulsive use" (p. 149).

   b. *Substance dependence*, defined by the *DSM-IV-TR*, is the psychological and physical response to substance use over a 12-month period that perpetuate substance use despite negative personal consequences. At least three of the following symptoms must be present:

      - tolerance: increasing amounts of the substance needed for the same effect;
      - withdrawal symptoms when the substance is no longer present in the body;

- compulsive use: taking the substance in larger amounts or for longer periods of time, despite the physical or psychological problems it produces;
- craving: a persistent desire for the substance or unsuccessful attempt to cut down on its use;
- curtailment or abandonment of social activities;
- more time devoted to obtaining substances; and
- continued use despite the substance having a negative impact on one or more areas of a person's life.

Substance dependence is a more serious condition than substance abuse, indicating that the individual continues to use the substance despite significant problems related to its use (Adesso et al., 2004; Hood & Johnson, 2002).

Prevalence Rates of Substance Abuse and Dependence

Substance abuse and dependence are major health problems in the United States. The *lifetime prevalence* of alcohol or drug abuse or dependence has been estimated variously at between 19% and 25%—meaning that at some point during the lifetime, substance abuse or dependence will become a clinically significant problem for up to a quarter of the population (Brems, 2000; Hood & Johnson, 2002). The term *prevalence* is used in epidemiological studies to refer to the number or proportion of individuals in a population with a disorder at any given time (Wicks-Nelson & Israel, 2006).

According to the 2001-2002 National Epidemiologic Survey on Alcohol and Related Conditions conducted by the National Institute on Alcohol Abuse and Alcoholism, 17.6 million Americans met the criteria for alcohol use disorders (AUD) during that 12 month period (Grant, Dawson, Stinson, Chou, DuFour, & Pickering, 2006; NIAAA, 2006). According to the 2006 National Survey on Drug Use and Health sponsored by the Substance Abuse and Mental Health Services Administration (SAMHSA), an estimated 20.4 million Americans age 12 or older had used illicit drugs within the past month (SAMHSA, 2007). Illicit drugs included marijuana, cocaine, heroin, hallucinogens, inhalants, and prescription drugs used illegally. Many illegal drug users abuse alcohol as well (Adesso et al., 2004). Rates of substance-use disorders are especially high in individuals who have a co-occurring mental health disorder (Brems, 2000), as well as among those having chronic physical disabilities and traumatic injuries to the brain or spinal cord (Bombardier, 2000).

Since the 1970s, substance use rates of certain types of drug use by adolescents, such as hallucinogens, have either stabilized or declined, but rates of other substances, particularly alcohol, have been on the rise (Cavell, Ennett, & Meehan, 2001, Winters, Newcomb, & Fahnhorst, 2004). The lifetime prevalence rates for adolescent alcohol use remain disturbingly high. In one national survey, more than one-third of eighth-graders reported that they drank alcohol during the past year and nearly three-quarters of 12th-graders reported consuming alcohol during the past year (Winters, Newcomb, & Fahnhorst, 2004). The lifetime prevalence rates for marijuana use were almost 20% for 8th-graders and more than 41% for 12th-graders (Cavell, Ennett, & Meehan, 2001).

Binge drinking on college campuses has increased markedly in the last several years, as indicated by several highly publicized cases of lethal alcohol poisoning in college fraternities and sororities (Davis, 2004). Other negative social consequences of AOD misuse include auto accidents, suicide, unwanted pregnancies, sexually transmitted diseases including HIV infections, interpersonal violence, academic failure and school dropout, and occupational difficulties (Cavell, Ennett, & Meehan, 2001).

Brief History of Substance Abuse Treatment

Substance abusers have been treated since the mid-1800s in a variety of ways. Initially, treatment consisted of *hospital stays* to help people detoxify or "dry out" from alcohol. The Martha Washington Home, built by Charles Hull in 1869, was the first settlement house in the United States. It provided drug and alcohol treatment for individuals, with length-of-stay ranging from 2 to 4 months (Straussner & Attia, 2002).

The modern era of substance abuse treatment has its roots in the *self-help movement*, typified by Alcoholics Anonymous (AA), which was initiated in the 1940s. Self-help groups made a tremendous contribution in alcoholism treatment of people by focusing on the steps needed to attain and maintain sobriety. A basic premise of AA and similar 12-step programs is that no one can help a person with alcohol or drug problems as well as someone who has been there, and that once sober or clean, individuals further their own recovery by helping others to attain sobriety.

Following the introduction of AA, attempts were made to treat other populations with substance abuse problems, primarily those seen in the criminal justice system. The *therapeutic community movement*, which began in California in the 1950s, was also grounded in the idea that a group of peers could best treat a person with antisocial behavior and attitudes, as well as addiction. As a result, using professionals to provide substance abuse treatment services received little attention.

Methadone came into use in the 1960s to keep people addicted to heroin from going into withdrawal. Despite the controversy surrounding the replacement of one addiction for another (O'Connor, Esherick, & Vieten, 2002; U.S. Department of Health and Human Services, 1994), methadone has proved to be the most effective method of keeping people off heroin and away from the risks associated with heroin use.

In the late 1970s, treatment services for persons criminally charged with driving under the influence (DUI) of alcohol came about to address the needs of communities that were impacted negatively by drinking and driving. DUI treatment, aimed at keeping intoxicated persons from driving, has evolved over the years into highly specialized interventions in some parts of the country.

Over the past decade, the field of *offender treatment* has grown dramatically as alternatives to incarceration are becoming more popular for individuals convicted of drug offenses. Treatments for DUI and drug offenders both have been subsidized partially by the criminal justice system, either through criminal justice treatment grants or by self-funding of treatment paid for by clients as a part of their probation or parole requirements.

In addition to the treatment approaches described above, emerging research suggests that many individuals are able to use *natural recovery* methods, using their own coping skills and support networks to reduce and/or end their use of alcohol and other substances without the aid of any formal self-help or professional intervention (Cloud & Granfield, 2001). One barrier to using a natural recovery approach for clients seen in child welfare settings is that many parents have few social support networks in place, in addition to having poor coping skills to deal with multiple stressors.

Substance Abuse Assessments of Clients in the Child Welfare System

Historically, professionals in the field of substance abuse treatment and those in the child protection field had little involvement with each other, even though substance abuse occurs in an estimated one-third to two-thirds of child welfare cases (U.S Department of Health and Human Services, 1999; Young, Gardner, & Dennis, 1998). Despite this prevalence, most social service caseworkers typically did not receive specialized training in how to incorporate substance abuse assessments into case planning.

More recently, the connection between childhood trauma and the subsequent development of substance abuse and addiction problems in adulthood has been documented (U.S. Department of Health and Human Services, 2000). Further:

> Although parental use of illegal drugs, especially cocaine, has attracted the attention of policymakers in recent years [i.e., prenatal drug exposure], the far greater problem in child protection caseloads is alcoholism. Alcohol abuse also is a common factor in sexual abuse cases. (Melton et al., 1997, p. 470)

As the connection between parental abuse and neglect of their children and the parents' own history of substance use has become more apparent, a number of conflicts have arisen between the two systems, including conflicts over client confidentiality; whether substance abuse evaluations of parents who have neglected or abused their children should be clinical or forensic in nature; and whether parental self-reports of alcohol and other drug use can be considered trustworthy.

Case Scenario 6.1 is offered as an example of an adult client in the child welfare system who has been referred for a substance abuse evaluation. This case illustrates some of the conflicts that frequently arise between child protection and substance abuse treatment professionals that significantly complicate case planning decisions. The case is elaborated upon later in this chapter in the Sample Report and Case Planning Considerations.

Conflicts Over Client Confidentiality

Adults referred to a substance abuse treatment counselor for an assessment are protected under the confidentiality rules in the Code of Federal Regulations, Title 42, Vol. 1 (42CFR2.13), *Confidentiality of Alcohol and Drug Abuse Patient Records*. This law was enacted to prevent clients who seek substance abuse evaluation or treatment from having any information they reveal used against them in a subsequent criminal prosecution. The underlying rationale for this protection is that individuals are more likely to seek treatment when the fear of police involvement is removed.

Case Scenario 6.1

Ms. Waterton, a child protection caseworker from the Department of Human Services, requested a substance abuse evaluation for Tom Steele, age 35, father and legal guardian of 7-year-old Sam and 4-year-old Heidi. The children were the product of the father's long-standing common-law relationship with Susan Carrel, age 30. Approximately 4 months ago, the mother died in a single-car, alcohol-related auto accident. The children were removed from the father's custody 2 months later, following an incident in which the father left the children with a male roommate/friend, who was using alcohol and marijuana while babysitting.

In her referral, Ms. Waterton shared considerable family history with the substance abuse evaluator, including the significant behavioral problems the children were exhibiting in their current foster home placement. Although it was not known if either of the children had been exposed to alcohol or drugs during their prenatal development, Ms. Waterton believes that the long history of substance abuse problems by both parents and evidence of the father's continued use strongly indicate his permanently impaired ability to appropriately and safely raise the children.

Although requesting a clinical evaluation to determine an appropriate substance treatment program for father, Ms. Waterton stated to the evaluator that she was extremely skeptical that any treatment would be successful, given father's past failures to maintain sobriety. Privately, Ms. Waterton told her casework supervisor that she hoped the results of a drug and alcohol evaluation would buttress her case planning decisions. She was planning to recommend to the court that the father's parental rights be terminated if he once again fails to remain abstinent and sober.

Under this federal law, a substance abuse counselor or treatment agency may release information to an outside party only if the client consents in writing to the disclosure. The consent must contain language stating that the information to be disclosed is protected information, and that the client may revoke permission to disclose the information at any time. In addition to providing written notification, substance abuse counselors typically go over this point with clients as part of the standard assessment protocol, to make sure the clients understand that their written consent is required for the agency or counselor to disclose information about the client's evaluation or treatment. The confidentiality provision prevents counselors from disclosing information obtained during an evaluation or treatment regarding illegal or criminal activities in which clients may have engaged when using drugs.

Clinical Versus Forensic Evaluations

Substance abuse evaluations, like psychological evaluations, can be clinical or forensic in nature. Each type of evaluation involves different referral questions, sources of information, and methods of data collection.

Clinical Evaluations

Clinical evaluations are used to determine the most appropriate courses of treatment or intervention for clients, utilizing all available information including self-reports of their problems and concerns. In a clinical substance abuse evaluation of parents, referral questions include the following:

- What are the parent(s)' past and present substance use patterns—in terms of type of substances used and to what extent, chronicity, and severity of use?
- What co-occurring mental health problems are contributing to or exacerbating parent(s)' drug or alcohol problems?
- What forms of treatment are appropriate to help parent(s) reduce or abstain from further substance use?
- What are parent(s)' motivation for maintaining sobriety or staying clean, and what is the prognosis or likely outcome of parental drug or alcohol treatment?

In clinical evaluations, parent(s)' defensiveness (inconsistent or avoidant responses about alcohol and other drug history or current use) is the focal point of the evaluation. The treatment plans subsequently developed are aimed at the user's achieving and maintaining sobriety. Parenting skills, as negatively impacted by the substance abuse problems, would be addressed, but secondarily.

Forensic Evaluations

Forensic evaluations address a legal question rather than a treatment question. They are intended primarily to identify the extent of parent(s)' substance misuse to determine whether they can raise their children appropriately and safely. These forensic evaluations tend to emphasize objective data (standardized measures of alcohol or substance use; breath, blood, or urine analysis; absentee records from work or school; arrest records and convictions, etc.). Forensic evaluations typically minimize, discount, or exclude altogether clients' self-report data about the extent of use or misuse of drugs and alcohol, as the reports are assumed to be inherently unreliable. Referral questions in a forensic substance abuse evaluation involving parents being seen in a child welfare setting include the following:

- What harm have the children incurred in their development and current functioning as a result of parent(s) substance use?
- To what extent have the parent(s) substance history and current use impacted their present ability to provide safe and appropriate care for their children?
- If the children are in a two-parent family, are the substance use problems the same with both parents? Is one of the parents a more adequate caregiver?

The distinction between the two types of evaluations is important, given that the permanency planning decision facing the child welfare worker often concerns whether children can be returned safely to the care and custody of their parents. Child protection professionals, such as Ms. Waterton in the case scenario, often assume that parental substance abuse or dependence, *per se*, makes parents unfit to care for their children. Melton and colleagues (1997) caution against jumping from a diagnosis of parental alcoholism to conclusions about parental unfitness, or to assume "that parental drug use necessarily means that the situation cannot be made safe for the child or that the parent cannot recover" (p. 471).

Self-Report Versus Objective Data

Related to the above distinction between clinical and forensic evaluations, a major controversy between substance abuse professionals and child welfare professionals has arisen over whether self-reports by parents can be considered reliable and valid. When clinical drug and alcohol evaluations are sought by referring professionals or ordered by the court, the findings and recommendations from the reports subsequently may be discounted or even rejected by those who originally requested them because client self-reported data are suspect. In such cases, the referring professional or court may actually have had a forensic evaluation in mind—desiring a report that would solidify a case in which termination of parental rights is contemplated or to make sentencing recommendations for drug violations—rather than planning for appropriate treatment.

Investigations of the accuracy of client self-reports regarding drug and alcohol use are numerous. Adesso and colleagues (2004) indicated that, contrary to the perceptions among many referring professionals that substance-abusing clients minimize or deny their problems—the findings of several studies have shown that clients' self-reports of their substance use are usually accurate under certain conditions, such as when

- clients are free of alcohol or drugs;
- clients are assured of confidentiality;
- interviews are conducted in a clinical or research setting that promotes honest reporting; and
- interview questions are clear and understandable.

Client self-reports can be verified by obtaining collateral information from other non-using observers (such as peers, spouses or partners, or employers), as well as assessment of biological markers (blood or urine specimens).

Components of a Substance Abuse Evaluation

According to Adesso and colleagues (2004):

> All too often health and social service professionals fail to ask about substance use problems because they have no means of addressing these concerns or know of proper resources for referring individuals for specialized services. (p. 160)

Those authors suggest that substance abuse evaluations can be divided into several phases or steps: screening; brief evaluations; comprehensive evaluations; and diagnostic evaluations. Each of these types has different protocols and procedures, as discussed below:

Screening

Screening is a brief assessment approach that typically involves a binary (yes–no) process designed to determine whether a person may have a drug or alcohol problem. Screening instruments typically are client self-report measures that are easy to administer and score.

> Screening for substance use can be accomplished effectively in non-substance-use-specialty medical and social service settings where individuals are seeking non-substance-abuse or dependence services. Screening for substance-use problems while individuals are seeking other medical or social services can be seen as an

opportunistic event to engage individuals in primary or secondary substance-related programs. (Adesso et al., 2004, p. 156)

Table 6.1 lists several widely used screening tools for drug and alcohol abuse or dependence. If possible problems are identified through these tools, clients are referred for further phases of the assessment process, described next. If no problem is identified, further assessment typically is not warranted.

Brief Evaluation

If the preliminary findings from a screening instrument indicate possible AOD problems, the next step typically is to complete a more extensive but still abbreviated and circumscribed evaluation. Depending on the amount of time a referring professional and/or substance evaluator and the client each are willing to devote to addressing the substance abuse problems, the assessment might consist of brief structured interviews or questionnaires designed to obtain a "snapshot picture" of individuals' substance-use problems, their perceptions about the consequence of their use, and their motivation for change (Adesso et al., 2004; Winters, Newcomb, & Fanhorst, 2004).

The *motivational interviewing* technique developed by William Miller and David Rollnick (1992) is especially useful in this regard, because this approach focuses on the clients' own motivation for change. Clients' responses provide the basis for determining whether they are ready for change (by contemplating or initiating action), or are not yet ready (pre-contemplation). Motivational interviewing recognizes that relapse is part of the cycle of recovery from abuse and dependence. Hence, the goal of every session is to have another session (Obert, 2002), because an evaluator cannot complete an assessment and a counselor cannot provide substance abuse treatment if clients are not participating in the process.

Another brief assessment tool is to provide feedback to individuals regarding how their use of alcohol or other substances compares to the use of others with substance abuse problems (Adesso et al., 2004). This has been found to be helpful to individuals who are not aware of the extent of their AOD use.

Comprehensive Evaluation

This evaluation step involves a comprehensive assessment that examines *all the major areas of clients' life and functioning* as these are affected by

TABLE 6.1	Screening Tools for Alcohol And Drug Abuse
TYPE	**DESCRIPTION**
Brief screening tools	CAGE—an acronym s for *Cut Down/Angry/Guilty/Eye Opener*—is a screening tool used to make a decision about whether further assessment is warranted (Ewing, Bradley & Burman, 1998, 1999; Mayfield, McLeod, & Hall, 1974). It consists of only four questions, to which any "yes" response would indicate a need for a further assessment regarding possible drug or alcohol problems: • Have you ever tried to *cut down* on your use of drugs or alcohol? *(C)* • Has anyone made you *angry* by suggesting that they think you use too much (alcohol or drugs)? *(A)* • Have you felt *guilty* or worried about your use of alcohol or other drugs? *(G)* • Have you ever needed an *eye opener* in the morning (or needed to use to alleviate withdrawal)? *(E)* Each of these questions addresses the concerns about substance use in a slightly different way. Questions *C* and *G* examine whether the client has ever felt that substance use might be a problem. Question *A* focuses on whether *others* in the client's life have been concerned about the individual's possible AOD problems. For those who do not think they have a problem, it may be easier to remember being angry at the concerned party than to remember that they were concerned. Question *E* addresses whether the person has used enough to develop withdrawal or physical dependence on the substance. RAPS—an acronym for *Rapid Alcohol Problems Screen*—is similar to CAGE but is aimed specifically at identifying alcohol problems (Cherpitel, 2000). RAPS has been found to be a more effective instrument than CAGE in detecting alcohol dependence across gender and ethnic groups (Hood & Johnson, 2002). The four items are: • *Remorse* about drinking (R): Assesses guilt about drinking. • *Amnesia* episodes caused by alcohol (A): Assesses blackouts. • *Performance* problems (P): Assesses whether individuals failed to do what was expected because of alcohol. • *Starter—Needs an eye-opener or morning drink (S):* Assesses symptoms of withdrawal and dependence. A positive response to any of these questions indicate the need for further evaluation.
Screening inventories	Among several standardized screening inventories developed are: • the *Alcohol Use Disorders Identification Test* (AUDIT) is a 10-item questionnaire, focusing on the amount and frequency of drinking, alcohol dependence, and problems caused by alcohol.

(continued)

TABLE 6.1	(continued)

TYPE	DESCRIPTION
	• the *Michigan Alcoholism Screening Test* (MAST) is a 25-item questionnaire containing a broad mix of times about alcohol problems, drinking styles, symptoms of dependence, perceptions, and help seeking. It is the one of the most widely used screening instruments. • the *Drug Abuse Screening Test* (DAST-20) is a 20-item questionnaire intended to identify clients using psychoactive substances through responses to simple questions. It does not differentiate the type of drugs being used. These instruments can also be used with clients who have co-occurring psychiatric and substance use disorders. The *Substance Abuse Subtle Screening Inventory (SASSI)* was developed specifically to address concerns about the reliability of clients' self-report data. It collects responses to questions that do not address substance use directly, and then interprets the response sets to determine a 93% likelihood that the client has a substance use problem. Thus, the client is not asked directly about substance use and conclusions are drawn as to whether the client has a problem, based on the client's responses to other questions. The SASSI should not be used as a measure in the comprehensive assessment phase, as it is intended only to identify clients with possible substance abuse problems.
Child welfare specific screening measures	The *Connecticut Screening Tool* was developed by the State of Connecticut as a child-welfare specific screening tool that relies on case data and consists of a checklist for the worker to complete upon returning from a home visit or after concluding the initial investigation. It identifies 14 areas in which possible problems might be detected; a "yes" answer to any one item indicates a need for a more in-depth substance abuse assessment. This tool is a helpful way for child protection workers to document their concerns or, conversely, to document that no concerns exist regarding a parent's substance use.

Adapted from "Substance Abuse," by V. Adesso, R. Cisler, B. Larus, & B. Hayes, in *Psychological Assessment in Clinical Practice: A Pragmatic Guide*, edited by M. Hersen, 2004, New York: Brunner-Routledge; "Clinically Useful Assessments: Substance Use and Comorbid Psychiatric Disorders," 2002, *Behavior Research and Therapy*, 40, 1345–1361; "A Brief Screening Instrument for Problem Drinkers in the Emergency Room: The RAPS4," by C. Cherpitel, 2000, *Journal of Studies in Alcohol*, 61, 447–449; "Detecting alcholism: The CAGE questionnaire," by J. Ewing, 1984, *Journal of the American Medical Association*, 252, 1905–1907; "Screening for Alcoholism Use CAGE: Correction, by Ewing et al., 1999, *JAMA*, 281(7), 611; *Assessment in Counseling: A Guide to the Use of Psychological Assessment Procedures*, 3rd ed., by A. Hood & R. Johnson, 2002, Alexandria, VA: American Counseling Association; *ADAD Approved Evaluation Instrumentation for Substance Using Adults*, by D. Timken, 2001, Denver: Colorado Department of Human Services, Alcohol and Drug Abuse Division.

past substance abuse. The evaluator gathers information from various sources, including clients, knowledgeable others, and collateral information (reports and test results, treatment discharge summaries, psychological evaluations, etc.) to figure out the most helpful and appropriate treatment to address his or her specific needs. Widely used comprehensive assessment measures are described in Table 6.2, including multi-scale questionnaires, problem-focused interviews, and diagnostic interviews (Winters, Newcomb, & Fahnhorst, 2004).

Diagnostic Phase of Evaluation

A diagnostic assessment often is a component of comprehensive assessment. In addition to determining whether clients' substance use meets the *DSM-IV-TR* diagnostic criteria for substance-use or substance–induced disorders that were described earlier in the chapter, it often is necessary to ascertain whether clients have co-occurring mental health problems. Estimates of co-occurring mental health disorders among clients with substance use disorders range from 75% to 85% (Adesso et al., 2004). Male substance abusers have a much higher incidence of co-occurring antisocial personality disorders. Female substance abusers have a greater incidence of co-occurring depression and anxiety.

The diagnostic phase of the evaluation typically utilizes structured clinical interviews aimed at collecting information specifically about the client's substance use as this pertains to the diagnostic criteria spelled out in the *DSM-IV*. Some funding sources require a diagnosis of substance abuse or substance dependence in order to provide services for a client. These diagnostic interviews allow evaluators to examine the interplay between substance use or abuse and any co-occurring mental health difficulties. Table 6.2 (presented below) lists some of the structured interviews used in the diagnostic phase of a substance abuse evaluation. Arriving at an accurate diagnosis is crucial for proper treatment planning:

> Not assessing a client's substance use and its potential effects on her or his life (and behavior, cognition, and affect) may mean misdiagnosing clients as depressed, psychotic, or otherwise impaired, when in reality they are experiencing these symptoms as a result of their drug use. Clearly, the treatment implications differ greatly depending upon whether certain symptoms are manifestations of a pure psychiatric disorder or a substance-induced disorder. (Brems, 2000, p. 57)

TABLE 6.2	**Instruments or Structured Interviews in the Comprehensive Assessment and Diagnostic Phases**

INSTRUMENT OR PROCEDURE	DESCRIPTION
Addiction Severity Index (ASI)	The *ASI* is a structured formal interview designed to measure disruptions of life functioning in six areas. A number of states have adopted this instrument as the standard for assessing substance abuse problems in clients referred to their publicly funded treatment programs. Many child welfare clients, therefore, must be assessed using this instrument to access the treatment programs made available to them. The *ASI* consists of closed questions regarding a client's legal and arrest history, psychiatric and physical health history, employment history, social and family history, and alcohol and drug use history. The closed-question format allows for little elaboration on the client's part with respect to other issues that may affect the need for substance abuse treatment services. (In the hands of a skilled interviewer, these areas can be covered in more depth.) Inquiries into parenting beliefs and parents' attitudes about or relationships with their children are noticeably absent from this structured interview instrument.
Adult Substance Use Survey (ASUS)	The *ASUS* is a 64-item, multiple choice, Likert-scale, self-report instrument. It gathers an individual's self-assessment data regarding substance use involvement and disruption as a result of substance use, as well as mood difficulties, history of antisocial behavior and attitudes, perceptual defensiveness or reluctance to self-disclose, and motivation for treatment. Responses to these items yield scores on nine different scales, which have Internal Consistency Reliability scores between .71 (antisocial behavior and attitudes) and .94 (disruption as a result of substance use). The defensiveness scale on the *ASUS* serves a similar function to the lie scales in standardized personality assessment instruments. A high score on the defensiveness scale may indicate that the individual in question is minimizing any of the items on the other scales, and when taken together with the scores on the other scales, point to areas of inconsistency that can be clarified with the client before the initial assessment report is written. Particularly concerning is a high defensiveness score combined with low scores on all of the other scales, indicating that the client is working hard to present a positive image to the counselor and leaving out important information in the process. With time and experience, counselors may learn to look for additional information from the profiles gleaned from the *ASUS*, leading nicely into the assessment process from screening.

(continued)

TABLE 6.2   (continued)

INSTRUMENT OR PROCEDURE	DESCRIPTION
Structured Diagnostic Interviews: *Structured Clinical Interview for DSM-IV; Substance Dependency Severity Scale* (SDSS)	Diagnostic interviews, such as the SDSS, are patterned closely after DSM-IV diagnostic criteria, and consist of a series of questions aimed at teasing out the factors in the client's life that might warrant a diagnosis of abuse or dependence. Structured diagnostic interviews may be computer-administered or a structured interview.

Adapted from "Substance Abuse," by V. Adesso, R. Cisler, B. Larus, & B. Hayes, in *Psychological Assessment in Clinical Practice: A Pragmatic Guide*," edited by M. Hersen, 2004, New York: Brunner-Routledge, pp. 147–173; "On Beyond Urine: Clinically Useful Assessment Instruments in the Treatment of Drug Dependence," by K.M. Carroll & B.J. Rounsaville, 2002, *Behavior Research and Therapy, 40*, 1329–1344; *User's Guide to the Adult Substance Use Survey: The North Carolina Normative Group*, by K. Wanberg, 2000, Arvada, CO: Center for Addictions Research and Evaluation.

Qualifications of Substance Abuse Evaluators

The qualifications of substance abuse counselors vary from state to state, as each sets its own requirements for certification or licensure of substance abuse counselors. In most cases, to become certified or licensed as addiction counselors, substance abuse counselors are required to complete significant work experience and training specifically in substance abuse. Depending on state requirements, substance abuse counselors may or may not hold graduate degrees in a mental health discipline, in addition to their drug and alcohol certification.

In any case, the certification or licensing requirements for substance abuse counselors typically are separate from the licensing requirements for the mental health professions. (Licensing standards in psychology are discussed in chapter 2.) Thus, an evaluating psychologist or referring professional from another discipline who lacks certification as a substance abuse counselor license or certification may not have the training and experience needed to address substance abuse issues properly.

At the same time, substance abuse counselors may lack expertise when the scope of the evaluation extends beyond diagnosing substance abuse and recommending appropriate substance abuse treatment. Referring professionals from other disciplines may have to obtain additional consultation from domestic violence counselors, mental health professionals, or medical professionals to complete their assessments of clients with multiple co-occurring issues.

A Sample Substance Abuse Evaluation Report

Before proceeding further, readers may wish to review chapter 9, which provides a detailed examination regarding the features of good professional report writing. As noted there, the well-written, informative, and authoritative report should

- clearly state its purpose at the outset;
- be divided into logical and distinct sections;
- identify the sources of the information used in the assessment;
- delineate the methods by which the data were gathered;
- be congruent with and sensitive to clients' cultural backgrounds
- organize the evaluator's opinions, diagnostic statements, conclusions, and interpretations into a section separate from the assessment data itself; and
- have recommendations that logically flow from the assessment findings.

Next we will examine the unique components of substance abuse evaluations and reports.

Preliminary Considerations

In conducting substance-use evaluations and writing reports, several issues must be addressed up front:

1. Depending on the purpose of the evaluation (forensic or clinical), substance abuse evaluators will decide at the outset whether to gather client self-report data. As noted earlier, the primary value of self-reported data is that information is collected directly from clients regarding their views of the problem. Clients' readiness to disclose drug use information is dramatically influenced by their comfort level with the evaluator. Evaluators must balance the tricky process of establishing sufficient trust and rapport with clients so they will report honestly, while also nurturing and harnessing clients' internal distress over their AOD use so it can be used in subsequent treatment as motivation to change (Adesso et al., 2004).

2. Evaluators should expect that some referring professionals might be reluctant to supply or even withhold collateral or background information about clients for fear of *confirmatory bias*—that the information will cause evaluators to prejudge or presume that clients have drug or alcohol problems. Evaluators should plan ahead to address this by carefully documenting the data gathered, the steps evaluators took in developing and testing various clinical hypotheses about the meaning of the data, and the clear formulation of diagnostic statements, conclusions, and recommendations based on the data collected.

   Referring professionals who deliberately withhold relevant collateral information put their clients at risk of not being fully understood by evaluators. It is unrealistic, not to mention naïve, for referring professionals to expect that evaluators can determine "the truth" about clients' substance use based solely on the limited time they typically have with clients during the evaluation process.

3. The language used in reports can subtly (or not so subtly) blame clients for their problems without providing clarity or guidance about treatment interventions or case planning recommendations. An example is the term *denial*, which can be used (incorrectly from its original meaning in psychoanalytic theory as a largely *unconscious* psychological defense mechanism) to imply that clients are intentionally lying or are stubbornly unwilling to admit they have a drug or alcohol problem.

   Other terms or labels, such as using the terms *addict* and *alcoholic*, blur the distinction between the AOD problems of abuse or dependence and clients' personhood. These terms are means by which some evaluators distance themselves from clients who are seeking or needing help. Such pejorative labels are counterproductive, as they tend to alienate those who have the greatest need for assistance in dealing with their problems.

   Many clients object to being labeled an "alcoholic" or an "addict" because of the social stigma involved, but they might well agree with the evaluator's statements (especially if reports incorporate their own descriptors and terminology) that they have "chronic, persistent problems" with alcohol or other drugs that have caused "profound difficulties in many areas of their life functioning." In addition, evaluators can draw on concepts and terms from other theoretical approaches (such as the cognitive-behavioral term *perceptual defensiveness*) to describe clients' failure to perceive that they have AOD problems, without pejoratively labeling such behavior as "denial" (Wanberg & Milkman, 1998).

Special Aspects of a Substance Evaluation Report

A special subsection of the report should include a *complete substance use history* encompassing *each* major category of substance: alcohol, marijuana, cocaine, amphetamines, hallucinogens, opiates, "club drugs" (such as rohypnol, GHB, ecstasy, and ketamine), inhalants, tranquilizers, and barbiturates. Specific inquiries would address

- *first use* (age, circumstances, amount, and consequences);
- *most recent use* and *period(s) of heaviest use* (quantity per day/week/month, amount of money spent on the substance if quantity is unknown);
- *longest period of abstinence* from the substance;
- *style of use* (route of administration; used primarily in gregarious social situations versus used primarily when alone; binge or sporadic use versus continuous use; compulsive or casual style of use); and
- *perceived benefits* from use and *problems associated with use*, as well as *concerns expressed by others* regarding the client's use.

As part of the substance use data, it is also appropriate for the evaluator to document any concerns the client expresses regarding his or her own substance use, any attempts to quit or cut down on any of the substances in question, and any benefits the client perceives as stemming from continued use. Benefits from substance use often are part of a client's attempts to avoid painful feelings of grief and loss. These feelings must be addressed at some point in treatment to prevent the client from returning to AOD use.

Sample Report 6.1 is based on the client, Tom Steele, presented earlier in the chapter. Following the report, the chapter examines the evaluation's strengths and weaknesses.

Case Planning Considerations

Case planning decisions regarding clients, especially parents, who abuse or are dependent on alcohol and other drugs, are complex and challenging. Several of these complexities are explored in greater depth.

Determining the Level of Care

Referring professionals should become familiar with the patient placement criteria for adults and adolescents with alcohol and other drug

Sample Report 6.1

Substance Abuse Evaluation

Confidentiality Notice

This information has been disclosed to you from records protected by U.S. Government's *Confidentiality of Alcohol and Drug Abuse Patient Records* rules (42CFR2.13). The Federal Rules prohibit anyone receiving this report from making any further disclosure of this information unless further disclosure is expressly permitted by the written consent of the person to whom it pertains or as otherwise permitted in 42CFR2.13. A general authorization for the release of medical or other information is NOT sufficient for this purpose. The Federal Rules restrict any use of the information to criminally investigate or prosecute any alcohol or drug abuse patient.

Client Identifying Information

Name: Tom Steele
Date of Birth: 3/15/70
Date of Interview: 4/14/2007
Date of report: 4/16/2007

Mr. Steele is a 35-year-old Caucasian male, recently widowed following the death of his common-law wife, Susan Carrel, who died in an alcohol-related single-car automobile accident in December 2004. Mr. Steele is father of two minor children, Sam, age 7, and Heidi, age 4. Temporary legal custody of the children has been obtained by the Department of Human Services. The children were placed in foster care in February 2005. The precipitant for removing the children was Mr. Steele's leaving the children in the care of his roommate, Alfred S., who was using alcohol and smoking marijuana in the children's presence while babysitting them.

Referral Question and Purpose of the Present Evaluation

Mr. Steele was referred for a clinical substance abuse evaluation by his Department of Human Services caseworker, Ms. Jill Waterton. Ms. Waterton stated to the present evaluator that she believed Mr. Steele needed treatment for his substance abuse, and requested an evaluation to determine the appropriate level of care for his substance abuse problems.

Methods and Procedures

Data for this evaluation were obtained from a 90-minute interview with Mr. Steele. In addition, Mr. Steele was administered the *Adult Substance Use*

(continued)

Survey (ASUS). Ms. Waterton supplied additional collateral information regarding her prior contacts with the Steele family and children.

Mental Status Observations

According to Ms. Waterton, Mr. Steele is well known to the staff at the Department of Human Services. During the past month, he has arrived for supervised visits with his children on a motorcycle, dressed in black leather biker jackets and chaps, wearing aviator-style mirror-lens sunglasses. Ms. Waterton stated that he acted "threatening and intimidating" toward herself and other child welfare staff of the Department.

During the present evaluation, Mr. Steele appeared fully oriented, rational and coherent, and told his story in a logical fashion. His affect was generally appropriate to the information being discussed—with exceptions when discussing recent and past losses in his life. He denied any current suicidal or homicidal ideation and stated that he has never consciously tried to kill himself. Importantly, however, he did reveal that there was a period of time in the mid-1990s, following the death of his first child, when he was using large quantities of cocaine, With some prodding from the present evaluator, Mr. Steele indicated that "I am probably depressed" and "maybe want to die," but he cannot admit this to himself at the time.

As noted below, in the Psychosocial History section, Mr. Steele has had a number of significant losses in his life. In discussing these events (the death of a cousin during his childhood; the death of his firstborn child 10 years ago; and the recent death of Susan Carrel, his common-law partner of 12 years), Mr. Steele provided information in a matter-of-fact manner with no overt expressions of feelings, such as sadness, grief, anger, or anxiety.

Psychosocial History

Background History: Mr. Steele is the oldest of three children. His sister Kelly is 7 years younger, and his brother Jimmy is 14 years younger. Mr. Steele never knew his birth father and was raised by his mother and stepfather, whom he considers to be his father. He remembers being in trouble "a lot" when he was growing up but states that he was "rebellious, but not disrespectful." He felt closest to his mother and to some of his friends, and his happiest memories are of hunting with his stepfather. Mr. Steele denies experiencing any physical or sexual abuse during his childhood or adolescence but has stated that he sometimes was punished with a belt, although this did not work very well in getting him to obey limits.

Mr. Steele stated that he had no medical problems as a child. He said he is in good health at present.

(continued)

His first significant loss occurred when he was age 12, when his cousin of the same age died of leukemia. Mr. Steele provided little further information about this event, other than saying that he and his cousin "were close."

Mr. Steele reported that he earned average grades in elementary school, and that his favorite subject was math. He completed 2 years of regular high school, after which he was sent to a juvenile detention facility as a court sentence following an arrest and conviction for burglary and theft. He served 18 months in the juvenile facility and was released when he turned 18. He completed his GED while attending the juvenile detention facility.

Five years after his release from the juvenile detention facility, Mr. Steele met Susan Carrel, and they lived together in a common-law marriage for 12 years. This union produced three children. Their first child, Thomas, died approximately 10 years ago, when the child was age 2. Mr. Steele reported that Thomas drowned accidentally in their backyard pool. Two additional children subsequently were born to this union, Sam (age 7) and Heidi (age 4).

Ms. Waterton reported that there had been several incidents of alleged domestic violence between Mr. Steele and Susan but that no arrests ever were made by the police or substantiated by the Department. Mr. Steele admitted to periods of intense conflict with Susan but stated that he never physically harmed her in any way.

Arrest and Court History as an Adult: During the past 10 years, Mr. Steele has been arrested a total of 20 times, primarily for traffic offenses, including one DUI 12 years ago and another for driving under suspension. He was deemed a habitual traffic offender in 1998, after being arrested six times for driving under suspension. In 1999 Mr. Steele also received a 5-year sentence on the felony charge of distributing an imitation controlled substance. He was placed in Intensive Supervised Probation through the county's probation department (1999–2004). During this period he was able to maintain employment through a work release program, in which he spent evenings and weekends in jail but was released to work during the day. During this time, however, Susan was left as the solo parent, to raise the children on her own.

Employment History: Mr. Steele's current employment is as a heavy-machinery mechanic. Previously he worked at a variety of jobs in the construction industry.

Current Situation: Sam and Heidi currently are in foster care as a result of protective concerns that arose as a result of the father's alcohol and marijuana use and poor parenting decisions.

Mr. Steele expresses a great deal of anger regarding the children's placement in foster care, stating that he believes this placement is a result of a

(continued)

personal vendetta by Ms. Waterton, his caseworker. He stated that the children were at much greater risk several years ago when, admittedly, he and Susan were using speed intravenously, resulting in neglect of the children. He said that he and Susan had been able to get off speed and prior to her death had been working to correct their mistakes in parenting. He thinks the current placement of the children is undoing the progress he and the children had been making.

Substance Use Data

History of Alcohol and Drug Use:

- *Alcohol*: Mr. Steele's first use of alcohol was at age 13–14. His heaviest use of alcohol was three or four times per week, between 3 and 12 beers each time. His most recent use was February 2, 2005, when he had several beers and shots of whiskey on the day his children were removed from his custody. Mr. Steele's longest period of abstinence from alcohol has been approximately 6 months at a time, during the times when he was using other drugs.
- *Marijuana*: Mr. Steele first used marijuana at age 13. His heaviest use was during ages 15 to 16, when he smoked marijuana daily. His most recent use was the first weekend in March 2005. Because his children have been placed in foster care, he has agreed to random drug testing [urine analysis (UAs)] so his abstinence can be monitored. His longest period of abstinence from marijuana use was approximately 3 years, 1994–1997.
- *Cocaine:* His first use of cocaine was at age 17 or 18, and his heaviest use of cocaine was immediately after the death of his first child, Thomas. Mr. Steele stated that he was using cocaine intravenously daily for approximately a year following Thomas's death. His most recent use of cocaine was approximately 5 years ago, when he snorted a line. His longest period of abstinence from cocaine use was 5 years.
- *Hallucinogens:* Mr. Steele's first use of hallucinogens was at age 15, and he reported having used it four or five times in his life. His most recent use of hallucinogens was at age 18.
- *Amphetamines*: Mr. Steele's first use of speed was at age 23–24. His heaviest use of speed was between ¼ and ½ gram per day, just before he was placed in the Intensive Supervised Probation. He was using speed intravenously at that time. His most recent use of speed was 2 years ago. The year prior to this most recent use, he reports that he had returned to using between ¼ and ½ grams per day. His longest period of abstinence from use of speed was the 5 years when he was on ISP, which included approximately 3 to 6 months following his release from ISP.

(continued)

- *Inhalants*: Mr. Steele has used inhalants (street names: "rush" and "locker-room;" amyl and butyl nitrate, respectively) a "few" times as a kid, at age 14–15, but stated that he did not like it because it gave him a headache. He has not used inhalants since that time.
- *Other drugs:* He denies any use of opiates, tranquilizers, or barbiturates.

Problems/Symptoms Associated With Use: Mr. Steele has experienced loss of behavioral control, psychophysical withdrawal, and role disruption as a result of his use of drugs and alcohol.

Benefits of Use: Mr. Steele reports no significant benefits from use of drugs and alcohol, at this time; however, he states that drinking beer is a part of his lifestyle, in that he gets considerable business as a mechanic from other customers in the bar where he usually "hangs out" several nights a week, and if he were to stop drinking alcohol, he would lose business. He states that smoking marijuana is more of a social activity for him at this point, and that he does not derive any benefit from its use other than the social benefit of being included in this activity with others.

Style of Use: At present, Mr. Steele's style of use of alcohol and marijuana is occasional and with other people.

Prior Help: Mr. Steele went through outpatient treatment (a therapeutic community program) approximately 7 years ago, and through a DUI education and therapy program, as a condition of his getting his driver's license back. He reports that the outpatient therapy program was helpful and the DUI program was not helpful. Mr. Steele also reports a self-help effort in which he and Susan attempted to reduce their use of cocaine.

Concerns: Mr. Steele expresses no concerns at this time regarding his current level of alcohol and marijuana use, although he acknowledges that after Susan's death he was drinking "a little too much." He states that he is willing—although reluctant—to give up the use of marijuana, as he understands this to be a condition of his children's being returned to his custody.

Acknowledgment of Substance Abuse: Mr. Steele does not acknowledge a substance abuse problem at this time, although he does readily acknowledge that his past use of drugs and alcohol has created significant problems for him.

Summary of ASUS Test Scores:

Mr. Steele scored in the "low-medium" range on the ASUS scale measuring defensiveness. He scored in the "high" range on the scales that measure

(continued)

involvement in use, disruption as a result of use, and emotional difficulties. He scored in the "extremely high" range on the scale that measures antisocial behavior and attitudes.

Assessment Conceptualization:

1. *Emotional/mood stability*: Mr. Steele's apparent difficulty in expressing appropriate feelings of sadness and grief related to the loss of Susan are strongly suggestive of clinical levels of both underlying depression and anxiety. These feelings appear to be exacerbated by the children being placed in foster care and his sense of powerlessness at being able to do anything about this. There appear to be considerable unexpressed layers of grief regarding numerous significant losses earlier in his life. Paradoxically, however, depression may be an asset in his subsequent treatment. His ASUS profile indicates that, perhaps for the first time, he has begun to consciously experience the conflicts in his life rather than projecting blame for his troubles onto other people. If his inner distress and emotional discomfort can be harnessed, his prognosis for success in treatment might be considered more hopeful. One potential obstacle to treatment is his continuing anger at the court and the Department of Human Services and long-standing need to defy the external authorities, whom he perceives as "always trying to run my life." His anger and oppositionality may obfuscate his emerging ability to tolerate painful feelings.

2. *Family*: Mr. Steele's role in his family-of-origin seems to be that of the rebellious kid who got into trouble a lot and challenged authority—a pattern that began during his adolescent years. This continuing pattern makes it difficult for him to model prosocial behavior for his own children—behaviors congruent with the values held by mainstream society. Mr. Steele identifies with the "biker" subculture, particularly its defiance of the law and its celebration of illegal drug use. It will be important for him to reconcile his identification with this subculture with his role as a parent, a part of which includes socializing his children in a way that will allow them to get along in society.

3. *Job stability/productivity*: Mr. Steele seems to have adequate job skills to enable him to support himself and his children.

4. *Associations with friends and peers*: As stated above, Mr. Steele's peer group seems to consist primarily of other people who adhere to the values and behavioral norms embraced by the biker subculture. He expresses a great deal of loyalty to his friends, particularly Alfred, the roommate/friend who babysat his children while impaired. Mr. Steele will have to resolve the conflict between his loyalty to his friends and his role as a parent so he can continue to socialize with and get support

(continued)

from his friends and at the same time assist his children in learning how to get along in the world without manifesting a disruptive relationship with authority figures.

5. *Compliance with rules and laws*: Mr. Steele's high score on the "antisocial behavior and attitudes" scale of the ASUS, while definitely of concern, should be judged in terms of the reality of his life so far. Although he has had numerous traffic violations, the revocation of his driver's license, and one felony conviction resulting in a jail sentence and extended period of intensive probation, he has managed to avoid more serious legal troubles during the past 18 to 24 months, after completing the Intensive Probation program. His avoiding serious criminal activity during this recent time period suggests that he can exercise control over his behavior and has good decision-making skills—notwithstanding the ingrained pattern of conflict with and defiance of legal authorities. This strength can be put to good use in helping his children learn to make good decisions for themselves, if he can separate his own antisocial attitudes from the attitudes that would be most constructive for his children to embrace.

6. *Substance use*: Mr. Steele has an extensive history of poly-substance use, which has interfered with his life on all levels. In his attempt to be an appropriate parent to his children, it is vital that he maintain *total abstinence from all use of drugs and alcohol* so he can use all of his mental and emotional faculties to attend to their needs and behaviors. Mr. Steele reports having benefited from his participation with the therapeutic community outpatient program, which is structured and confrontational. (The program is designed specifically to serve men with antisocial tendencies.) He has the basic tools necessary for recovering from substance use, but he may need a "refresher" course of this outpatient treatment to further utilize the concepts of recovery to assist him in parenting his children. With his oppositional relationship to authority figures (and this will most likely extend to any treatment providers with whom he comes into contact), it will be important to process for himself the applicability of the concepts he learns in treatment, rather than being forced or required to accept these concepts at face value.

7. *Parenting/child custody*: Mr. Steele's children are manifesting some concerning behaviors (e.g., difficulty in forming positive attachments to the foster parents; persistent disobedience; stealing, and physical aggression), of which Mr. Steele has to be aware prior to their return to his custody. He seems to regard the reports about the children's problems as fabrications of Social Services for the sole purpose of keeping his children from him. He will have to examine these assumptions carefully rather than assuming that no damage has been done to his children as

(continued)

a result of the lifestyle he and their mother led prior to the children's placement in foster care.

Mr. Steele reports some concerns of his own that are congruent with the concerns expressed by the Department of Human Services. Both he and his children could benefit greatly from a careful examination of those concerns, as well as an ongoing forum in which he can discuss these issues with someone with whom he has established trust.

If the children are returned to Mr. Steele's custody, he can greatly enhance his own skills as a parent by participating in some counseling and parenting education, as well as some interactive treatment with his children, focused upon his learning to read their nonverbal behavioral cues as well as their verbal statements regarding their perceptions of their relationship to him.

Recommendations:

1. Mr. Steele should abstain from all use of drugs and alcohol so he can utilize his own feelings as necessary feedback to what is happening in his relationships with his children. Mr. Steele's abstinence from drug and alcohol use should be monitored through use of random UAs and breathalyzers for a minimum of one year. If he is unable to maintain abstinence from use of drugs and alcohol, he should be reassessed to determine what level of treatment would be most beneficial to him.

2. Mr. Steele should be referred for a comprehensive psychological evaluation for assessment of anxiety, depression, and antisocial behaviors as they have interacted with his drug use. His drug treatment must be supported by concurrent mental health treatment, given that his long-standing pattern of responding to major losses in his life seems to have numbed his emotions with alcohol and other drugs.

3. Mr. Steele should participate in parent education and counseling to address the conflict between the values he embraces and his role as a parent. In this counseling (which would be most effective in a group setting), he should explore the relationship between his behaviors and the well-being of his children. At this time, the most appropriate forum for this process would seem to be a group for men, as many of the concepts utilized and discussed in this forum are similar to those that Mr. Steele could benefit from addressing.

4. Mr. Steele's concern for his children, as well as the strengths discussed above, should be utilized as the primary motivation in changing his behaviors, as any attempt to point out to him that continuing drug or alcohol use is inherently wrong is likely to trigger his oppositional, antisocial tendencies.

(continued)

5. With respect to custody of his children, Mr. Steele's abstinence from use of drugs and alcohol should be a condition of their return to his home from foster care, as well as their remaining in his custody.

Strengths and Weaknesses of the Sample Evaluation Report

The above report has a number of strengths.

1. The report contains Mr. Steele' self-disclosures regarding the details of his substance abuse history, as well as tentative first steps in acknowledging his feelings of depression and loss (e.g., revealing that his heavy cocaine use after the death of his first child might have been a form of attempted suicide). This information suggests that the evaluator's skill in establishing safety and rapport *and* the confidentiality protections afforded him in this evaluation under federal statute were critical elements in allowing him to provide reliable and valid information about his AOD use and his unmet mental health needs.

2. The substance abuse evaluator clearly documented Mr. Steele's polysubstance abuse history from his early adolescent years through his current mid-30s adult years, and drew attention to the pattern of his heaviest AOD use occurring as maladaptive responses to multiple losses and unresolved grief. In addition, the report highlighted the father's antisocial tendencies. The evaluator's report provides an excellent foundation for a referral for subsequent psychological evaluation on Mr. Steele. A psychological evaluation would be essential in determining more clearly the severity of his depression, anxiety, and possible personality disorder co-occurring with his drug and alcohol problems.

   The evaluator did call attention to father's strengths (such as his efforts to curtail cocaine use) and his caring for his children, without minimizing his past problems. The balance in this report of addressing problems and highlighting strengths provides evidence of the evaluator's efforts to be fair and objective.

3. The evaluator reviewed Mr. Steele's previous AOD treatment interventions and incorporated the father's views about which treatment approaches were helpful and which were not. This information suggests that the father already has begun moving from the precontemplation stage of recovery to the contemplation stage, in that Mr. Steele can identify what has worked for him in the past.

   The evaluator's report also highlighted for the referring professional, Ms. Waterton, the specific case management approaches to take in supporting the father's continuing motivation to maintain sobriety, such as

(continued)

emphasizing the importance of the father's being the consistent parent in the lives of his children, and which approaches to avoid, such as expressing condemnation for his drug use or being a "bad father."

4. Finally, it should be noted that the evaluator did not provide a DSM-IV diagnosis of Mr. Steele's substance abuse problems. This omission is consistent with the point made earlier—that professionals in this field typically see clients' substance abuse as being on a continuum, ranging from nonuse to dependence, rather than falling into simplistic and/or arbitrary diagnostic categories. Nevertheless a formal diagnosis may be a requirement for Mr. Steele's admission to a treatment program and, thus, the lack of diagnosis ultimately may prove to be problematic.

A few weaknesses in the report are worth noting.

1. Given the circumstances of the case (i.e., the father's extensive drug history, continuing use of alcohol and marijuana, resulting poor parenting decisions that placed his children at risk for significant harm), the evaluator might have probed more deeply into the initial referral question posed by the child welfare caseworker, Ms. Waterton. The evaluator seems to have taken at face value that the referring professional was seeking a clinical evaluation to determine the most appropriate form of drug and alcohol treatment for the father. But Ms. Waterton's expressed skepticism as to the likelihood that Mr. Steele would stick with and/or benefit from another round of drug and alcohol treatment should have tipped off the evaluator that the caseworker's true interest was in obtaining evaluation findings that would buttress a recommendation to the court regarding termination of the father's parental rights.

2. The report, while providing the standard written legal notification about client confidentiality and prohibitions against further disclosure without the client's written permission, does not make clear whether the substance abuse evaluator clarified up front with the referring caseworker that information in the evaluation is protected under the federal confidentiality provisions (42CFR2.13). (Child welfare professionals may assume that the state laws mandating the reporting of suspected child abuse also override federal confidentiality rules and the prohibitions against a drug and alcohol evaluation in a criminal investigation.)

   Failure to clarify the referral question and the federal confidentiality protection may result in the referring professional who originally made the request for substance abuse evaluation being disappointed in the report, or even rejecting its findings and conclusions. In this scenario, the caseworker was clearly looking for a substance abuse report that would provide the needed documentation to support her intended recommendations to the court that Mr. Steele's parental rights be terminated.

(continued)

Child welfare professionals also could react negatively to the report by dismissing the substance abuse data and assessment sections as inaccurate because the evaluator had solicited and reported information directly from Mr. Steele. As will be discussed in chapter 7, referring professionals and examining evaluators have to be clear about the referral question and purpose of the evaluation.

3. Finally, the report does not include a detailed discussion of the ASUS scales, nor does it provide the numeric score. Thus, the reader is unable to judge the severity of the scores. As will be noted in chapter 9, reports that are most informative provide both quantitative and qualitative data about assessment results and findings.

problems developed by the American Society of Addiction Medicine (ASAM). For each age group five broad levels of care are specified: early intervention, outpatient, intensive outpatient/partial hospitalization, residential/inpatient treatment, and medically managed intensive inpatient treatment (ASAM, 2004). The admission criteria address

- the severity of addictions and related problems, such as intoxication/withdrawal;
- biomedical conditions and complications;
- emotional, behavioral, or cognitive conditions or complications;
- readiness to change;
- relapse, continued use, or potential for continued problems; and
- the recovery environment.

Considering Gender in Case Planning

Gender-specific substance abuse treatment needs should be addressed as part of an evaluation and any recommendations for treatment. In the sample evaluation report, the evaluator addressed gender issues in several places, such as by noting that the treatment group from which Mr. Steele had benefited was specifically for men with similar antisocial tendencies, and by placing considerable emphasis on Mr. Steele's role as a father (and sole remaining parent) as the leverage needed to keep him engaged actively and appropriately in the upbringing of his children.

Likewise, an evaluation of a female client with substance abuse problems would take into consideration the specific treatment needs for women, such as programs that offer female-only groups, collateral services to partners and family members, linkages to additional services addressing domestic violence and trauma (in addition to any co-occurring mental health disorders), medical services including family planning, as well as concrete services such as access to transportation, child care while the woman is in treatment, and baby and child-care items such as diapers and formula.

An evaluation of a female client's need for treatment should take into account the multiple roles that she may play as mother, daughter, wife, friend, caregiver, and employee with the people in her life, as well as how her substance use has affected her performance in those roles. A middle-class woman who uses methamphetamine, for example, may report a perception that this drug helps her to keep up with the many tasks she has to perform each day. A woman involved in prostitution may use drugs to overcome shyness or inhibitions, and/or it may be a means of chemical coercion and oppression forced upon her by male pimps. In any case, drugs and alcohol likely play a prominent role in whatever work she does, and treatment approaches will have to address those broader issues, such as feelings regarding sexual exploitation and victimization.

Empowering Clients

Progress in treatment is more likely when clients are motivated to address at least one issue that is contributing to their problems or current difficulties. Frequently, however, what is of most concern to clients is not the same as what most concerns the evaluating or referring professionals. When possible, treatment approaches that *first* address clients' perceptions of their need often allows them to become engaged more readily in the treatment or change process, following which the course of subsequent treatment or other interventions can be modified or adjusted to address their additional needs. This encourages clients to be more in charge of their treatment.

Coordinating and Prioritizing Multiple Interventions

In addition, case managers should tailor their services from a variety of agencies to meet clients' needs. Referring to the case scenario, probably no single all-encompassing treatment program can address all of the major problematic areas in Mr. Steele's life: drug treatment; mental health treatment to address his unresolved feelings of grief and loss; a monitoring and compliance program to demonstrate sobriety and accountability to the Court and Department of Human Services; and a program teaching parenting skills. In the real world, services might be drawn from several systems, including drug dependency, mental health, a probation agency, and a parenting program with hands-on mentoring or coaching.

The Role of Urinanalysis in Case Planning

Many caseworkers rely on the results of urinanalysis testing (UAs) rather than request a more thorough assessment to determine whether intervention into a parent's substance use is warranted. UA may be an unreliable indicator because individuals can use substances in other ways, enabling them to provide a clean urine sample for testing (Paliani, 1998). This creates a practice dilemma because the focus of child welfare professionals' contact with parents becomes the contents of the urine rather than the problematic parenting that brought the parents to the attention of the child welfare system in the first place. When case planning is directed primarily to urinanalysis testing, the implication is that if the UA comes back clean, the caseworker will not inquire further about the parent's substance use.

Therefore, referring professionals must ask themselves, prior to making a referral for a UA: What will I do if this UA comes back negative for drugs and/or alcohol? If the referring professionals' suspicions were strong enough to warrant the request for a UA, they likely are based on enough information to warrant a full-blown assessment and could probably be documented on one of the screening or assessment instruments discussed previously. Careful psychological assessment of the *extent of cognitive impairment* that clients have incurred from chronic drug use is imperative.

Also, sensitive language can prevent misunderstandings and even tragedies. It is much more effective to say to someone, "You'll have to stop using alcohol and drugs, and to be sure you're abstinent, we'll set you up on a schedule of random UAs to show that you're not using" rather than, "You have to drop three clean UAs before you can visit with your children." Some clients with severe cognitive impairments may not know what you are referring to when you say "clean UAs." In one tragic case, a woman injected a combination of bleach and bathroom cleaner into her veins to give her "clean UAs" so she could retain custody of her 18-month old daughter (S. Adams, personal communication, November 6, 1996).

Additional Resources

The following information is provided to interested readers who desire to learn more about the screening or assessment instruments discussed in this chapter.

Screening Instruments

1. *Alcohol Use Disorders Identification Test (AUDIT).* Information on the AUDIT can be obtained from Thomas F. Babor, Alcohol Research Center, University of Connecticut, Farmington, CT 06030-1410.
2. *Cut Down/Angry/Guilty/Eye Opener (CAGE).* The CAGE originally was published in the article, "The CAGE Questionnaire: Validation of a New Alcoholism Instrument," by D. Mayfield., G. McLeod, and P. Hall, in *American Journal of Psychiatry, 131* (1974), 1211–1223.
3. *Drug Abuse Screening Test (DAST).* Information on the DAST can be obtained from the Center for Addiction and Mental Health, Marketing Department, 33 Russell Street, Toronto, Ontario, Canada M5S-2S1; Phone 1-800-661-1111.
4. *Michigan Alcoholism Screening Test (MAST).* Information on the MAST can be obtained from Melvin L. Selzer, MD, 6967 Paseo Laredo, La Jolla, CA 92037.
5. *Substance Abuse Subtle Screening Inventory (SASSI).* Information on the SASSI can be obtained from the SASSI Institute, Rt. 2, Box 134, Springfield, IN 47462; Phone 800-726-0526.

Assessment Instruments

1. *Adult Substance Use Survey (ASUS).* Information on the ASUS can be obtained from the Center for Addictions Research and Evaluation (CARE), 5460 Ward Road, Suite 140, Arvada, CO 80002; Phone 303-421-1261.
2. *Addiction Severity Index (ASI).* Information on the ASI can be obtained from the Treatment Research Institute, 600 Public Ledger Building, 150 S. Independence Mall W., Philadelphia, PA 19106; Phone 215-399-0980.

Patient Placement Criteria

The American Society of Addiction Medicine (2nd Edition, Revised) of Patient Placement Criteria (ASAM PPC-2R) can be ordered from ASAM

Publications Distribution, PO Box 101, Annapolis Junction, MD, 20701-0101; Phone 1-800-844-8948; Fax: 301-206-9789. The main office for the American Society of Addiction Medicine is 4601 North Park Ave., Arcade Suite 101, Chevy Chase, MD, 20815; Phone 301-656-3920; Fax: 303-656-3815; Web: www.asam.org

Federal Confidentiality Rules

The federal confidentiality rules can be found in the Code of Federal Regulations, Title 42—Public Health, Chapter I: Public Health Service, Department of Health and Human Services, Part 2: Confidentiality of Alcohol and Drug Abuse Patient Records, available online: www.access.gpo.gov/nara/cfr/waisidx_02/42cfr2_02.html

Conclusion

This chapter is intended to give professionals a working knowledge of substance abuse evaluations. Particular attention has been directed to evaluating substance abuse in parents enrolled in the child welfare system—because these clients have either been under-served or served inappropriately in the past. A comprehensive assessment examines substance abuse along with other concerns, problems, or disorders that may be co-occurring in a client's life. Effective case planning requires attention to all of these issues so clients can make the needed changes in their lives and their abilities as parents.

Chapter 7

Developing Referral Questions for Psychological Evaluations

*Basic to the psychological report
is the referral question.
Before beginning the
evaluation process,
the referral question
should be considered.
The referral question
should again be contemplated
before beginning to
write the report.
If the referral question
has not been addressed,
then the report will not
achieve one of its major objectives
(i.e., to answer the
referral question).*

(Wolber & Carne, 1993, p. 3)

I n this and the next three chapters, we turn from the work of

OVERVIEW

psychologists and substance abuse evaluators to the work of referring professionals. These chapters examine the following key competencies needed by informed consumers of psychological assessments.

- Writing clear referral questions
- Preparing clients for the evaluation process
- Evaluating the quality and usefulness of psychological reports
- Integrating strengths-based and problem-based assessment data in formulating comprehensive and effective case plans

This chapter reviews the process of developing referral questions and suggests sample referral questions appropriate for professionals working in mental health, school, divorce and custody (parenting time) disputes, and child protection settings. (Referral questions for substance abuse evaluations were introduced in chapter 6). In addition, we examine several types of problematic referral questions.

The Process of Developing Referral Questions

Developing well-formulated referral questions and organizing referral materials are major tools of referring professionals in shaping the psychological assessments for their clients. The referral questions posed and the clinical judgment of evaluating psychologists provide the framework within which appropriate assessment strategies, tests, and protocols are selected to address the issues that have been raised.

Merrell (1994) observed that referral decisions tend to be based on three interdependent perspectives:

1. Whether clients' behaviors are seen as departing significantly from the norms about what constitutes acceptable functioning or appropriate behavior in the *broad society-at-large*. For example, children or

adolescents who demonstrate violent behaviors toward others usually are seen as violating overall societal standards.

2. Whether clients' behaviors are seen as a significant departure from the norms of *smaller social units within society*—specific cultural groups, neighborhoods, or various societal institutions such as schools and religious organizations. Complicating the referral and subsequent case planning process is that what constitutes acceptable behaviors in one social unit may be seen as unacceptable in another. For example, a child's assertive or aggressive behavior may be praised and reinforced at home as "standing up for yourself" or as an appropriate response to oppression and prejudice, whereas displays of the same behavior in another setting, such as schools, may be perceived as a form of "acting out" or labeled as a conduct disorder.

3. Whether clients' behaviors are seen as a significant departure from the *expectations of others in specific settings* in which they have face-to-face interactions, such as with their families and in classrooms. Thus, the context-specific expectations of parents, teachers, and others determine whether the behavior is considered to be appropriate.

The tolerance for specific client behaviors varies greatly. Referring professionals should understand that there is no standard "one size fits all" psychological assessment protocol or series of tests. A good psychological evaluation is one that addresses the specific referral question posed to it. The more specific the question, the more attention the assessment and feedback will be directed to the professional making the referral (Kissel & Freeling, 1990). As recommended by Wodrich and Kush (1990) with additions from other authorities (Merrell, 1994; Goldman, L'Engle Stein, & Guerry, 1984; Ownby, 1997; Wolber & Carne, 1993), referring professionals should consider the following process when making referrals for psychological evaluation.

1. Formulate *behavioral statements* of the clients' problems for which you are seeking further information. Generally, the more specific the information that psychologists receive about client problems, the better able they are to design appropriate evaluation strategies. Because social workers, physicians, teachers, and other health and human service professionals typically have more extensive contact with clients than evaluating psychologists do, they usually are able to provide information about the frequency, chronicity, and intensity/duration of problems and the settings or contexts in which the problem behaviors are manifested.

2. Organize your own assessment data and thinking into *clinical hypotheses* about the factors that may be contributing to the formation and maintenance of problems. Share with evaluating psychologists your own diagnostic thinking as to how you understand clients' problems and functioning. Consider as many different explanations as possible. The assessment reports developed by professionals from other disciplines offer a valuable guide to psychologists about the referral agents' perceptions and concerns. These reports include

   - psychosocial, health, and medical histories;
   - report cards about grades and samples of academic performance;
   - work performance evaluations;
   - previous diagnostic and treatment reports; and
   - observations of clients' functioning at home, work, school, or community.

3. Ask an *explicit referral question.* "If the referral agent cannot think of at least a one-line referral question, the case is inappropriate for psychological testing" (Wodrich & Kush, 1990, p. 22). Psychological assessments can contribute best to case planning decisions when they address clients' *present functioning.* Generally speaking, psychological evaluations cannot answer questions about etiology or the origins of problems. They may be able to address prognosis questions (predictions about the likelihood of future behavior) regarding clients' functioning, if evaluators state clearly the limits of the scientific certitude underlying their conclusions and opinions.

4. Obtain an *initial consultation* with the evaluating psychologist about the case being referred (Wolber & Carne, 1993). Upon receiving the referral, evaluating psychologists are likely to take some time to clarify the referral questions. Referral questions are the starting place for evaluating psychologists to begin to generate hypotheses and alternative explanations about clients' problems.

   > The clinician is wise to begin by taking referral questions at face value, but to consider other possibilities as the material develops. No purely mechanical use of assessment procedures will substitute for the active clinical judgment of the psychologist. (Goldman et al., 1983, p. 118)

In completing the assessment, more complex hypotheses often emerge regarding clients' functioning, problems, and strengths.

Obtaining an initial consultation with psychologists at the time the referral is made can help to establish a strong interdisciplinary working relationship between psychologists and referring professionals (Wolber & Carne, 1993). This may pay significant dividends later when the evaluation is completed and when referral agents desire a follow-up consultation. Because a collaborative relationship has been established, evaluating psychologists may participate more productively in treatment planning meetings with referring professionals and/or with clients regarding how to implement the assessment recommendations into effective case plans.

The above steps in formulating appropriate referral questions for psychological evaluations are illustrated in the case scenario. This case provides an example of how the referring professional's careful description of a client's behaviors, the professional's own diagnostic and evaluation procedures, and specific referral questions enabled the evaluating psychologist to conduct a comprehensive psychological evaluation of the client, and to propose an effective treatment plan.

As can be noted in the case scenario, the physician's referral questions guided the psychologist's evaluation of Mrs. Leibowitz. Those questions, in turn, were based on the treatment planning decisions her physician was facing. Because no medical basis was found for her physical symptoms, might psychotherapy in conjunction with closely monitored psychotropic medication be of benefit to her? Dr. Rubin looked to the evaluating psychologist to shed light on whether Mrs. Leibowitz was suffering from mental health problems and, if so, to recommend a possible course of treatment.

The case scenario also provides an example of a psychologist going beyond the specific referral questions to provide valuable information for the referring professional to consider in the case planning decision. In this case, the psychologist provided three additional pieces of information that were not asked directly in the referral:

1. The evaluating psychologist identified sources of the client's strength and resilience, as well as existing resources in her social environment.
2. The psychologist crafted a culturally appropriate treatment recommendation. Although marital and/or family treatment involving her husband and daughter could have been considered as a treatment option, the psychologist knew that Mrs. Leibowitz initially would feel more comfortable working individually with a Jewish therapist when

Case Scenario 7.1

Dr. Rachael Rubin, a family physician, has provided ongoing medical care for Doreen Leibowitz, age 55, during the past several years. Mrs. Leibowitz initially came to see the doctor complaining of general fatigue, weakness, and pain in her arms and legs, along with periodic abdominal cramping. She said that initially these symptoms occurred once or twice per month but recently have progressed to several times a week. Each episode typically lasts several hours, most frequently in the evening or at night. In several episodes Mrs. Leibowitz felt severely ill and incapacitated all day, eventually resulting in emergency-room visits to the local hospital.

Despite conducting numerous diagnostic tests and medical evaluations, to date Dr. Rubin has been unable to determine a physical illness or injury that would account for her symptoms. Mrs. Leibowitz has been evaluated for several medical conditions, but the results of all of the tests have been negative. Nonetheless, she has remained adamant that all her problems are related to an undiagnosed medical disease that so far has eluded detection. Based on the consistent negative medical test results, Dr. Rubin subsequently recommended that Mrs. Leibowitz obtain a psychological evaluation, to which she reluctantly agreed.

In referring Mrs. Leibowitz to Dr. Francine Rothstein, a clinical psychologist at the Jewish Family Center, Dr. Rubin shared the above medical history and current medical test results and also noted that the patient currently was experiencing a number of psychosocial stressors: a difficult marriage to a husband with long-standing problems with alcohol; the recent arrest of her oldest daughter for drug possession; and the threat of being fired from her job because she had missed numerous days of work as a result of her recurring physical symptoms. The referral to the psychologist asked the following questions:

- Are Mrs. Leibowitz's somatic symptoms and distress indicative of a mental health disorder, and if so, what kind?
- Would psychotherapy likely be beneficial to her? If so, what kind of therapy or intervention would most likely be successful?

Using these questions as a guide, Dr. Rothstein developed a multi-part assessment strategy that included individual interviews with Mrs. Leibowitz; joint interviews with her and her husband; collateral consultations with her employer and the juvenile justice officials involved with her daughter; and the administration of several psychological tests, including standardized inventories for anxiety and depression and substance use screening evaluation.

(continued)

The results of this evaluation led the clinical psychologist to conclude that Mrs. Leibowitz's somatic symptoms were attributable to co-occurring mental health disorders of anxiety and depression, expressed somatically. Results of the substance abuse screening measure were negative, with no indication of a past history of alcohol or other drug abuse. The clinical interviews revealed several areas of strengths: Mrs. Leibowitz was motivated to retain her present employment, had great concern for her daughter's welfare, and had established a well developed social support network with friends and members of the local Jewish temple.

Dr. Rothstein's treatment planning recommendation was for Mrs. Leibowitz to participate in a trial of time-limited psychotherapy. Specifically, the psychologist recommended a combination of behavior stress-reduction techniques along with cognitive therapy, to help her reframe some distortions in her thinking. The clinical psychologist also addressed the pros and cons of medications. While noting that anti-anxiety and anti-depression medications are beneficial to many clients in reducing their distressing symptoms, the psychologist expressed caution that medications could reinforce Mrs. Leibowitz's beliefs in physical/organic causes of her difficulties.

As a result of these recommendations, a collaborative treatment plan was developed with the client, the family physician, the evaluating psychologist, and a clinical social worker who was also working at the Jewish Family Center. Mrs. Leibowitz agreed to a trial of psychotherapy with the social worker, and to have her physician closely monitor her psychotropic medications. Over the course of individual treatment during the next 3 months, the episodes of somatic distress decreased markedly, as did her absences from work, accompanied by less demand for medical care.

At the conclusion of the 3 months, Mrs. Leibowitz completed a second set of standardized inventories for anxiety and depression, which Dr. Rothstein scored and interpreted. The scores confirmed the client's self-report and the social worker's behavioral observations—that her presenting problems of depression and anxiety were much improved. Mrs. Leibowitz also indicated that she felt better able to deal with her husband and daughter. In addition, she no longer felt the need to continue taking medications.

sharing sensitive personal and family information. The psychologist recommended cognitive and behavioral interventions because of their empirically demonstrated effectiveness in treating depression and anxiety, and also because they could be presented in a culturally congruent manner—as a means by which Mrs. Leibowitz could free up her natural energies to deal more effectively with the problems at home and work.

3. The psychologist added a caution about psychotropic medications, which normally might be used in conjunction with psychotherapy to treat anxiety and depression.

All of these additional sources of information substantially assisted in the client's treatment planning.

Sample Referral Questions

The following are commonly asked referral questions in a variety of settings in which an evaluation might be requested. These examples are meant to be suggestive rather than comprising an exclusive or exhaustive list. Just as there is no "one-size-fits-all" battery of psychological tests, no one-size referral question fits all types of clients, problems, and settings (Wodrich, 1997). Referring professionals will have to develop their own specific referral questions for each case for they wish to obtain psychological consultations. The following lists of sample generic referral questions might be asked in a variety of practice settings and are gleaned from the American Psychological Association (1994, 1998), Dyer (1999), Kissel and Freeling (1990), and Melton, Petrila, Poythress, and Slobogin (1997). The questions listed for mental health/substance abuse cases could be included among the referral questions asked in the other settings as well.

Mental Health and Substance Abuse Referral Questions

- Does the client have a mental health disorder or disturbance? If so, what is the severity or extent of disturbance?
- Does the client have a thought disorder (difficulty distinguishing what is real from what is not)?
- To what extent do the client's mental health problems interfere with his/her adaptation or functioning at home, school/work, or community?
- Has the client had a change in functioning compared to a previous point in time (an earlier evaluation)?
- What are the relative contributions of learned behavior and organic/neurological brain functioning to the client's difficulties?
- What is the differential diagnosis of the client's problems (mental health, substance abuse, mental retardation, or developmental delay)?

- What is the nature and extent of the client's dependence on, or addiction to, drugs and/or alcohol? How motivated is the client to make changes in his/her substance use?
- What is the client's degree of impulse control and tolerance for frustration?
- What are the major current stresses, coping styles, and sources of strength in the client's life?
- Do any cognitive, affective, and behavioral factors indicate that the client may pose an imminent danger to self or others?
- What risks do the client's present mental health problems pose to his/her future development or functioning if the problems are untreated?
- What are the client's strengths and capacities and environmental resources that he/she can draw upon to help cope with severe and persistent mental illness?
- Can the client benefit from psychotherapy? What type of therapy should be recommended?
- What accounts for the client's lack of expected progress in the therapy currently offered? Is another form of intervention needed?

School Referral Questions

- What is the child's or adolescent's current level of intellectual functioning? What are his/her cognitive strengths and weaknesses?
- Does the child or adolescent have a cognitive processing problem? Are intellectual limitations contributing to his/her poor school performance?
- What is the child's or adolescent's current level of academic achievement? What are his/her current academic strengths and weaknesses?
- What are the child's or adolescent's learning style, attitudes toward school, and motivation for learning? Are motivational issues contributing to poor school performance?
- To what extent are memory or attention problems interfering with the child's or adolescent's capacity to learn? Does he/she have attention deficit hyperactivity disorder (ADHD)?
- What are the child's or adolescent's relationships with peers?
- Are interpersonal or emotional difficulties contributing to withdrawn or disruptive behaviors in the school setting?

- Does the child or adolescent have an educational handicap (learning disability, speech/language disability, significant limited intellectual functioning, emotional or behavioral disturbance) that can be addressed in the general education school setting and/or would qualify him/her for special education services?
- What instructional methods and educational programming are needed to ensure success in school?
- Would the child or adolescent benefit from placement in a program for the gifted and talented?

Parenting Time/Custody/Visitation Disputes Referral Questions

- What are the adult caregivers' capacities for parenting (knowledge, attributes, skills, and abilities)? To what extent are mental health or substance abuse problems interfering with parent(s)' relationship to the child and ability to provide appropriate care?
- What are the psychological and developmental needs of the children involved in the custody or visitation dispute? What are the children's wishes about shared parenting, custody, and visitation?
- What shared parenting and visitation arrangements would be in the best psychological interests of the child?

Child Protection Referral Questions

- What have been the developmental consequences to the child from maltreatment (i.e., physical, emotional, or sexual abuse, or neglect)?
- What are the nature and strength of the attachment and emotional bond between child and parent(s)?
- Does a parent(s) have a mental health or substance abuse problems that has interfered with the ability to provide appropriate care for the child?
- What therapeutic interventions would be helpful for the child?
- Can the parent(s) show sufficient progress and improvement within a specified period of time?
- What would be the psychological effects on the child if he/she were returned to the care and custody of the parent(s)? What would be the effects if the child were separated from the parent(s)?

- Would out-of-home placement be beneficial for the child? If so, what kind?

Other Questions

Obviously, a host of additional questions could be asked in other practice settings. For example, in criminal hearings, referring professionals may ask psychologists to evaluate whether clients are capable of understanding the court proceedings and assisting in their own defense. Other forensic questions might include asking psychologists to evaluate the client's state of mind at the time of the offense. Interested readers may wish to consult Melton et al.'s (1997) *Psychological Evaluations for the Courts* for further discussion of these forensic issues.

Problematic Referral Questions To Avoid

Several types of referral questions should be avoided. These can be classified as vague referrals, requests for overly specific tests, and biased questions.

Vague Referrals

Many referrals to psychologists for evaluations are vague, nonspecific, or amorphous, such as when the referral party says, "I need a psychological evaluation on this client" without providing further information (Dyer, 1999; Eyde et al., 1993; Wodrich & Kush, 1990). This may happen in a number of circumstances. For example, in certain legal proceedings (e.g., termination of parental rights, commitment hearing, competency determinations), clients' due process rights may automatically trigger requests for psychological evaluations as procedural safeguards before a case planning decision can be made (Dyer, 1999).

An additional complication in these circumstances is that attorneys' requests or judges' orders for evaluation may be overly broad, based on the belief that, because standardized test scores are quantifiable, psychological evaluations can provide inherently more objective or accurate information about clients, or that greater scientific certitude is available to support the determination of difficult case planning decisions (Melton, Petrila, Poythress, & Slobogin, 1997).

A referral for psychological testing *may* be appropriate in such cases, assuming that there is a clear referral question. As noted earlier, testing data comprise only one component of a comprehensive psychological assessment. Thus, testing data should not be the only information upon which referring professionals base their case planning decisions.

Overly Specific Testing Requests

The opposite problem has been pointed out by Wodrich and Kush (1990): Some referral agents inappropriately ask for specific tests rather than deferring such decisions to the clinical judgment of the evaluating psychologist. For example, in one of the training sessions on using psychological assessment data in child welfare case planning, a forensic clinical psychologist complained of the numerous referrals he received from judges and attorneys representing either the Department of Human Services or the children in the department's custody requesting neuropsychological evaluations. He noted the inappropriateness of these types of referrals, in that information from neuropsychological examinations (assessing brain-behavior relationships) usually contributes little to difficult case planning decisions such as whether to remove or return children from the care of their parents or legal guardians.

As has been noted in this book, the clinical judgment of evaluating psychologists should be what determines the selection of specific assessment protocols and tests. Referring professionals should not ask for or order specific tests to be conducted.

"Hidden Agenda" and Biased Referral Questions

Katz (1985) discussed several problems in dealing with referral sources who "really like" or "really hate" their clients (pp. 164, 185), and who make referrals for psychological testing primarily to gain confirmation of their preconceived notions about the client or to back up the predetermined case planning decisions they want to make. (See the case scenario in chapter 6 for an example.) Although psychologists are appropriately asked to provide an independent second opinion about clients' current function, diagnosis, or prognosis, making hidden agenda or biased referrals is likely to result in evaluating psychologists' recognizing that their professional integrity and objectivity are being severely compromised.

Obviously, this situation will increase psychologists' mistrust of referring professionals and reduce their motivation for collaborating on treatment planning recommendations and decisions with other clients in the future. Given the time and expense of a psychological evaluation, time should not be wasted with these types of inappropriate referral questions.

Case Planning Considerations

Before deciding whether to seek the added value of a psychological evaluation, professionals should think carefully about what they know and what they do not know about a given case. The process of developing referral questions can be beneficial in its own right, for it enables referring professionals to clarify their own thinking and to decide if the psychological assessment is likely to add important diagnostic information about clients and/or result in effective recommendations for treatment or interventions. In some cases, obtaining an initial consultation with psychologists when making a referral may be all the help that professionals from other disciplines need in deciding on an appropriate course of action or intervention.

Referring professionals often have unrealistic expectations about what psychological evaluations can contribute to the case planning process, such as making unerring predictions about clients' future behaviors. Psychologists can offer useful diagnostic information about clients' functioning in a variety of domains, but ultimately many of the case planning decisions faced by referring professionals (e.g., is the client dangerous? Are the parents fit to care for their child?) are outside the province of what psychological assessments legitimately can offer (Melton et al., 1997). Therefore, referring professionals should ask themselves the following guiding questions before making a referral for psychological evaluations:

- Why do I want a psychological evaluation for the client?
- How will it add to my present knowledge of the case?
- What specifically do I hope to gain from it?
- Will the client benefit from this information?
- How will it aid the case planning decision making with and for my client?

Additional Resources

Interested readers may learn more about the process of developing referral questions from the following resources.

American Psychological Association. (1994). "Guidelines for Child Custody Evaluations in Divorce Proceedings." *American Psychologist, 49*, 677–680.

American Psychological Association. (1998). *Guidelines for Psychological Evaluations in Child Protection Matters,* Washington, DC: Author.

American Psychology–Law Society. (1991). "Specialty Guidelines for Forensic Psychologists." *Law and Human Behavior, 15*, 655–665.

National Association of School Psychologists. (1999a). *Position Statement on Early Childhood Assessment.* Available from National Association of School Psychologists, 4340 East West Highway, Suite 402, Bethesda, MD 20841.

National Association of School Psychologists. (1999b). *Position Statement on School Psychologists' Involvement in the Role of Assessment.* Available from National Association of School Psychologists, 4340 East West Highway, Suite 402, Bethesda, MD 20841.

Conclusion

A key competency for referring professionals from other disciplines in becoming informed consumers of psychological and substance abuse evaluations is to learn how to develop well formulated referral questions. The questions and accompanying information from the referring professional regarding his or her own thinking about the client's problems and strengths are a major source of input that guides the psychologist in evaluating the client. Vague, poorly formed, or biased referral questions are likely to result in psychological evaluations that will be of limited value in aiding referring professionals with their case planning decisions.

Chapter 8

Preparing Clients for Psychological Evaluations

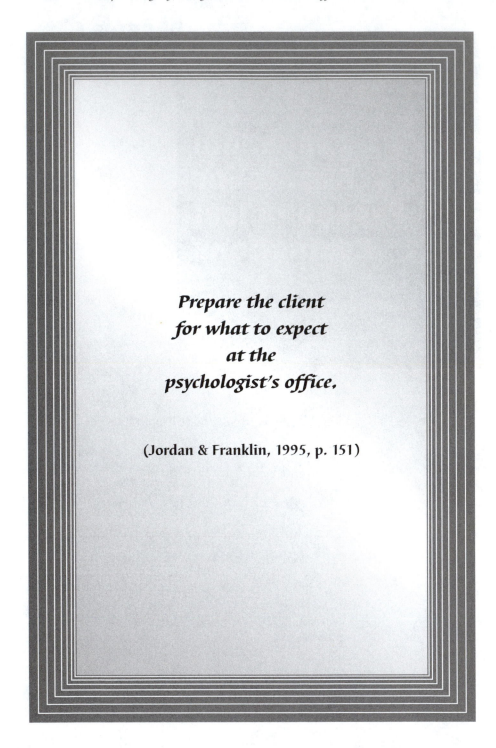

*Prepare the client
for what to expect
at the
psychologist's office.*

(Jordan & Franklin, 1995, p. 151)

This chapter offers guidance to refer-ring professionals regard-

OVERVIEW

ing the key competency of preparing clients for psychological assess-ments. The problems that can arise when clients are not prepared for evaluations are illustrated using a personal reflection of the author. Referring professionals must understand the rights of clients taking psy-chological tests and the responsibilities of helping professionals (includ-ing both psychological evaluators and referral agents) in preparing clients. The special issues involved in client preparation in clinical, research, edu-cational, and forensic evaluations are examined in detail.

When Clients Are Not Prepared

Helping professionals, be they psychologists, social workers, or other health and human service workers, are trained in a variety of practice methods and procedures that guide their work with clients. These methods rarely are transparent to clients, either because they have not been explained or because helping professionals (consciously or uncon-sciously) have a need to maintain a position of power over their clients (Pinderhughes, 1989).

When clients are uncertain about what to expect from their encounters with helping professionals, their usual behavior and typical abilities may be affected. For many clients an evaluation by a psychologist is an unfa-miliar and even threatening experience, especially if it is involuntary. Therefore, clients must be educated about the reasons for the evaluation, what to expect, and what will happen as a result of the evaluation.

To illustrate the problems that may arise when clients are not pre-pared, a personal experience touches on typical problems in the assess-ment process.

The personal incident provides a glimpse into what being referred for and undergoing a psychological assessment looks like to someone who does not understand what it is all about. Today's elementary and high

Author's Reflection

The summer before I entered the eighth grade, my parents decided that I should have my intelligence tested. They didn't fully explain the reason for this testing, even though I asked them repeatedly. In the absence of a clear explanation, I concluded that, as a student with a less than stellar academic record during elementary school, my parents thought I was dumb. (Looking back on it now, this episode was just prior to when the standardized high school entrance placement examinations were administered to all eighth-graders in parochial elementary schools. My parents probably wanted to gain some idea about my ability to succeed academically in a competitive high school environment.)

Through my father's work contacts, he arranged to have me tested privately by a school psychologist he knew. On a summer morning I reluctantly took the city bus to the school psychologist's home. I had no idea what to expect from the man I was supposed to meet. I only knew that I desperately wanted to be elsewhere—with my friends, playing ball, riding bikes, swimming, or doing something fun. The psychologist lived about 4 miles away in a first-floor apartment of an old brownstone house. He answered the door, seemed like a nice man, and with little conversation led me down a long, dimly lit hallway to the kitchen at the back of the house, where we sat at the kitchen table. I remember the tall white walls, the cooking odors left from an earlier meal, and the pile of dirty dishes in the sink.

I spent about 2 hours there while the psychologist gave me (what I now know to be) a standardized intelligence test, consisting of vocabulary test, math test, and block design puzzles. I recall that he was patient and encouraged me to perform well. About midway through, we took a break. He asked if I was thirsty and gave me a glass of water from the tap. At the conclusion of the testing session, I said good-bye, walked across the street to the bus stop, and waited for the bus to take me back home.

A week later I asked my Dad about the test results. Even though I was fuzzy about the meaning of "IQ," I wanted to know my IQ. Because the testing situation turned out to be not nearly as bad as I had imagined it to be, my imagination now had gone to other extreme. I was convinced that the test results would show that I tested at a genius level! (If the psychologist had administered a projective or personality test, he would have discovered that I suffered from *Pubescent Delusions of Grandeur*—a category soon to appear in a diagnostic and statistical manual near you!) Alas, I was informed that my intelligence was "normal," and that I didn't have to spend any more time thinking about it or pestering my parents with any more questions about it.

school students take many more standardized achievement tests than I did while growing up, but the personal anecdote is a reminder that everyone, young and old, constantly make meaning from their experiences.

In the absence of clear information from referral professionals or evaluating psychologists, clients will make up their own explanations about the purpose and nature of psychological assessments—which often will not be accurate. Children and even adults conclude that the reason they are being referred to a psychologist is because they are "dumb," "retarded," "crazy," "mental," "a head case," "deviant," "disturbed," "addicted," or "bad." Needless to say, when clients are not prepared, the influence of *person factors* (e.g., test anxiety and test-taking skills) and *situational factors* (e.g., unfamiliar, noisy, or distracting testing site) likely will have a negative impact on clients' performance.

Client Preparation in Clinical, Counseling, and Educational Settings

The American Psychological Association (1998b) developed a set of practice guidelines regarding clients' rights as test takers and the responsibilities of evaluating psychologists: *Guidelines on the Rights and Responsibilities of Test Takers*. These guidelines define "tests" broadly to mean psychological and educational instruments that testing personnel use in schools, clinical practice, counseling, and other human services settings for the purpose of client assessment. The section on client rights seems most applicable to situations in which clients are participating in an evaluation voluntarily. The section on responsibilities applies both to *test developers* and to *test users*.

Test Developers

The APA practice guidelines state that test developers have a responsibility to inform test takers of their rights and responsibilities. Typically, this entails providing evaluating psychologists with clear guidance regarding proper administration of the tests. As noted in chapter 3, when constructing standardized or criterion tests and/or clinical psychological instruments, developers typically conduct a variety of studies in support of the measure's development and ultimate use in practice. Through these studies developers gain considerable experience in how the subjects in these studies experienced the testing situation and responded to test instructions. These experiences typically are translated into administration instructions for evaluators and test instructions for clients. Obviously, this type of preparation, though important, is generic and indirect because it cannot address how to prepare a client who has a specific concern or a question about the evaluation or testing process.

Client Rights and Responsibilities as Test Takers

The APA guidelines address client rights and responsibilities as test takers. According to these guidelines, clients who take psychological tests should expect the following.

Client Rights

- To be informed of their rights and responsibilities
- To be treated with courtesy, respect, and impartiality regardless of their age, disability, ethnicity, gender, religion, sexual orientation, or other personal and cultural characteristics
- To be tested with appropriate measures used for the purposes and populations intended
- To be informed ahead of time, orally or in writing, about the purposes of the testing, the kinds of tests to be used, whether the test results will be available to the client, planned uses of the results, and whether testing accommodations are available
- To know ahead of time when tests will be administered, if the results will be made available, and if so, when, and whether there is a fee for testing
- To have the test results interpreted by an appropriately trained psychologist who practices within the psychology ethical code
- To know ahead of time if taking the test is optional, and any consequences for not taking or completing the test
- To have test results communicated orally or in writing within a reasonable amount of time after the test has been completed, and in reasonable, understandable language
- To have test results remain confidential, except as provided by law
- To have the opportunity to raise concerns about the testing process and to receive information about the procedures to be used in addressing those concerns

Client Responsibilities

- Asking questions if they do not understand the testing process
- Following test instructions carefully
- Informing evaluators if they require test accommodations
- Following test instructions carefully and answering test items honestly
- Paying for the testing, if required
- Understanding the consequences of not taking the test
- Presenting their concerns about testing in a timely manner

Many clients, however, are not sufficiently knowledgeable about the testing process and/or self-empowered in their interactions with psychologists to assertively claim either their rights or to actively fulfill all of their responsibilities as test takers. As noted earlier, in many instances clients who are referred for psychological evaluations are vulnerable and usually not in a position of power to ask questions or raise concerns. Referring professionals and evaluating psychologists share a joint responsibility for making sure that clients know what their rights and responsibilities are in testing situations.

Preparation by Psychological Evaluators

Both the psychology ethical code of conduct and the APA practice guidelines for testing repeatedly emphasize the importance of informing clients ahead of time about various aspects of the assessment and testing process (American Psychological Association, 1998b, 2002). Typically, this is done through *informed consent procedures* that typically involve both a written form that clients (or their parents or guardians) sign and psychologists' verbal instructions or descriptions to clients about their rights and responsibilities as test takers prior to the assessment getting underway. The required and optional information about psychological testing that should be shared with clients as part of the informed consent process is summarized as follows (APA 1998b).

Required Information

- Clients' rights as test takers, including the right to receive a written or oral explanation of test results within a reasonable timeframe, in commonly understood terms without the use of negative labels or comments that are "likely to inflame or stigmatize the test taker" (APA, 1998b, p. 6)

- Whether test preparation materials are available
- What reasonable accommodations for testing can be provided if clients have a qualified disability as defined by the Americans with Disability Act (ADA) or other legislation
- The nature of the test, whether the results of the tests will be given to them, and the planned use of the results (assuming that sharing the latter information does not conflict with the purpose of the testing)
- Whether specialized equipment (calculators, computers, etc.) is allowed or required and whether test takers will be given an opportunity to practice using the equipment prior to the testing
- What type of feedback and interpretation of test results are provided routinely, and whether additional information can be provided for a fee.
- Test administration procedures, including who will administer the test and how much time the testing will take
- Whether questions will be permitted during the test
- When the tests will be administered, and whether a fee is required for the testing
- Why clients are being asked to take the test, whether the test is optional, and the consequences for not taking or completing the test
- An explanation if the testing professional decides to depart from the previously agreed upon testing plan (e.g., administering a different test or an alternative test)
- How clients can question the results of the testing if they do not believe the test was administered properly or scored correctly, or if they have other concerns
- How to appeal decisions that are based in whole or in part on the results of psychological tests

Optional Information Available "Upon Request"

- Information about the examining professional's qualifications
- Sources used in interpreting test results, such as technical manuals, technical reports, norms, a description of comparison groups, and any additional information about the test taker
- What measures have been taken to safeguard the accuracy of test scores
- General information about appropriateness of the test for its intended use

- Information about retesting, including whether retaking the test is possible, and if so, under what conditions and timeframes, whether retesting is likely to improve their scores, or how test results might change if clients elect to take the test again
- How test results will be scored
- How to obtain a second opinion regarding interpretation of test results
- Who will have legitimate access to test results (when clients are identified individually) and in what form

The APA guidelines indicating that additional information can be shared "upon client request" puts the burden on clients' knowing enough about the evaluation process to be able to ask for the additional information. As noted earlier, referring professionals can help clients become more empowered consumers of evaluation services by helping them secure this additional information.

In addition to following these practice guidelines, psychologists typically spend time building rapport with clients at the outset of the evaluation process. This may involve getting to know something about clients' backgrounds and interests and learning about their expectations and feelings regarding the psychological examination. When psychologists are able to address clients' concerns by describing what to expect during the evaluation, their anxiety is likely to decrease and their motivation to cooperate is likely to increase.

Client Preparation in Research Settings

The federal government has developed a set of mandatory rules that investigators conducing biomedical and behavioral research studies must follow to ensure the protection of people participating as research subjects—Title 45, Code of Federal Regulations, Part 46: Protection of Human Subjects (45CFR 46). These regulations require that the organization sponsoring and funding the research and/or employing the investigators develop an Institutional Review Board (IRB) to ensure that all studies conform to the federal policies and regulations regarding the protection of human subjects. Among other things, the federal procedures require an *informed consent form* containing the following information.

- The name and contact information of the person(s) conducting the research. If an undergraduate, graduate, or doctoral-level student is conducting the research, the name and contact information of the faculty member supervising the student's research.

- The name and contact information for the faculty chair of the IRB and/or the IRB compliance officer—included if clients had questions or concerns about the research or were unable to research the principal investigator.
- A description of the purpose of the study.
- A statement describing the *risks* and *benefits* to the individual participating in the research study.
- A statement about how the research results would be used, and whether the information would be treated confidentially. In behavioral research studies the informed consent form would include a statement that if clients disclose certain types of information, such as child abuse, suicide, or homicide, investigators may be required to report this information to the appropriate authorities.
- A statement describing how individuals can withdraw their previous consent to participate.
- A statement authorizing the use of certain procedures, such as audiorecording or videorecording client interviews, or administration of any experimental procedures.
- A statement indicating whether the student will receive a copy of the results or findings of the study.
- A place at the bottom of the form for the signatures of the research subject and a witness, and for the date of the signature, by which formal consent to participate in the research study is given. If the individual participating in the study is a minor (under the age of 18 years), a parent's or legal guardian's signature would be required.

Some biomedical research organizations also require that investigators obtain written "assent" from children—indicating their voluntary and informed agreement to participate, even though individuals under age 18 do not have the legal right to give their own consent.

Client Preparation in Mandated Educational Testing Situations

Testing in educational settings, particularly mandated academic testing of elementary, secondary, or college students, presents an entirely different set of circumstances about clients' preparation and their protection than has been discussed previously. Case Scenario 8.1 describes one such example.

Why did this "reasoning test" not provide the customary safeguards required of biomedical and behavioral researchers under the federal rules for protecting participants of research? The answer lies in the fact that the study was part of an *internal research study* at this college, assessing the progress of a cohort of students in achieving institutional outcomes. As an internal program evaluation study, the reasoning test is exempt from federal government policy and regulations regarding the protection of human subjects.

Increasingly, colleges and universities are required to complete these types of internal assessments by accrediting organizations and/or accountability mandates from federal and state governments that want to learn about educational outcomes, teacher effectiveness, and the effectiveness of specific instructional methods. Even though these types of studies are a form of behavioral research, they remain exempt from the requirements to protect human subjects as long as they do not focus on individual student behavior.

Let's imagine that this same group of faculty members wants to do the same kind of study as a form of research on college students as individuals rather than a study of educational outcomes. They might use the same reasoning test, recruit the same sample of college freshmen, collect data on the same phenomenon of interest—the reasoning process of college students as they think about a variety of controversial issues—and analyze their data in the same way. Everything would be the same, with the exception that the investigators would be required to develop and gain the approval of an informed consent form before they could conduct their research.

Students involved in these "high stakes" mandated testing situations are not accorded the same level of protection when they are evaluated internally as they would be if they were human subjects in a program of individual research. Adequate preparation likely would reduce students' anxiety and secure their cooperation in completing tests correctly. Presumably, this would provide researchers with more reliable and valid results.

Unprepared clients do not care much about the niceties of reliability and validity. Rather than answering questions honestly and thoughtfully, some clients respond randomly or arbitrarily, especially when they feel frustrated, disrespected, or coerced. Choosing to exact a measure of

Case Scenario 8.1

About midway through his first academic term in college, a student was told by his advisor that all freshmen had to take a mandatory, online "reasoning test" developed by two counseling psychology faculty members in the Education Department. According to the advisor, the test is one way by which the college tracks students' progress over the course of their studies.

A few days later the student logged on to the college website to take the test. After reading the directions and answering the first several questions, he became concerned as to whether he understood the true purpose of the test. What was labeled as a "reasoning test" seemed to him to be an underhanded means of ascertaining students' attitudes about a variety of controversial topics, such as attitudes about dating, homosexuality, drinking among college-aged students, gun control, and so on. Because he concluded that what the test was said to elicit was deceptive and that his privacy had been violated, he eventually stopped answering the questions and asked his parents what he should do. After reviewing the test on-line, the parents also had the following concerns.

- The test instructions contained only a brief, general description of the purpose of the test. No information was given about the benefits or risks of taking the test, nor was information provided about who would have access to the test answers or how the test results were to be used subsequently.
- Names of the researchers/test developers were listed at the top of the page but with no phone number or e-mail address regarding how to contact them with questions or concerns.
- No explanation was given for why the test was mandatory, nor was any option given to students who may have wished not to take the test.
- No provision was made for anonymous testing, because students' name, address, and college identification number were required.

As a result of these concerns, the student was encouraged to go back to his advisor and ask for clarification regarding the intent of the test. Although sympathetic, the student's advisor (who was not involved in development or administration of the test) eventually just shrugged and said in a humorous tone that the college "assessment police" would be after him if he didn't take the test, adding that students who refused would be barred from registering for courses for the following academic term.

Ultimately the student was faced with the ethical decision of whether to complete the test. (He eventually did—choosing to comply with the institutional mandate rather than take on the college bureaucracy as a freshman.) From the student's perspective, however, no information was provided about how this would benefit him in his educational experience.

revenge against the test developer or test administrator may be their only perceived recourse, and clients may not care if this renders their scores useless and invalid. Even when deception as to the true purpose of test is a legitimate part of the assessment process, evaluators are ethically bound to debrief clients immediately following the testing situation (American Psychological Association, 2002a).

Client Preparation in Forensic Evaluations

Forensic evaluations present another unique set of issues regarding client preparation. Forensic evaluations routinely involve disclosure of information to judges and attorneys, in the form of written reports, depositions, or court testimony. Hence, the confidentiality privilege that normally would apply to clients' communications in clinical situations (except in certain situations such as child abuse or danger to self or another) does not apply to forensic evaluations.

"Forensic evaluators must advise clients of reasonably foreseeable disclosures and uses of information that in nonforensic context would be considered confidential" (Melton, Petrila, Poythress, and Slobogin, 1997, p. 87). These authors suggest the following minimum standards for notifying clients about the limits of confidentiality in forensic investigations:

- Who the helping professional is conducting the evaluation for (person or agency), and to whom the evaluator's report or testimony will be disclosed
- The legal issue that will be addressed in the evaluation
- The kinds of information most likely to be relevant to the evaluation, and the techniques proposed to gather that information (interviews, tests, etc.)
- The legal proceeding in which the evaluator anticipates having to provide testimony
- The kinds of information that may require special disclosure to third parties, such as an admission of child abuse, and the possible consequences for the person being evaluated
- Whether the person being evaluated has the right to decline or limit his or her participation in the evaluation, and any known sanctions for declining

The standards help clients in forensic evaluations make informed decisions about whether to participate and what kinds of information to provide. The objective of this disclosure is to encourage clients' involvement through an informed dialogue.

If a client is facing criminal charges, the evaluator should be aware that any statements the client makes could become incorporated into the clinician's reports (Dyer, 1999). This includes information that clients may wish to divulge "off the record." Interested readers are referred to Melton and colleagues (1997) for further discussion of forensic evaluations and clients' constitutional rights, such as the right to remain silent (Fifth Amendment) and the right to counsel (Sixth Amendment).

Case Planning Considerations

The APA guidelines address only the preparation activities of psychologists. I am adding below my own suggestions for how referring professionals also may play a significant, albeit secondary, role in client preparation. Wherever possible, referring professionals should collaborate and coordinate their activities with evaluating psychologists to provide clients with uniform, consistent information. One or more of the following steps by referring professionals may be appropriate:

1. Explain to clients who is requesting an evaluation and for what purpose. Describe the referring professional's role in requesting the evaluation, his or her relationship to the evaluating psychologist, the referring professional's prior experience with other clients who have found psychological evaluations to be helpful, and how the information from the psychological assessments will assist in case planning decisions.
2. Help clients identify an issue or concern that an evaluation may address. Clients and referral agents often disagree about the need for psychological assessments. For example, teachers or parents may believe that a child's academic or social difficulties warrant a psychological evaluation to determine whether the child would benefit from special education services. The child, however, may deny any cognitive or behavioral difficulties and instead blame others for being unfair, overly demanding, rejecting, mean, biased, and so on.

    Referring professionals can adopt a neutral, facilitating stance by initially not challenging the child's depictions. Rather, the child can be helped to see that meeting with the psychologist is one way by which parents, teachers, and children themselves can learn how to make things go better at school.

A similar approach might be taken with adult clients. For example, a child welfare caseworker may point out to defensive parents the potential benefits of participating in a psychological evaluation such as discovering underutilized parenting strengths in themselves; gaining new insights about their children's feelings and behaviors; learning new parenting strategies to employ in raising children safely and appropriately; or (at the very least) ending the court's or Department of Social Services' involvement with the family as quickly and as appropriately as possible.

3. Assist the evaluating psychologist in the logistics of the assessment, which may include obtaining clients' signed informed consent form and signed releases of information; making sure that evaluating psychologists receive all relevant previous cumulative educational records, diagnostic reports, social histories, treatment plans, progress reports, client observations, case notes, and the like in a timely manner; ensuring that clients appear for scheduled sessions; and, when necessary, transporting clients to and from the psychologist's office for evaluation sessions.

4. Adopt an advocacy role with evaluating psychologists to ensure that clients' rights as test-takers are honored.

5. If clients do not understand or disagree with the test results and/or the psychologists' conclusions and recommendations, assist them in obtaining follow-up consultations with psychologists.

6. Become familiar with DHHS policies and regulations regarding the protection of human subjects. Become a member of an Institutional Review Board (IRB) in research and higher education institutions, which establishes policies and procedures regarding the protection of human subjects in voluntary biomedical and behavioral research.

7. Become a member of a Student Assessment Committee in elementary, secondary, and postsecondary education institutions that develop policies and procedures regarding the (involuntary) assessment of student progress, instructional methods, program effectiveness, educational outcomes, and so forth.

Additional Resources

The APA *Guidelines on the Rights and Responsibilities of Test Takers* document is available either as a brochure or from the APA website (www.apa.org/science/ttrr.html). To order the brochure, write to the

American Psychological Association, 750 First Street NE, Washington, DC, 20002-4242.

Information on the federal regulations regarding research on human subjects (45CFR46) can be obtained from the Office for Human Research Protection, Department of Health and Human Services, 1101 Wootton Parkway, Suite 200, Rockville, Maryland, 20852; Phone 301-496-7005. The regulations are available online at either of the following websites: www.llnl.gov/HumanSubjects/appendices/Appendix03.pdf; or www.hhs.gov/ohrp/humansubjects/guidance/statute.htm.

The practice of psychology is legally regulated by the states, and as noted in chapter 2, states may vary considerably regarding what information is required to be disclosed to clients at the beginning of their work with psychologists. The state licensing board is the source for state regulations about mandatory disclosure information that must be given to clients at the onset of the delivery of professional psychological services.

Conclusion

This chapter has examined the process of educating and preparing clients for what to expect from a psychological evaluation. Examining psychologists and referring professionals alike have a significant role in this enterprise. In addition, test developers, professional organizations in psychology, and state laws regulating the practice of psychology make significant contributions. The type of preparatory information shared may differ among clinical evaluations, research studies, educational testing, and forensic evaluations.

Chapter 9

Judging the Quality of Psychological Reports

*Judging test findings is,
for most consumers, a matter
of being able to understand
and use the results.
What makes findings useful
is when the referral question
is answered, information is
reported in language that
avoids jargon,
limitation of the results
are clearly expressed,
and programming
recommendations are
included for the referral agents.*

(Wodrich, 1997, p. 337).

I n clinical, counseling, educational, voca-tional, medical, and legal

OVERVIEW

settings, written and oral reports from evaluating psychologists provide crucial information to referring consumers in their case planning work with clients. In chapter 6 we reviewed the structure and components of alcohol and drug assessment reports. In this chapter we will address the topic more broadly, reviewing the purpose of psychological reports, prin-ciples of report writing, and common characteristics or usual features of written psychological reports.

In addition, this chapter delineates a variety of problems in report writing that have been identified in the psychology literature and provides samples of full reports and report excerpts to help consumers distinguish between those that are problematic and those that are written better. Further, the chapter presents a variety of formats in which assessment results can be communicated to referring professionals and their clients, both in writing and orally.

The later part of the chapter suggests a number of ways by which referring consumers can obtain consultation from psychologists and pro-vide feedback to psychologists about the quality and usefulness of their reports. The case planning discussion suggests a procedure for holding an interdisciplinary case planning/treatment planning conference with exam-ining psychologists and clients.

Purpose of Psychological Reports

Ownby (1997) observed that "the primary reason for writing a report is to persuade someone to accept or do something that the psychologist believes will benefit the client" (p. 5). Based on a review of the research and pro-fessional literature on report writing, he suggested that most authorities in the field agree that the purposes of psychological reports are to

- describe the client and problem or area of concern that was assessed,

- report the results of tests for future use,
- communicate test results to interested readers (e.g., referring professionals, clients), and
- recommend appropriate courses of action that should be taken with or for the person being evaluated.

Typical Features of Written Reports

The written psychological report has been described as an "x-ray of the personality" (Wolber & Carne, 1993, p. 1). That is to say, the intellectual and emotional functioning of individuals is evaluated in detail and is typically compared to the functioning of other individuals (the normative comparison group) to derive an integrated and coherent picture of the client and to assist in achieving appropriate, effective case planning.

The organization, structure, length, and specific sections of psychologists' reports are influenced by a host of factors including

- purpose of the evaluation (i.e., referral questions the psychologist has been asked to address) and practice setting in which the evaluation took place (e.g., clinical, counseling, educational, vocational, and forensic);
- number of tests or assessment procedures administered;
- theoretical orientation of the examining psychologist and model of report-writing being used;
- intended audience for the report;
- amount of time that has elapsed between completion of the assessment procedures and the date of the report writing;
- participation, if any, of testing assistants who may have administered and scored the test and/or supervising psychologists who may have overseen the evaluation;
- use of computer-assisted programs or services for test scoring and/or interpretation purposes;
- external reporting requirements and mandated deadlines;
- report writing proficiencies of psychologists; and
- whether the psychologists' time for writing reports is reimbursable.

Despite these variations, consumers might reasonably expect a number of usual features or characteristics in psychologists' written reports. These are summarized in Table 9.1.

TABLE 9.1 Organization and Structure Frequently Found in Written Psychological Reports

REPORT ELEMENTS	INFORMATION USUALLY INCLUDED
Report title	Reports typically begin with an identifying heading, such as *Psychological Assessment, Psychological Report*, or *Forensic Psychological Evaluation*. Confidentiality notices (see below) also may be stated just under the title, describing the access or restrictions to disseminating the report.
Examiner's information and qualifications	The examiner's name, degree(s), licensure, and contact information are listed on the title page of the report. Certain types of reports, such as forensic psychological evaluations, may require more detailed information regarding the evaluator's specific training and experience.
Identifying client information	Identifying information includes the client's name and address, age, gender, race/ethnicity; occupation or school status (e.g., school or grade attended); marital status and/or name and address of parents or legal guardian(s); names and ages of members of immediate family (or household); and other information as relevant.
Source and reason for referral	The report identifies the referring agent and specific referral questions the psychologist has been asked to address in the evaluation.
Purpose of evaluation	An explicit statement gives the specific purpose of the report, as this has been shown to be a prerequisite to determining its effectiveness. For example, the report may seek to answer a specific referral question and also to communicate information discovered in the course of the evaluation that may be relevant to consumers in working with clients.
Evaluation procedures	The report lists all the assessment procedures, tests, and protocols used in the evaluation, including contacts with collateral sources used in the evaluation and/or reviews of prior evaluations or other client records consulted as background for the present evaluation, and dates of evaluation appointments.
Background information on the client	A concise summary covers the client's history as relevant to the present evaluation, such as psychiatric history (e.g., symptoms and/or previous treatment), educational history, vocational or career history, developmental or psychosocial history, medical or rehabilitation history, sexual history, drug/alcohol history, and arrest record or criminal history, etc. The summary also includes current educational, health, social service agencies or legal systems currently involved with the client.

(continued)

TABLE 9.1   (continued)

REPORT ELEMENTS	INFORMATION USUALLY INCLUDED
Behavioral observations	Descriptions of the client's "presentation" during the evaluation include appearance, mental status at the time of evaluation, relevant cultural or cross-cultural characteristics that may be influencing the client's manner of communicating or interacting with the examiner, extent of cooperation or defensiveness in completing the assessment procedures or tests, etc.
Situational factors	Descriptions of the testing situation may be especially important in certain types of evaluations, such as forensic assessments.
Test results	Test results include intellectual, personality, and other measures administered both through numeric scores and narrative statements indicating the meaning or significance of the test result.
Interpretation and discussion	The report integrates and interprets of all test scores, interview data, and information obtained from other procedures into a meaningful, coherent whole. The evaluator's theoretical orientation may be used explicitly to tie the client's test scores into psychological constructs used to interpret the meaning of the information. Any limitations, cautions, or qualifications of test results or assessment findings are identified and explained.
Diagnosis (or diagnostic impressions)	Where required, diagnostic concepts or formal classification systems (e.g., DSM-IV) are used to label and group the client's present symptoms or functioning into one or more recognizable clusters of mental health disorders, psychological impairments, or educational handicaps. This includes delineating differential diagnosis, and/or additional information needed to rule in or rule out alternative diagnoses.
Recommendations	Based on the assessment and test results, the report suggests programming intervention in the home, educational, mental health, legal, or vocational settings in which the client has difficulties. For referring professionals, the recommendations section typically is the most important section of the report.
Prognostic statements	Where required, prognostic statements render an opinion or professional judgment by the evaluating psychologist regarding the client's future behavior, performance, adjustment, recuperation, recovery, etc., or the client's anticipated response to intervention or treatment, etc. that can reasonably be expected, based on the test results, assessment findings, or inferences made by the psychologist.
Confidentiality notice	The report must include statements delineating the persons who are granted access to this report, and specification of

(continued)

TABLE 9.1   (continued)

REPORT ELEMENTS	INFORMATION USUALLY INCLUDED
	restrictions on the dissemination, release, or duplication of the report to persons not authorized to read it. (As noted in chapter 6, in drug and alcohol evaluations, this notice appears at the beginning of the report rather than near the end.)
Summary	A brief concluding statement summarizes the referral question, major findings of the assessment, and recommendations resulting from the evaluation. The summary may contain a statement from the evaluating psychologist regarding whether the psychologist will be available to answer additional questions about the evaluation or be available for consultation with consumers and/or clients.
Signature of report author(s)	The report author's name and signature are included at the end of the report. Typically, the author's terminal degree, license or other professional credentials, and institutional affiliation (if any) are listed. Contact information (name, address, phone, email, fax) of the evaluating psychologist is included here, if not listed already on letterhead. In the event that the evaluation was conducted by an unlicensed psychologist or trainee, the report includes the name, signature, license number, and contact information of the supervising psychologist.

Sources: *Assessment in Counseling: A Guide to the Use of Psychological Assessment Procedure* (3rd ed.), by A. Hood & R. Johnson, 2002, Alexandria, VA: American Counseling Association; *A Practical Guide to Psychodiagnostic Testing*, by L. Katz, 1985, Springfield, IL: Charles C Thomas Publishing; *Psychological Reports: A Guide to Writing in Professional Psychology*, by R. Ownby, 1997, New York: Wiley; *Assessment of Children* (3rd ed.), by J. Sattler, 1988, San Diego: Jerome M. Sattler Publishing; *Clinical and Forensic Interviewing of Children and Families: Guidelines for Mental Health, Education, Pediatric, and Child Maltreatment Fields*, by J. Sattler, 1998, San Diego: Jerome M. Sattler Publishing; *Diagnosis and Treatment Planning in Counseling*, by L. Seligman, 2004, New York: Kluwer Academic/Plenum Publishing; *Forensic Psychology: From Classroom to Courtroom*, by B. Van Dorsten, 2002, New York: Kluwer Academic/ Plenum; *Writing Psychological Reports: A Guide for Clinicians*, by G. Wolber & W. Carne, 1993, Sarasota, FL: Professional Resource Press; *Clinician's Thesaurus: The Guidebook for Writing Psychological Reports* (4th ed.), by E. Zuckerman, 1995, New York: Guilford Press; & *Clinician's Thesaurus: The Guidebook for Writing Psychological Reports*, by E. Zuckerman, 2000, New York: Guilford Press.

Principles of Good Report Writing

Ownby (1997) noted that consumers in clinical settings often criticize reports for both their content (over- or underinterpreting the psychological data) and the style in which the report was written, which may result in these reports not being used in treatment planning. He cautioned that psychological information used in educational settings can bias teachers' expectations and attitudes about children's capacity for learning, ability to benefit from instruction, and eventual classroom success. Part of the problem seems to be that, during the course of psychologists' education and training, most of their attention is directed to the mechanics of test administration and scoring, at the expense of guidance in writing informative, coherent, and concise reports. Drawing on several authorities in psychology, the following principles have been extracted as benchmarks in judging the quality of written reports.

1. Reports typically are organized into distinct paragraphs or sections to present information in a logical, sequential manner. Well written reports are concise, designed to succinctly convey essential information about clients in an informative manner (Zuckerman, 1995, 2000). (Forensic evaluation reports are an exception; they often are lengthy and detailed and include extensive verbatim quotes from clients.)
2. The report ideally is written in jargon-free language. Technical terms and acronyms, if used, should be fully explained in understandable language (Hood & Johnson, 2002).
3. Reports should provide a clear picture of the person being evaluated —his or her strengths, current capacities, deficits, and potentials— rather than detailing the tests or measures administered or the psychologist's theoretical orientation (Katz, 1985; Wolber & Carne, 1993). Reports that describe clients' performance in functional terms are easier for the nonpsychologist consumer to understand and interpret than reports that deal predominantly with tests and scores (Ownby, 1997).
4. All evaluation procedures and protocols and collateral sources of information used in preparing the assessment report should be specified clearly at the outset. Wodrich (1997) suggested that the title of a test often is a poor or misleading indicator of what the test actually measures. Hence, test scores should be accompanied by a brief description of what the test is measuring.
5. The report should clearly explain the strengths and limitations of the tests and the process by which tests are scored (Hood & Johnson, 2002). The report should convey to the reader the psychologist's extent of certitude in the reliability and validity of the test scores upon which diagnostic and prognostic conclusions subsequently may be based and case planning recommendations formulated (Sattler, 1988, 1998).

6. Test results should be reported in a separate section from the psychologists' interpretation of the meaning of these results (Zuckerman, 1995).

7. Test results should be related to and integrated with other sources of information, such as interview data, behavioral observations, psychosocial case histories, medical/physiological data, and results of previous evaluation results (Sattler, 1998; Seligman, 2004).

8. The sources of data used in arriving at a diagnosis and in making treatment recommendations should be clearly evident (Zuckerman, 2000).

9. Conclusions, recommendations, and prognostic statements should be written in probabilistic language, rather than written as definitive pronouncements (Wodrich, 1997).

10. The timeliness of the report is a key factor in whether the assessment information ultimately is used in case planning with clients (Wolber & Carne, 1993).

Identifying Problems in Reports

Despite a growing number of resources developed for psychologists about how to write informative, clinically useful reports (Lichtenberger, Mather, Kaufman, & Kaufman, 2005; Ownby, 1997; Zuckerman, 1995, 2000), report writing still seems to be a significant weakness in the repertoire of many evaluating psychologists. Table 9.2 lists some of the common problems in report writing that have been identified in the psychology literature.

TABLE 9.2   Common Problems in Report Writing

TYPE OF PROBLEM	DESCRIPTION
Reports overusing jargon	Many authorities identify overuse of jargon as one of the major weaknesses in psychological report writing.
Reports failing to meet the needs of the referring consumer	The following fail to meet these needs: failure to answer the referral question, failure to incorporate crucial client information provided by the referring consumer, telling the consumer what he or she already knows without adding anything new, avoiding making recommendations or failing to take a stand on the referral questions or issues, making unrealistic treatment recommendations, failure to back up treatment recommendations with facts and clinical reasoning, failure to provide consumers with the significance of the findings.

(continued)

TABLE 9.2   (continued)

TYPE OF PROBLEM	DESCRIPTION
Reports lacking interpretation	Some reports provide test results in great detail but without an interpretive or organizing section that pulls all the data together. This may mean that psychologists either lack confidence in their diagnostic abilities or avoid their professional obligation to offer interpretations and make predictions based on the test results. In addition, overly descriptive reports of test findings may lead to misunderstandings by clients who read their scores but do not understand their meaning.
Reports lacking supporting data	Reports with an overly theoretical interpretation often do not provide enough information about clients' actual test results, leaving the referring consumer in the dark as to how the psychologist arrived at his or her conclusions, diagnosis, prognosis, or treatment recommendations.
Poorly written, disorganized, and/or erroneous reports	Reports with misspelled words, poorly constructed sentences, or incorrect grammar lack credibility. They also may contain contradictory information, lack clear organization, intermix test results with background information and client history, and/or intermix the description of test score results with interpretation. These reports are difficult to read and also make it difficult to discern how clients actually performed. Reports that overuse "qualifiers" ("some," little," "very," etc.) are, in Zuckerman's (1995) evocative view, "leeches that infest the pond of prose, sucking the blood of words" (p. 326). In addition, reports that contain blatant errors (e.g., misidentifying the client's name, age, gender, race, or ethnicity) quickly begin to raise questions about the overall competence of the evaluating psychologist.

Adapted from *Responsible Test Use: Case Studies for Assessing Human Behavior*, by L. Eyde, G. Robertson, K. Krug, A. Roberston, K. Moreland, et al., 1993, Washington, DC: American Psychological Association; *A Practical Guide to Psychodiagnostic Testing*, by L. Katz, 1985, Springfield, IL: Charles C Thomas Publishing; *Psychological Reports: A Guide to Writing in Professional Psychology* (3rd ed.), by R. Ownby, 1997, New York: Wiley; *Assessment of Children* (3rd ed.); *Children's Psychological Testing: A Guide for Nonpsychologists* (3rd ed.), by D. L. Wodrich, 1997, Baltimore: Paul H. Brookes; *Clinical Interpretation of the Wechsler Adult Intelligence Scale*, by I. Zimmerman & J. Woo-Sam, 1973, New York: Grune & Stratton; & *Clinician's Thesaurus: The Guidebook for Writing Psychological Reports* (4th ed.), by E. Zuckerman, 1995, New York: Guilford Press.

Sample Reports and Excerpts

The chapter now turns to analysis of several psychological reports and excerpts, to help consumers differentiate problematic report writing from better report writing. Material has been extracted from several different sections of reports to help readers develop a critical eye in judging the quality. These excerpts come from published reports in the psychology literature and from composites of several evaluation reports. All client and practitioner information has been disguised and altered to preserve confidentiality.

Example A: The Case of the Disappearing Psychologist.

Psychologists are professionals in positions of privilege and power over client populations that typically are vulnerable and at risk. One of the ways by which this power and privilege are misused, intentionally or unintentionally, is when psychologists write reports that edit their own behavior out of the report. Table 9.3 compares two different excerpts from the behavioral observations section of the report.

Example B: "Killing Me Softly" With Test Score Minutia

As noted earlier, a common problem in psychological report writing is in providing detailed test score results without interpreting how the information

TABLE 9.3	Comparison and Analysis of Behavioral Observations Report Excerpts
PROBLEMATIC EXCERPT	**ANALYSIS**
"James (age 12) presented in a defensive, guarded manner. He complied with all the test requirements, although reluctantly some of the time. He was well oriented and his affect was blunted. His speech was disjointed, circumstantial and difficult to follow. Often he contradicted things he said previously. He asked many hostile questions masked as humor, and frequently challenged the relevance of the testing materials or procedures. He repeatedly asked if he were dumb, wanted feedback about the questions and spoke without thinking. When he did not know an answer, he made excuses unrelated to the task."	No information is provided about the psychologist's own behavior. Thus, it remains unknown as to what effort or steps were taken to build rapport, reduce anxiety, and obtain cooperation from the client. The client's presentation of self may be taken out of context, or the client's behavior may be misinterpreted as enduring *trait* characteristics, rather than a temporary *state* of anxiety about the evaluation.

(continued)

TABLE 9.3   (continued)

MORE INFORMATIVE EXCERPT	ANALYSIS
"Robert (age 9) presented as a small boy who appeared physically to resemble a five-year-old. He was pleasant and cooperative and appeared motivated to work as hard as he could to please the present writer. To that end, while working with the examiner, he managed to clean up the waiting room by himself, putting all the toys away in the hall closet. This kind of behavior is highly unusual for a nine-year-old boy and is suggestive of children who need to please adults. However, throughout the evaluation, his behavior was highly guarded and secretive. When asked to draw a picture of his family, he refused to let the examiner watch him as he drew, stating that it makes him "nervous" to have someone look over his shoulder while he draws. People who watch him were said to make him nervous because he feared they might 'hurt him.'"	The client's presentation of self can be seen in the context of the evaluator's behavior and reactions. The evaluator succinctly conveys information about the child's motivation and degree of cooperation during the evaluation, provides a description of the child's physical appearance and behaviors that appear to be atypical for his chronological age, gives several behavioral examples that provide the basis for the evaluator's judgment about the child's compulsive behavior and suspiciousness (e.g., the need to put all the toys away in the playroom and the mistrustful, secretive response to a benign request to do a family drawing).

contributes to a meaningful, holistic understanding of the client. The report in Table 9.4 is an example.

Example C: Differentiating Measures From Frameworks

Psychologists typically conduct their evaluations within a conceptual framework based on both human behavior theories and empirical research. Sometimes, however, reports are written in such a way as to present the evaluator's conceptual framework as if it were an empirical instrument. Consider the excerpts in Table 9.5 in which two different authors report the use of Arnold Lazarus' (1981) Multimodal Behavioral Therapy conceptual assessment framework in their written reports.

Example D: "The Devil is in the Details"

When projective measures are used in an evaluation, it is helpful to provide the reader with a flavor of the client's responses to specific inkblots

**TABLE 9.4   Psychological Report Excerpts of a
Child Evaluated for Attention Deficit
Hyperactivity Disorder (ADHD)**

ORIGINAL REPORT INFORMATION	ANALYSIS
Procedures Section • Clinical Interview • Consultation with Teacher • Conners Questionnaire • ADD-H Comprehensive Teachers Rating Scale (ACTeRS) • Child Behavior Checklist (CBCL-Parents; CBCL-Teacher Report Form) • Gordon Diagnostic System	• The assessment procedures and tests are listed, but without any explanation as to their relative merit or weight in contributing to the evaluation of ADHD. The evaluator fails to indicate that the Conners Questionnaire and ACTeRS are both behavior rating scales that specifically assess problems with attention and hyperactivity, whereas the CBCL is a behavior rating scale that assesses hyperactivity plus a broad range of internalizing and externalizing behavior problems as well as assessing prosocial behavior, and the Gordon Diagnostic System is a continuous performance test that is a direct measure of a client's capacity to organize and focus attention while being presented with tasks requiring vigilance (i.e., maintaining concentration while being exposed to computer-generated distractors). • No details are provided regarding the Clinical Interview or the Consultation with Teacher. It is unknown with whom the clinical interview was conducted (i.e., with one or both parents, with or without the child), whether the interview and consultation consisted only of the informants filling out rating scale forms or whether parents or teacher were actually interviewed, or whether the child was observed directly by the psychologist in the classroom.

ORIGINAL REPORT INFORMATION	ANALYSIS
Results Section * Note: Higher scores indicate greater degree of problems; t-scores above 70 are significant.	• The evaluator fails to note that the Conners behavioral ratings of father, mother, and teacher frequently do not agree. All of the father's ratings place the child in the clinically significant range of behavior problems, with the exception of anxiety.

Conners Scales

	Father	Mother
Conduct Problem	.71	.49
Learning Problem	.95	.91
Psychosomatic	.80	.61
Impulsivity/Hyper.	.76	.68
Anxiety	.60	.53
Overall Index	.90	76

The mother notes significant problems primarily with learning, although her rating of impulsive/hyperactivity approaches significance.

The teacher, in contrast, does not rate the child as having conduct or hyperactive problems but does endorse problems of inattention that approach the clinically significant range.

(continued)

TABLE 9.4   (continued)

ORIGINAL REPORT INFORMATION	ANALYSIS
Conners Scales	• The Gordon Diagnostic System, the one direct measure of the child's distractibility, does not reveal significant problems with vigilance or distractibility. Interestingly, the evaluator did not provide the actual scores (which are markedly different from the detailed reporting of all the other test score results), but reports only whether the scores were nonsignificant.

Conners Scales

	Teacher
Conduct Problem	.45
Hyperactivity	.58
Inattentive-passive	.68
Overall Index	.60

Gordon Diagnostic System

Delay Task:	NS (Not Significant)
Vigilance Task:	NS
Accuracy Index:	NS
Distractibility Task:	NS
Accuracy Index:	NS

ORIGINAL REPORT INFORMATION	ANALYSIS
Behavioral Observation Section "The child was able to attend and perform relatively better in this one-to-one, quiet, novel setting with minimal distractions, as compared with a classroom situation. Her performance in this assessment and the reports indicate variability in her attention abilities, with increasing levels of visual and/or auditory and other stimulation resulting in increasing difficulty."	• The context or length of the behavioral observation is not clear. Was the activity or interaction between the child and the psychologist simply the completion of the Gordon Diagnostic System tasks, or were other activities involved? • The evaluator's statement that the child was able to attend "relatively better" in the one-to-one setting does not provide the comparative context that the evaluator is using to make this judgment.

ORIGINAL REPORT INFORMATION	ANALYSIS
Diagnosis Section "Attention Deficit Hyperactivity Disorder (ADHD) is confirmed at a mild level."	• The evaluator's basis for the ADHD diagnosis is not firmly supported by the test results. The evaluator made no effort to consider alternative hypotheses or explanations for the data. This raises the possibility of the evaluator's *confirmatory bias*—finding what one expects to see rather than evaluating the evidence objectively.

(continued)

TABLE 9.4   (continued)

ORIGINAL REPORT INFORMATION	ANALYSIS
Recommendations Section "1. Given the diagnosis of ADHD, consideration should be given to a trial on stimulant medication. Parents have been requested to discuss this with their physician. 2. Parents and the child should attend family therapy to address the behavioral and scholastic issues, which persist. 3. Parents should join the Attention Deficit Advocacy Group, for additional information regarding ADHD related issues, events, and Parent Support Group meetings."	• The psychologist's primary recommendation of a trial of stimulant medication has several problems. First, it is not the psychologist's role to determine which class of medications may be appropriate. This should be determined by the psychiatrist or a medical prescriber. Second, the psychologist fails to address any environmental changes or increased structure at home or school that might assist in the child's adjustment and performance. Encouraging parents and teachers to increase external structure would be an essential recommendation with children diagnosed with ADHD, regardless of whether medication is prescribed. Third, no educational programming recommendations are offered to teachers regarding management of possible deficits in the child's attention. • The recommendation for family therapy appears generic and nonspecific to the treatment of ADHD.

ORIGINAL REPORT INFORMATION	ANALYSIS
Disclaimer Statement "This assessment was limited to those factors most relevant to ADHD. It does not constitute a full psychological evaluation, which would include other assessment areas (for example, learning disabilities and psychopathology)."	• This disclaimer is particularly problematic given that the one area of consensus in the behavioral ratings of mother, father, and teacher is that all three view the child as having significant learning problems, either in addition to or as a component of whatever attention and hyperactive problems may be present. Because ADHD frequently co-occurs with both learning disabilities and disruptive behavior disorders, the evaluator seems to be remiss in not assessing the child's cognitive functioning or possible emotional and behavioral contributors to the child's current functioning.

* The Results Section has been abbreviated. Only data from the Conners Scales are reported. Scores from the ACTerS and the CBCL-Parent Report Form and CBCL-Teacher Report Form were similar to those of the Conners Scales.

TABLE 9.5   Comparison and Analysis of Procedures Section Excerpts

PROBLEMATIC EXCERPT	ANALYSIS
"Tests Administered to Mr. E., Sr. BASIC-ID Assessment: The BASIC-ID is an acronym that describes a client's seven modalities (behavior, affect, sensation, imagery, cognition, interpersonal relationships, and drugs/biology). I assessed Mr. E. in each of these modalities" (Sapp, 2002, p. 149).	The BASIC-ID assessment is listed as the first item under the section heading "Tests Administered," as if it were an empirical test similar to the other objective and projective measures given to this client, rather than being the evaluator's organizing theoretical framework. The evaluator does not make clear that the data reported in the BASIC-ID assessment section is essentially a combination of semi-structured interview and observation data, not an empirical instrument. Also problematic in this report, the BASIC-ID assessment data were not used in making case planning recommendations.

MORE INFORMATIVE EXCERPT	ANALYSIS
"Lazarus' model enables counselors to take a systematic and comprehensive look at a person, determine areas of strength and weakness, and develop a treatment plan designed to have a multifaceted impact ... [The model assumes] that change in one aspect of a person will affect and be encouraged by change in other aspects of the person. . . .[A] seven-fold model, represented by the acronym BASIC I.D. [is used] for assessing the person and planning the treatment. Assessment of these seven areas leads to the development of a Structural Profile to guide the counseling process" (Seligman, 2004, p. 209).	Clearly, the BASIC-ID is an overarching conceptual framework, not an empirical instrument. Also, the purpose is clear, as are the organization of data and how the client's profile will be used in the treatment planning process.

or story cards rather than just a global summary of their responses to ambiguous material, regardless of whether the responses formerly are scored or not. Compare the two report excerpts in Table 9.6.

Example E: Is the Profile Valid?

Recall from chapter 3 that certain objective personality tests, such as the MMPI, have statistical means to assess whether a client is responding honestly or is defensive, and also can determine whether the client responded randomly to the test items. Before interpreting the clinical scales on the MMPI, psychologists must inspect the validity scales to

TABLE 9.6 Comparison and Analysis of Results Section Excerpts (Projective Test)

PROBLEMATIC EXCERPT	ANALYSIS
"Her Rorschach responses were consistent with her intelligence scores. She tends to see things in overly simplistic, black-and-white terms that make her prone to conflict with others. Her emotional expression tends to be dramatic and intense. She is less responsive to emotionally laden situations than most people. Mistrustful of others, she nonetheless expects that interpersonal interactions will be collaborative. She is likely to protect her personal space strongly and maintain superficial relationships."	• The psychologist does not provide the details of which inkblot cards the client responded to, or describe the specific images or themes that may have emerged from the projective testing. Rather, the psychologist provides summary statements and conclusions about the client's projective responses but does not indicate the basis upon which these were made. • Given the large number of probabilistic statements in this report segment (e.g., "tends to see things in overly simplistic, black-and-white terms" ... "emotional expression tends to be dramatic and intense" ...."likely to protect her personal space strongly"), the client's Rorschach responses likely were scored by computer testing software or services, whose "interpretive report" is being used as the basis for these statements, rather than the interpretations being formulated by the psychologist.

MORE INFORMATIVE EXCERPT	ANALYSIS
"One-half of her responses to the Rorschach cards included skull responses (some with blood on them). Other responses included spiders and a dead mouse. It is a highly unusual finding for a child who is developmentally age five to produce this number of 'skull' responses. The affect accompanying the production of these responses was also highly unusual in that Julie appeared to get lost in her own responses, disengaging emotionally from the setting and appearing to be preoccupied with her own internal processing of these responses. Responses to TAT cards were unusual in that one story was about a lady who became so distraught about her father dying that she remained at his gravesite, not eating or drinking until she died. A second story described a husband asking to be buried alive with his dead wife."	• Multiple projective measures were employed— both the Rorschach inkblot test and the TAT picture story card test. The child made similar unusual responses to each, which give credence to the psychologist's conclusion that the client is preoccupied with inner images of harm, danger, and death. The client's responses to specific cards or specific story productions are reported with enough detail to convey the strength of the preoccupation. • The observation of the client's apparent detachment from immediate reality when responding to the inkblots suggests that the projective data were scored personally by the psychologist rather than being generated by a testing service. The two projective tests together convincingly convey a picture of a client who has been exposed to a number of overwhelming experiences that seem to have resulted in an overgeneralized, extreme fear reaction.

assess clients' attitude toward the testing process—particularly whether they have been honest and cooperative in responding to the questions (Hood & Johnson, 2002). The report should contain information regarding whether the test scores are considered valid, as well as provide information on the results of the clinical scales. Compare the two report excerpts in Table 9.7 regarding reporting of MMPI results.

A plethora of scales and norms have been developed for the MMPI and its successor, the MMPI-2. Much interpretive significance often is

TABLE 9.7   Comparison and Analysis of Behavioral Observations Report Excerpts

PROBLEMATIC EXCERPT	ANALYSIS
"In his response to personality tests, Mr. Jones gives evidence of moderate levels of emotional problems. He did not give any test results which would suggest a serious mental illness.... He reports significant symptomatology on the MMPI.... Test findings indicate the presence of both significant anxiety and depression, but depressive symptoms appear to be more important and more long-standing" (Katz, 1985, p. 153).	The psychologist does not provide any information about the client's attitude or degree of defensiveness about taking this personality inventory. Thus, we do not know whether the clinical test scores were considered valid. Scale elevations are presented descriptively, without reference to the specific subscales themselves.

MORE INFORMATIVE EXCERPT	ANALYSIS
"Ms. B. obtained significantly high L and K t-scores. [The L scale measures conformity and denial. The K scale measures defensiveness.] In fact, she attempted to under-report her psychological concerns.... These results support earlier data which stated that Ms. B. wanted to present herself in the most positive light possible.... In summary, the results of the MMPI-2 suggest that Ms. B. lacks psychological sophistication and insight; in addition, she presented herself in a defensive manner.... Finally, Ms. B. had elevations on the clinical scales 4 and 5, which suggest that she does not like to conform or obey authority" (Sapp, 2002, pp. 145–146).	The psychologist begins by reporting the validity scales of the MMPI-2, which provides a clear picture of the client's attempts to minimize psychological problems. As Hogan (2003) notes, if one or more of the validity indexes are grossly atypical, the clinical scales may not be reported at all. Specific scale elevations and their meaning then are presented together.

attached to the "two point code types"—meaning the two MMPI clinical subscales with the highest elevations (Hogan, 2003). Interpretation of the meaning of these code types is based on actuarial data accumulated over many years regarding the characteristics of individuals with certain code type profiles. Interpretive statements based on these actuarial data are inevitably written in probabilistic language, such as: Persons with this code type "appear to be," or "tend to be," or "are likely to be" such and such. In their written reports, evaluating psychologists address how close a fit their individual client is to the aggregate code type profile generated from the actuarial data. But, as Horn, Wanberg, and Foster (1990) note:

> The law of individual differences powerfully limits the interpretive value of general principles. Although thinking of individuals in terms of "types" is helpful, true understanding of an individual must be governed as much by how the individual deviates from the type as by the type itself. (p. 51)

Written and Oral Formats for Communicating Results

A variety of written and oral formats for communicating assessment results may be used by evaluating psychologists and/or specifically requested by referring professionals. These formats include: the narrative report, the evaluation letter, and the face-to-face interpretive conference with evaluating psychologists in which results are reported orally to referring professionals and/or to clients. The format selected likely is based on the nature of the evaluation, the report's intended audience, and the customary reporting practices of evaluating psychologists. As discussed below, each format has advantages and disadvantages. Also, written and oral reporting can be combined.

The Narrative Report

Ownby (1997) describes two versions of the traditional written report—the brief narrative and the lengthy narrative. The brief narrative is a short written report, two to three pages in length, communicating the essence of the evaluation findings and detailing programming recommendations (Katz, 1985). A major advantage of brief reports is that they can be written or dictated quickly, resulting in rapid dissemination to referring professionals and clients. Teachers, for example, may benefit from immediate feedback on children's performance that can be used in developing new instructional or behavior management approaches in the classroom.

The lengthy report is simply an expanded and more detailed written account of the brief evaluation. It may give a more detailed account of the client's background; describe more fully clients' performance or behavior on various assessment measures, interviews, or observations; employ more extensive use of the evaluator's theoretical constructs or organizing frameworks to explain and interpret client behavior or performance; place greater emphasis on differential diagnosis; and provide an expanded discussion on treatment planning recommendations (Ownby, 1997). In addressing legal or forensic questions (e.g., evaluation of child abuse, malingering, competency to stand trial, custody evaluations, and fitness to parent), the lengthy report may well be the preferred format.

The organization and structure of a lengthy report were outlined in Table 9.1, earlier in the chapter. Advantages of the lengthy report are that they document test score results, interpret the meaning of the test scores integrated with other non-test data, make diagnoses, render prognostic opinions, and provide recommendations for intervention. The chief disadvantage is the length of time required to write such a report. (An example of a lengthy report is the drug and alcohol assessment presented in chapter 6.)

Ownby (1997) outlined three general models of narrative written reports (either brief or lengthy) regarding how reports are organized. These are the hypothesis-generated report, the domain-oriented report, and the test-oriented report.

Hypothesis-Oriented Reports

Hypothesis-oriented reports present one or more hypotheses about the client that the assessment data seek to answer. For example, evaluating a client referred because of "lack of relatedness to others" might generate several hypotheses, such as: "Is the client depressed?" "...experiencing schizophrenia or psychosis?" "Does the client have a personality disorder?" "...mental retardation?" "Has the client experienced a trauma?" "Has the client had an attachment disorder?" These hypotheses can be tested systematically through various tests and assessment procedures, and the results used to confirm or disconfirm the various hypotheses.

Domain-Oriented Reports

Domain-oriented reports are organized into different broad or narrow domains of client abilities or functioning. Broad domains include Cognitive Abilities, Academic Achievement, and Personality Functioning. Each of those broad areas can be broken down into smaller domain areas. Cognitive Abilities, for instance, could be subdivided into the domains of sensory/perception; sensorium (i.e., orientation to time, place, and person); concentration and attention focus; intellect; memory, and so forth (Wolber & Carne, 1993). In forensic evaluations, the reporting of domains of clients' abilities is typically subsumed under the specific legal questions the psychologist has been asked to address.

Test-Oriented Reports

In test-oriented reports the test results are "presented sequentially by assessment measure used" (Ownby, 1997, p. 77). [Or, to make a bad pun—as a psychologist in Shakespeare's time might say: "measure for measure."] For example, the full scale and subtest scores from *Cognitive Test A* are reported, followed by those from *Cognitive Test B*, followed by scales from *Projective Measures X, Y,* and *Z,* and so forth. Contemporary authorities on report writing discourage this model because of its emphasis on tests, not the persons being evaluated. Nevertheless, as shown earlier in Table 9.4, this type of report still is produced by many psychologists in practice.

The Evaluation Letter

An alternative written format is to summarize the evaluation findings and recommendations in the form of a letter. The letter might be addressed to another professional or, more commonly, to clients themselves and/or their parents or guardian. In circumstances in which formal psychological reports are not required, referring professionals might consider requesting evaluating psychologists to communicate their findings in the form of a concise letter rather than a lengthy report. Two examples of evaluation letters are provided.

Example F: Letter to Parents

In Sample Evaluation Letter 9.1, a psychologist crafted a report in the form of an evaluation letter for parents who were relocating out of state and had not yet determined the school district in which their son would be

Sample Evaluation Letter 9.1

Dear Mr. and Mrs. Eldridge:

I am writing to summarize the results of the psychological evaluation I conducted with your son, Greg, in March and April of this year. The purpose of the present evaluation was to determine his level of current school functioning and to assess his readiness for the second grade. Greg was 7 years and 3 months old at the time of the current evaluation. Tests administered included:

Wechsler Intelligence Scale for Children-IV (WISC-IV)
Wide Range Achievement Test—3rd edition (WRAT-3)
Bender-Gestalt Test of Visual-Motor Integration
Draw-A-Person Test
Rorschach Test
Thematic Apperception Test (TAT)

A comparison of current intellectual performance with past testing conducted when Greg was in kindergarten revealed his current performance to be quite different from his performance a year ago. That is to say, previous testing showed Greg to be functioning at the low end of the Average Range of Intellectual Abilities with little variability noted between scores. The current results again show Greg to be functioning in the Average Range of Intellectual Abilities in terms of overall functioning but with a highly significant discrepancy noted between verbal and nonverbal intellectual skills.

Current testing places Greg's nonverbal intellectual skill functioning in the Superior Range of Abilities, or the top 9% of the 7-year-old population. His verbal intellectual functioning is in the Low Average Range of Abilities, with a 39-point difference noted between these two scores. A difference of close to two standard deviations would suggest that his intellectual performance is quite variable and subject to influence by a number of factors. Performance on individual subtests scores range from a low score of 3 (mean of 10) to a high score of 19, which is off the high end of the scale. Again, his scores range between close to three deviations below the mean to three standard deviations above the mean.

Within-subtest functioning was also seen to be quite variable in that his performance was characterized by failure on easy items and success on harder examples of the same task. Findings related to the variability of his performance suggest that Greg's level of performance can vary on a daily basis. Tasks that he has mastered on one day may not be able to be produced on another day.

Strengths related to intellectual abilities include his abilities to process and organize information when it is presented visually. When given several

(continued)

manipulative tasks where abstract thinking was involved, he performed at an extremely high level. This finding suggests that, with appropriate academic interventions aimed at remedying areas of difficulty, Greg has the potential to perform at a high level of intellectual ability.

A number of factors seem to account for his variable performance. First, verbal intellectual skills are affected by his thinking style, which is highly concrete in nature. When given a task where he was asked to relate two objects, Greg was unable almost 100% of the time to describe any similarities between events. This thinking style is developmentally appropriate for a four-year-old child. Besides an inability to describe the relationships between events, Greg's thinking is subject to intrusions of emotional material related to what goes on inside of him. Preoccupations, particularly with aggressive impulses, seem to interfere with his ability to think in a clear fashion. This finding suggests that on days when he is preoccupied with issues not related to school functioning (e.g., a visit to the doctor) his performance is likely to be more disorganized. Instructions provided to him about school tasks should be presented in a clear fashion to negate any need for him to abstract information from the context.

Greg presents as a highly distractible child. He is easily diverted by events happening around him. He seems to have difficulty sitting for extended periods of time. It is helpful for him to be able to walk around between academic tasks. This distractibility is believed to be a function mainly of organic interference rather than a purely behavioral problem. Medication for this condition is not recommended for a variety of reasons, including the fact that Greg needs to feel that he is in control of his own behavior. He can be managed with interventions such as clear expectations about his behavior and positive reinforcers for appropriate behavior. He can be easily redirected if presented with challenging but manageable tasks. An individualized behavioral contract directed to specific behaviors that are disruptive in the classroom would be a helpful intervention for him in the second grade.

Writing is a difficult task for Greg. In part, his difficulty with writing is a motivational issue related to the fact that he knows this is hard work for him and it is difficult for him to put energy into tasks that he thinks he will fail. His fine motor skills appear variable. A Bender Gestalt Test places him a little over five years of age (versus his current age of seven years and 3 months). A Berry Test given to him by Dr. H in the early part of this year found him to be at a six and one-half year level. In any case, Greg finds the task of writing frustrating because of his fine-motor difficulties. Use of a computer for written assignments and the use of other methods for presenting his ideas is suggested especially to reduce the current level of frustration Greg feels about this communication modality.

Greg's academic skills appear to be delayed by approximately one year. He can read letters and a few words that he has memorized. He reverses

(continued)

letters consistently, such as *eat* for *cat*, and seems not to understand sound–symbol associations. Because of his difficulty with reading, one would expect his spelling skills to be less well developed. Results of the WRAT-3 demonstrate that his spelling skills are pre-first grade. Remedial interventions aimed at helping Greg develop basic reading and writing skills will be difficult because of his combination of strengths and weaknesses in the use of auditory and visual skills.

Significant emotional intrusions interfere with his ability to use cognitive skills in the most efficient fashion. Fears related to abandonment and concerns about the predictability of events are close to the surface. Greg is aware himself that he is easily triggered by aggression outside of him. His aggressive impulses are close to the surface and, once triggered, he has few ways of gaining control over his feelings and calming himself. He evidences some of the organic qualities of "emotional liability"—meaning a biological/neurological-based difficulty in controlling his aggressive impulses (rather than solely due to emotional conflicts or psychological maladjustment).

This is an important issue in terms of understanding that, at this point in time, Greg needs a considerable amount of help from adults to assist him in ways to both structure and control his behavior. For the most part, Greg's aggressive behaviors cover his feelings about being scared or anxious about what is going on in front of him. He needs a great deal of structure and predictability to help him learn to develop his own ways to cope with issues related to growing up. Greg could benefit from some individual psychotherapy to develop techniques for controlling his impulses. Gaining greater control over how he expresses his feelings will help him feel more confident about his abilities to succeed.

In summary, Greg presents as an engaging child who is quite invested in accepting help to deal with his problems. He presents a complicated picture of a child with a number of different learning problems. His academic skills are delayed by at least a year. Writing is a particularly difficult and frustrating task for this child. His thinking style is highly concrete. He may have some underlying language-processing problems, which should be explored with further testing. His visual-perceptual skills are excellent. He presents with both organic and emotional contributors to variable performance. Problems in his control of behavior should be addressed systematically, including clear communications between home and school concerning expectations about his performance and clear rules as to acceptable behavior and consequences for unacceptable behavior, particularly at school.

I hope this letter will be helpful to you and the school district in planning appropriate educational interventions with Greg. Once your relocation is complete, I will be happy to talk further (with your permission) with Greg's teacher, school principal, school psychologist, or a mental health therapist about the results of this evaluation. Best wishes for success for Greg and your family.

attending. Because of the severe nature of the child's chronic medical problems and accompanying academic and emotional difficulties, the psychologist decided that a letter would be a more effective way of communicating results to the parents, and might expedite the child's receiving appropriate educational and treatment services once the family's relocation was complete.

Strengths and Limitations of the Evaluation Letter

This evaluation letter has noteworthy strengths and some limitations, as outlined below. The strengths are as follows:

1. The report is written for a specific audience (parents and school officials), and for a specific purpose (primarily, to make recommendations regarding the child's academic programming in a new school; and secondarily, to offer parents support and encouragement for continuing the child's psychotherapy once their relocation is completed). In addition, the letter format itself may be a less threatening manner of communicating results to parents while maintaining useful objective information to teachers, school officials, and prospective therapists.
2. The report is a concise summary rather than the lengthy, detailed report written in the third-person and divided into distinct section headings (the format outlined in Table 9.1). The psychologist succinctly summarizes and integrates the evaluation procedures, test results, behavioral observations, interpretation, and educational and treatment recommendations into an informative letter. The report generally is free of jargon, and the meaning of the intelligence tests scores are explained clearly.
3. The psychologist was able to compare and contrast the present evaluation from a previous evaluation, which helped identify areas of functioning that seem to have declined or deteriorated over time, as well as those that have been maintained at a steady level. A clear picture of the child and the child's cognitive abilities in an academic setting emerges, identifying strengths and weaknesses.
4. The psychologist was able to integrate the findings from intelligence and achievement tests with projective test information in a coherent manner that gives parents and teachers a clear idea about how the child feels about learning, identifies which academic subjects are sources of reward and/or frustration, and offers helpful teaching strategies that are likely to be effective given the child's cognitive needs and learning style.

5. The report highlighted specific emotional triggers, both within the classroom environment and within the child, that are likely to lead to a loss of behavioral self-control; underlines the importance of adults at home and in school establishing consistent expectations for his behavior; and suggests behavior-management techniques.

6. The report gave a rationale for why medication, which normally might be contemplated for a child with disruptive behaviors, was not recommended in this case.

7. The psychologist was able to document the clear need for special education services and continued psychotherapy treatment while avoiding a diagnostic label of psychopathology or educational handicap.

8. The psychologist's willingness to provide subsequent consultation with school officials or treatment professionals is specified clearly.

Some limitations in the evaluation letter can be identified as well.

1. The psychologist makes reference to a test administered by another evaluator (the Berry Test given by Dr. H.) but does not clarify the purpose of the test or the results.

2. The behavioral observations, test results, and the psychologist's interpretation of the results sometimes are blended together, making it impossible to differentiate among the sources. For example, a helpful comment would have been to explain how the following interpretive statement was reached: "Significant emotional intrusions interfere in his ability to use his cognitive skills in the most efficient fashion." The psychologist does not make clear if that conclusion was based on behavioral observations, the results of cognitive testing, the results of projective testing, or from other sources. If this conclusion was derived from multiple sources—test and non-test—that information would be helpful to subsequent professional and lay readers of the report.

3. The report omits information regarding the family dynamics or contributions by parents to the child's behavioral and learning difficulties. This omission no doubt occurs because the primary intended professional audience consists of the teachers, school principal, and special education officials, who likely are most interested in information relevant to classroom performance. Also omitted is information about parenting style, or areas of psychological stress or dysfunction experienced by family members that normally would be included in a more formal report (or if the intended audience of the letter was another

therapist or clinician who had begun working with the child and/or family).

4. Likewise, the letter does not provide a formal psychiatric diagnosis or educational disability. This omission potentially could be an obstacle to the child's receiving needed education or treatment services. The psychologist may have concluded, however, that putting such a label in the letter would not have been helpful to the parents. The invitation extended to the school district officials or new therapist to contact the psychologist for further information may have been one way around this.

Example G: Letter to an Attorney

In the following example, a psychologist reported assessment findings on an adolescent injured in an auto accident. The evaluation was requested by the attorney representing the teenager in a personal-injury lawsuit against the driver.

Sample Evaluation Letter 9.2

Dear Mr. Duran:

At your request, I am writing to summarize the results of my psychological evaluation of Beatrice ("Bea") Gonzales, age seventeen (BD 10/6/88). This evaluation was completed on January 31, 2004.

In general, Beatrice presented as a delightful young woman who had made a near miraculous recovery from serious injuries sustained when an automobile hit her. Her speedy physical recovery appears to be attributed to the excellent medical care and rehabilitation services she has received, along with ongoing psychological support from her parents. Bea herself also presented as determined to put this accident in her past.

Mr. and Mrs. Gonzales and Bea herself agree that she has had ongoing emotional problems since the accident. Beatrice continues to have nightmares, now three months after the accident. She is unable to drive by herself after the accident and insists that her parents drive her to school. Bea often expresses fears of being alone. She is reluctant to leave the house and has withdrawn from almost all of her usual social contacts with peers, as well as from numerous extracurricular activities after school.

Beatrice was found to be of average intellectual ability, with the potential for above-average cognitive functioning. Although her strong conceptual skills have possibly helped her to organize her perceptions of the accident,

(continued)

her verbal skills seem variable. The intrusion of fearfulness into her thinking appeared to be inhibiting her ability to use her cognitive skills to the best of her ability.

She appeared to be a teenager on the verge of young adulthood who is preoccupied with being hurt. For example, she was so anxious in her first meeting with me that she was unable to perform many simple tasks. She was, however, able to mobilize and be productive in subsequent sessions. Results from projective testing showed that she continued to be fearful about being hurt again. Nine of ten responses to the Thematic Apperception Test (TAT) cards produced stories about people dying or being killed. When given a blank card and asked to make up her own story, Beatrice told a story of her own death in a car accident and her mother crying because she lost her daughter.

In summary, Beatrice was seen to be a delightful young woman with many internal and external resources that accounted for her speedy physical recovery. She was also found to be preoccupied with conscious fears that a car might hit her again. Individual psychotherapy was recommended for Beatrice, in conjunction with a behavioral program to help her deal with her fears about driving and the resumption of normal social activities outside of the home. Short-term group therapy with other clients who also have experienced psychological and physical trauma from an unexpected injury would be beneficial.

Strengths of this second example letter are that

- it focuses on the single issue requested by the attorney who made the referral for psychological evaluation—ascertaining the adolescent's cognitive and emotional capacities for recovery from a traumatic auto accident;
- it conveys a clear picture of the teenager's current level of recovery and extent of family support; and it details the intensity and persistence of her fears and anxieties; and
- it describes the type of mental health interventions that would aid in her ongoing recovery.

The major weakness of the letter is that the evaluation procedures and tests administered are not clearly specified. Although both intelligence testing and projective testing were completed, only the TAT projective test (Murray, (1943) is identified specifically, and the responses reported in detail.

The Face-to-Face Interpretive Conference

Wodrich (1997) observed that

> There is nothing inherent in the assessment process itself or psychological tests that indicate programming recommendations to make. That is, tests do not make program recommendations, psychologists do. (p. 335–336)

Thus, the interpretive conference, in combination with a brief narrative report, "is probably the format of choice for communicating most psychological assessments" (Ownby, 1997, p. 113). This reporting format is suitable for communicating assessment results in many educational, vocational, or rehabilitation settings.

The interpretive conference approach with clients present is based on the assumption that clients' understanding of test results and assessment findings is what is of paramount importance, not evaluating psychologists or referring professionals (Hood & Johnson, 2002). Although many of the same principles discussed earlier about quality written reports have relevance to the interpretive conference (e.g., avoiding the use of jargon), Table 9.8 outlines some benchmarks for evaluating psychological reports that are particularly relevant for the face-to-face meeting with clients.

TABLE 9.8 Evaluating the Quality of Psychologists' Oral Reports in Interpretive Conferences

CRITERIA	DESCRIPTIVE INDICATORS
Showing respect to clients	Psychologists should communicate respect and confidence in clients' ability to understand and use the assessment findings and test data. For example, they should acknowledge that clients may feel anxious at the start of an interpretive conference. Framing the purpose of the conference is one helpful way to provide clients with information they need in facing current concerns or decisions in their lives.
Using "person first" language	Psychologists should use language that begins with the personhood of the client, not with the label of the client's disability, disorder, or disease—for example, referring to a client as "a person with Down syndrome" or a "person with a hearing impairment" or "a person who has quadriplegia," or "a person with a drug addiction," rather than referring to the client as "retarded," "deaf," "quadriplegic," or "an addict."

(continued)

TABLE 9.8   (continued)

CRITERIA	DESCRIPTIVE INDICATORS
Eliciting clients' perceptions and questions	Psychologists should solicit feedback from clients regarding how they felt about the assessment and/or tests they took. Psychologists should encourage clients to ask questions about any aspect of the test results and their interpretations.
Reminding clients about the tests administered	Psychologists should refresh clients' memory about what tests they took and what the tests measured.
Using visual aids	Psychologists may choose to use graphs, charts, tables, etc. as supplemental visual aids to further clients' understanding of test results in addition to psychologists' verbal description.
Integrating test results with other data	As with written reports, psychologists should offer interpretations of test results by integrating test and non-test data into a coherent whole.
Involving clients in the interpretation process	Psychologists should invite clients to offer their own insights or meanings to the assessment findings.
Summarizing test findings often	Psychologists should summarize test findings frequently throughout the interpretive conference. Psychologists should allow time for discussion and clarify misunderstandings.
Attending to clients' verbal and nonverbal reactions	Psychologists should listen and respond to clients' verbal and nonverbal reactions to test results, especially when the results are not what clients expected.
Future actions	Psychologists should help clients connect assessment findings with options or choices or pathways in the future.

Adapted from *Assessment in Counseling: A Guide to the Use of Psychological Assessment Procedure* (3rd ed.), by A. Hood & R. Johnson, 2002, Alexandria VA: American Counseling Association.

Consultation and Feedback with Psychologists

Feedback about the quality and usefulness of psychological evaluations ideally is a reciprocal, two-way street between referring professionals and evaluating psychologists. But, as is the nature of human communication—even among professionals specifically trained in working with people—problems often arise between referring professionals and evaluating psychologists.

Referring professionals may be reluctant to bring up problems with evaluating psychologists (Katz, 1985). This may stem from a variety of factors including fear of offending the evaluator, the desire to avoid conflict with professionals they perceive as having higher status or power, or lack of confidence in how to present their concerns. Thus, evaluators may not hear from the referring professionals unless they have a major complaint, and hence receive little positive feedback or constructive criticism about the quality of their reports. Evaluators most likely are curious about whether the report was found to be useful and was used subsequently in case planning with clients; if so, what was most helpful; and if not, the barriers or obstacles that prevented it from being used.

The reciprocal feedback process can be initiated in a variety of ways. Informal means might consist of a phone call, an e-mail exchange, or a personal meeting with an evaluator to discuss specific aspects of the reports, such as asking for clarification of findings and/or the proposed recommendations. A more formal feedback mechanism was developed by Ownby and his colleagues (Ownby, 1997; Ownby & Wallbrown, 1983). They attach a brief questionnaire to the psychological report, asking for feedback on whether the report answered the referral question, provided new information about the client; suggested new ideas about working with the client; made helpful and realistic recommendations; and was found to be useful. Separate versions of the questionnaire have been developed, depending on whether the referral agent is a teacher, therapist or psychiatrist, parent, or another psychologist. The questionnaires contain a brief checklist and space for open-ended comments.

Katz (1985) pointed out the importance of obtaining regular feedback between referring professionals and evaluating psychologists, to establish a firm foundation of trust and mutual respect and to provide a forum for handling disagreements or differing views about clients. This process should begin at the time of the initial referral for a psychological evaluation. At the outset, referring professionals should inquire as to the customary reporting format and the usual time expected for completing reports. In addition, the psychologists should state their reporting format preferences in terms of what they have found to be most useful with clients, and explain the due dates or time constraints in case planning decisions. If the expectations differ markedly, disagreements can be negotiated.

Further, referring professionals should determine whether the psychologists will be available for subsequent consultation by phone or in person to clarify questions about their evaluations, and whether the psychologists are receptive to feedback about their evaluation referral.

Referring professionals can also ask psychologists for feedback regarding the appropriateness and clarity of the referral question and the thoroughness and accuracy of any information or material provided to the psychologist. Establishing mutual openness and reciprocal transparency between referring professionals and evaluating psychologists is vital in developing effective case plans with clients.

In forensic evaluations, too, communication and feedback are important, given that reports may be entered as exhibits in court and/or psychologists may be called to testify as expert witnesses about their findings, subject to cross-examination. In some situations, attorneys do not want a written report, to avoid disclosing fully in advance the psychologist's expert opinion to the other side (Van Dorsten, 2002). Determining the specific reason for the evaluation at the outset and then having a debriefing following the conclusion of the legal dispute will help keep open the lines of communication between referring professionals and forensic psychologists. It should be kept in mind, though, that in forensic evaluations, reports are written for the court, regardless of who hires the psychologist.

Case Planning Considerations

The most appropriate manner of reporting results in many settings may be a combination of a brief written narrative report and a face-to-face interpretive conference with evaluating psychologists, referring professionals, and clients themselves. Conferences between clients and a large number of professionals, however, can be intimidating and often do not go well.

As a side note—a social work colleague referred to the typical special education staffing attended by parents as a "parentectomy," likening it to an emotional appendectomy in which parents sit through a meeting in which all the professionals (e.g., teacher, school psychologist, social worker, and speech and language specialist) take turns describing what's wrong with the child (and sometimes, by not so subtle implication, what's wrong with the parents)—a gut-wrenching experience!

The following case planning considerations are drawn from a variety of sources to suggest ways in which referring professionals can aid all parties—clients, evaluating psychologists, and other helping professionals—to contribute to a more productive and helpful conference (Ownby, 1997; Orton, 1997; Sattler, 1998; Wolber & Carne, 1993):

1. Prior to the conference, prepare clients about what to expect from the interpretive conference: who will be in attendance; what each person's

role in the evaluation has been; how the results will be shared; what opportunities will be available to ask questions; their rights in the case planning decision-making process; and the approximate length of the conference.

Coach clients on the importance of listening and taking a nondefensive stance. Remind clients that if they expect professionals to listen to them, they have to demonstrate good listening abilities themselves. Further, clients can practice assertive communication skills to avoid defensive reactions, verbal attacks, aggressive or argumentative threats, or sarcastic statements.

Help clients develop a list of questions they would like to have addressed in the conference, identify topics that are touchy for the client, develop a "game plan" about how to handle those reactions if they come up during the conference, and/or schedule a debriefing time to process those feelings after the conference. The overall goal of pre-conference preparation should be to develop an attitude of partnership among the client, the evaluating psychologist, and the referring professional.

2. Begin the conference by making sure that attendees are introduced to each other, then state clearly the purpose or agenda for the conference. Emphasize that the information from the psychologist has a bearing on the client's present needs and/or the case planning decisions currently facing the client and referring professionals.

3. Briefly review the concerns and processes that led to the decision to seek a psychological evaluation.

4. Invite the psychologist (and other evaluating professionals, if present) to share their results. This should be done in a supportive manner without using technical jargon. Start with an area of strength, then move to a difficulty, then back to another strength, then to another difficulty, and so forth.

5. Encourage clients to react to what has been presented. Support clients in expressing their concerns and questions. Help clients stick to the topic. Acknowledge the impact of the evaluation findings and recommendations on them, and allow time for them to process their feelings.

6. Ask all participants for their interpretation of the assessment results.

7. Review each recommendation in terms of how clearly it is tied to the problem areas and sources of strength identified in the report. Determine if recommendations are provided for each problem identified, and whether the recommendations are presented in sufficient detail to realistically carry out. Determine if the recommendations

answer the referral question, provide new information, and suggest new approaches to working with the client.

8. Incorporate the psychologist's recommendations and those of other professionals into an intervention plan.

9. Develop goals and specific objectives regarding implementation of the intervention, in terms of who is going to do what, with whom, by when, for how long. Ascertain who will be responsible for completing each of the assigned tasks related to the recommendations.

10. Establish a timeline for monitoring progress toward the goals.

11. Conclude the meeting by summarizing the major findings and recommendations of the psychological evaluation and any case planning decisions that have resulted. Set up future or follow-up meetings as necessary.

12. Arrange, as necessary, additional debriefing times between client and referring professional to review the report.

13. Provide post-conference feedback to the psychologist about the quality and usefulness of the evaluation report and/or conference.

Additional Resources

To learn more about psychological reports and conferences, referring professionals may wish to consult the following sources.

Lichtenberger, E., Mather, N., Kaufman, N., & Kaufman, A. (2005). *Essentials of Assessment Report Writing.* New York: Wiley and Sons.

Ownby, R. (1997). *Psychological Reports: A Guide to Report Writing in Professional Psychology* (3rd ed.). New York: Sage.

Sattler, J. (1998). "Guidelines for the Post-Assessment Interview," in *Clinical and Forensic Interviewing of Children and Families: Guidelines for the Mental Health, Education, Pediatric, and Child Maltreatment Fields.* San Diego: Jerome Sattler Publishing.

Wolber, G., & Carne, W. (1993). *Writing Psychological Reports: A Guide for Clinicians.* Sarasota, FL: Professional Resource Press.

Zuckerman, E. (2000). *Clinician's Thesaurus: The Guidebook for Writing Psychological Reports* (5th ed.). New York: Guilford.

Conclusion

For the referring consumer, the written report and interpretive conference are major means for learning the findings and recommendations of the evaluating psychologist. The chapter has examined the purposes and usual features of psychological written reports. This includes the principles of good report writing that have been developed in the profession of psychology, and it has summarized some of the common problems identified in psychological reports. Several reports or excerpts were examined to discern those that were problematically written from those that were better written. Various of reporting formats were examined, followed by strategies for offering and receiving feedback from evaluating psychologists. A case planning approach to an interdisciplinary case conference with clients was presented.

Chapter 10

Integrating Strengths-Based and Problem-Based Assessment Information in Comprehensive Case Plans

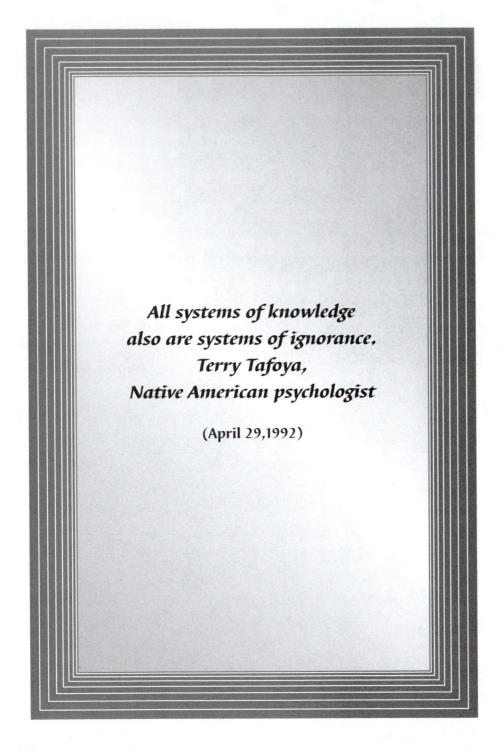

*All systems of knowledge
also are systems of ignorance.*
Terry Tafoya,
Native American psychologist

(April 29,1992)

T he social work pro-fession (and per-haps other disciplines as

OVERVIEW

well) have viewed psychological assessments skeptically because they typically focus on clients' problems and pathologies (Hepworth, Rooney, & Larsen, 1997). Indeed, some authorities in social work have asserted that the emphasis on problems is a form of oppression because clients are treated in an objectifying, dehumanizing manner. This accusation is held most fervently by the developers of the strengths-based perspective in social work practice, which firmly deemphasizes client problems (Rapp, 1998; Saleebey, 1996, 1997, 2002). Further, clinical practitioners who have traditionally utilized information on client problems and pathologies in their case planning decisions have been charged with being more inter-ested in maintaining their positions of power, privilege, and expertise than in honoring clients' strengths and capacities (Cowger, 1997; Goldstein, 1990, Saleebey 1998).

Yet, integrating assessment information on clients' problems and pathology with assessment information on their strengths, resources, and capacities is essential in treatment planning. Treating the two perspectives as polar opposites and antithetical to each other makes the task of integra-tion exceedingly difficult. The aim of this chapter, therefore, is to exam-ine ways by which case plans can be directed at enhancing client strengths, coping capacities, and personal resources, while also address-ing the problems in one or more domains of psychological functioning.

An Exercise in Reconciling Opposites

Tsang (2000) has suggested that one way to treat opposing theories or frameworks is through *dialectic thinking*—generating contradictions in producing new knowledge and change. In dialectics there always is a *thesis* (or affirmation), which later is contradicted by an *antithesis* (negation), followed ultimately by a creative *synthesis* of the opposing viewpoints. Dialectics holds that all things contain conflicting and contradictory elements. Furthermore, these contradictory elements are embraced, not denied or given a negative connotation.

The coexistence of opposites is what bestows a sense of power, conflict, and change on professionals who are seeking to make a difference. Table 10.1 summarizes the theses and antitheses (key points of difference) between the problem-based and strengths-based assessment frameworks. A conceptual synthesis between these two opposing frameworks can be achieved by valuing the contradictions and conflicts between them. The table illustrates how this synthesis is developed.

By simultaneously holding multiple, contradictory theories and viewpoints about human behavior and the social environment, practitioners learn to be cautious of assessment reports or case/treatment planning approaches that rely on a single lens or theory. This helps them identify assessment reports that point to clients' pathology without acknowledging their strengths, or assessment reports that point out clients' strengths without recognizing their problems, or assessment reports that focus exclusively on intrapsychic or interpersonal factors while ignoring social, cultural, or environmental contributors (or vice versa). A synthesis of viewpoints helps in identifying what is missing in assessment reports.

The price for achieving theoretical orthodoxy all too often is a professional with a diminished capacity to critically analyze his or her own presuppositions and/or the ability to decenter from his or her own worldview (Yalom, 1989). The ability to hold multiple, even contradictory, theories does not mean falling into the trap of muddle-headed eclecticism or flying by the seat of your pants, borrowing treatment goals or case planning techniques indiscriminately. Indeed, seeing the relativity of theories and assessment frameworks and the convergence and divergence of their concepts is a hallmark of advanced clinical thinking and practice (Robbins, Chatterjee, & Canda, 1998; Saari, 1989).

A synthesis recognizes that the concepts of "strengths" and "pathology" are *social constructions*, that is, social artifacts or products of cultural, symbolic, linguistic, and historical interchanges among people (Goldstein, 1990). Each term, then, contains a value base and a worldview that remains worthy of attention only as long as it serves varied social, adaptive, and professional purposes. A synthesis recognizes that neither strengths nor pathology can truly be understood without reference to the other.

In its broadest usage, psychopathology does not mean the objective and dehumanizing study and classification of illnesses of the mind, as many of the strengths-based writers have alleged (Cowger, 1997; Rapp,

TABLE 10.1   Comparisons of Problem-Based and Strengths-Based Assessment Frameworks

PROBLEM-BASED FRAMEWORK	STRENGTHS-BASED FRAMEWORK
Conceptualization	*Conceptualization*
• A problem or pathology perspective focuses on identifying the things that *trouble or cause pain* to clients and/or *interfere* with their strivings to achieve their full potential.	• A strengths-based perspective focuses on identifying clients' *unique strengths, traits, talents, and resources*, rather than their deficits and limitations.
• Problems are viewed as a *natural part of existence*. Everyone is assumed to have experienced problems at some time in life. A *natural optimism* views problems as amenable to management, relief, and alleviation.	• Practitioners unwittingly oppress clients when they focus primarily on client problems or psychopathologies because it *dehumanizes and objectifies* people as having an "illness," "disorder," or "case."
• The pain and suffering associated with problems acts, in part, as a *source of motivation* for clients to undertake the arduous process of change and growth in themselves and their environments.	• Emphasizing the pathology and diagnostic labels *obscures the personhood of clients* and sets up practitioners' *negative expectations* about clients' potential for growth and change.
Practice Principles	*Practice Principles*
• The purpose of precisely defining problems or classifying pathology in the assessment process is to *partialize problems* so as to make them more manageable or less overwhelming, and to see them in their social context.	• Clients are regarded as *experts* in their own lives. Clients' personal accounts of their experiences are essential in effecting change. Clients have the power to bring about changes in themselves and their environments.
• The basic steps in the problem or pathology model of practice are: (a) to identify problems through assessment; (b) to explore the nature of those problems with clients; (c) to develop goals to alleviate or remedy the problems; (d) to develop tasks, strategies, or interventions to address problems and achieve the goals; (e) to evaluate effectiveness of the interventions; and (d) to terminate this process.	• Assessments should focus on the search for *exceptions to the problem*, such as times when clients coped more successfully with the problem and/or times when problems had less impact on clients' lives.
	• Past problems in childhood are *not predictive* of problematic behavior in later life. Problems may strengthen or weaken clients.

(continued)

TABLE 10.1   (continued)

PROBLEM-BASED FRAMEWORK	STRENGTHS-BASED FRAMEWORK
Empirical Evidence	*Empirical Evidence*
• A large body of research in social work and in psychotherapy indicates that the more precisely that problems are defined in the assessment and the more concretely the treatment goals are specified in the case planning process, the more effective client outcomes will be following clinical interventions.	• Research on effectiveness of the strengths-based perspective is still emerging. At present, few large-scale, multi-site, randomized studies have been done. Although some studies show positive changes in clients (i.e., reductions in use of inpatient hospitalization), a potential confounding variable seems to be the low caseloads of strengths-based practitioners, which afforded frequent contact and intense involvement with clients.
• The most consistent finding across different problem-oriented therapeutic approaches to working with clients is that the quality of the helping relationship between clients and practitioners appears to be a key element in client improvement.	• Thus, the extensive worker–client contacts and quality of the relationship, rather than the strengths perspective framework itself, may be what accounts for positive changes.

Adapted from *Evaluating Practice Guidelines for the Accountable Professional*, by M. Bloom, J. Fischer, & J. Orme, 1995, Boston: Allyn & Bacon; "An Annotated Review of the Evidence Base for Psychosocial and Psychopharmacological Interventions with Children with Severe Disorders," by B. Burns, S. Compton, H. Egger, E. Farmer, & E. Robertson, *Community Treatment for Youth: Evidence-based Interventions for Severe Emotional and Behavioral Disorders*, edited by B. Burns & K. Hoagwood, 2002, New York: Oxford University Press, pp. 212–276; "Assessing Client Strengths: Assessment for Client Empowerment," by C. Cowger, 1997, *Social Work*, 39, 262–268; "Strengths-based Social Work Assessment: Transforming the Dominant Paradigm," by C. Graybeal, 2001, *Families in Society*, 82(3), 233-242; "Ending Social Work's Grudge Match: Problems vs. Strengths," by J. McMillen, 2004, *Families and Society*; *The Strengths Model: Case Management With People Suffering From Severe and Persistent Mental Illness*, by C. Rapp, 1998, New York: Oxford University Press; *The Strengths Perspective in Social Work Practice*, 2nd ed., by D. Saleebey, 1997, Boston: Longman; "The Road to Effective Child Psychological Services: Treatment Processes and Outcome Research," by S. Shirk, *Handbook of Psychological Services for Children and Adolescents*, 2001, edited by J. Hughes, A. La Greca, & J. Conoley, Oxford: Oxford University Press; "The Operationalization, Implementation, and Effectiveness of the Strengths Perspective: A Review of Empirical Studies," by M. Straudt , M. Howard, & B. Drake, 2001, *Journal of Social Service Research*, 27(3); *The Skills of Helping Individuals, Families, Groups, and Communities*, 4th ed., by L. Shulman, 2006, Belmont, CA: Thomson Brooks/Cole; *Interpersonal Process in Therapy: An Integrative Model*, 5th ed., by E. Teyber, 2006, Belmont, CA: Thompson Brooks/Cole; "Don't Throw the Baby Out with the Bath Water—In Defence of Problem Solving," by C. Trotter, 1999, *Australian Social Work*, 52, 51–55; and "Casework Effectiveness: A New Look at the Research Evidence," by K. Wood, Nov. 1978, *Social Work*, 437–458.

1998; Saleeby, 2002). The root word of "pathology" is the Greek word *pathos*, connoting suffering, endurance, and sorrow, which the ancient Greeks and modern-day existentialists alike argue are universal experiences of the human condition (Yalom, 1980).

Notwithstanding the strengths-based critique, a psychopathology orientation means having an abiding interest—based in both science and art—in all things that trouble and cause pain to the human spirit or soul. A psychopathology orientation focuses on the obstacles and suffering that humans encounter in our daily lives and the challenges we face in striving to achieve our full potential (Trotter, 1999). Particular attention is directed not just to the classification of diseases or disorders of the mind but also to the subjective or personal elements of psychosocial suffering (Yalom, 1980, 2002). This view acknowledges the courage and grace required to endure and continue living in the face of obstacles and limitations. It also means drawing on the qualities of compassion when assisting others—based on an authentic relationship. Empathy and compassion are the cornerstones of professional helping relationships (Perlman, 1979; Shulman, 1999, 2006).

According to Goldstein (1990), the strengths-based perspective is interested primarily in "normalcy"—what is average or what can be expected from people according to given moral standards within particular contexts and cultures. The problem/pathology perspective, in contrast, is interested in understanding serious or severe departures from normalcy. Ultimately, however, both perspectives converge because abnormal behavior cannot be evaluated unless normative behavior has been conceptualized and measured. Likewise, strengths cannot be evaluated without understanding weaknesses and deficits. Neither perspective makes sense alone. Both are essential in developing comprehensive, integrated case plans and effective interventions with clients.

A synthesis promotes understanding that all theories of behavior and mental health counseling have significant weaknesses and limitations in understanding the human condition (Robbins, Chatterjee, & Canda, 1998). The strengths-based perspective has made a significant contribution to clinical practice by pointing out the limitations of the problem/pathology models of practice (i.e., its failure to recognize clients' strengths). Graybeal (2001) speaks of the vital role that the strengths-based model has had in transforming the dominant problem/pathology paradigm in mental health practice by opening up assessment procedures and practices to include new information on clients' strengths and possibilities. Such transformations challenge the dominant-paradigm thinking and exert influence well beyond the individual clinician and client.

A synthesis suggests that the strengths-based system must be examined as well. The strengths-based perspective must address how clients' pain, suffering, and sources of distress can be honored and acknowledged when practitioners shift their attention from addressing only clients' problems. It would be unfortunate, indeed, if the legacy of the strengths-based perspective is that it teaches practitioners to communicate to clients, unwittingly, the sole message: "I cannot hear your pain. What distresses you is not of interest to me. My agenda is to focus on your strengths."

Case Planning Considerations: Putting All the Steps Together

As should be apparent by now, case planning is a complex enterprise, involving multidimensional conceptual and pragmatic considerations. The preceding chapters have provided detailed guidance for referring professionals about a variety of topics, including the components of case planning; the branches of psychology and qualifications, ethical principles, and expertise of different types of psychological evaluators; the controversies and contributions of psychological assessments and tests; the assessment of multicultural clients and those with special needs; the process of writing referral questions; procedures for preparing clients for assessment; and the benchmarks for judging the quality of psychological reports. Outlined below are suggestions about how referring professionals can put all these steps together, once the reports from psychologists are received, in developing a comprehensive, integrated case plan with clients:

1. Read all assessment reports in their *entirety* (not just the section on recommendation)!
2. Recall the purpose for requesting the psychological evaluation and ascertain whether the *referral questions* have been answered in the reports. Have the main clinical, educational, vocational, or forensic questions that prompted the evaluation been answered to the referring professionals,' clients,' and other stakeholders' satisfaction? Are necessary pieces of the puzzle still missing or unclear?
3. Identify which observations, results, and findings within psychologists' reports are *congruent or consistent* with all the other information known about clients. Triangulation of data is especially meaningful when it is obtained from reports of professionals working

independently from one another, who conducted their evaluations at different points in time in different settings, used different methods or measures, and/or were guided by different theoretical perspectives. The robustness of evaluation findings boosts referring professionals' confidence that they are obtaining an accurate view of their clients.

4. Identify any assessment information that provides *new information or fresh perspective* on clients, including unique observations, outlier outcomes, or atypical performances by clients—markedly better or worse—than seen by other evaluators or professionals. Determine whether the context, method of evaluation, relationship with examiners or other professionals, or some other factor may have influenced clients' performance.

5. Identify any *internal contradictions* within psychologists' reports, such as test interpretations, diagnostic/prognostic statements, and recommendation not supported by the evaluation data and test results in the body of the reports. Do the tests and measures seem to be used according to their intended purpose? If there is any confusion or uncertainty, seek consultation from evaluating psychologists to clarify their findings and recommendations.

6. Treat contradictory evidence among different evaluators or professionals as a *valuable source for clinical hypothesis testing*. Ongoing contact with clients usually will clarify which of these hypotheses should be retained and which should be revised and/or discarded.

7. In reviewing assessment results with clients, *ascertain clients' reactions* and readiness for change. What are clients' ideas regarding the starting place? What do clients think is most urgent to change, or easiest, or presents the greatest obstacle? How do clients' views match those of the referring professionals or other providers or systems of care currently involved in the case? Will the recommendations offered by psychologists and/or other evaluators fulfill the legal mandates, requirements, or court orders under which clients have been placed?

8. Consider the relative weight that psychologists' findings and recommendations will have on the case plans that are finally developed. Recall from chapter 3 that the greater the impact on clients' lives that psychologists' reports are likely to carry, the greater is the need for psychologists to use measures that demonstrate high reliability. Reports that use *multiple measures* in the assessment of clients' intellectual abilities, achievement, aptitudes, vocational interests, personality functioning, psychopathology, and so forth are to be preferred over single sources of information. Likewise, reports that include

behavioral observations of clients drawn from *multiple contexts or settings* are preferred over observations made in a single setting and/or on a single occasion, especially if those single observations are gathered in time-limited, high-stakes, analogue settings.

9. Consider the contributions that psychological reports make to understanding and *building upon clients' strengths as well as understanding the duration, severity, and extent of their problems.*

10. Formulate case plans that

   a. incorporate the human behavior theories that offer the best means for understanding clients' current functioning;

   b. provide hope to clients for positive growth and change;

   c. are respectful of and congruent with clients' cultural background;

   d. target problematic symptoms or behaviors to decrease, as well as the strengths or prosocial behaviors to increase;

   e. identify obstacles as well as resources in clients' environments that must be addressed for interventions to succeed;

   f. set goals that are realistically achievable in both the near term and the long term, given the anticipated length of time of intervention and resources brought by clients and professionals;

   g. use intervention techniques that match clients' needs and strengthen their self-efficacy and empowerment, and that fall within the skills and competencies of the treating professionals; and

   h. provide for periodic review and evaluation of their effectiveness.

11. After completing all of the above steps, be prepared to face—and embrace—the ambiguities and uncertainties in implementing the case plans. To paraphrase Yalom (1989), if case plans are helpful to clients at all, it is because they help to assuage the referring professionals' anxieties, not merely clients' anxieties, in facing the myriad unknowns of clinical practice. The more that referring professionals are able to tolerate the anxiety of not knowing, the less need we will have to devise rigid, inflexible treatment plans with and for our clients.

Additional Resources

Interested readers may find the following resources helpful in obtaining further information on reconciling strengths-based and problem-based assessment frameworks:

Bendor, S., Davidson, K., & Skolnik, L. (1997). Strengths-pathology dissonance in the social work curriculum, *Journal of Teaching in Social Work*, *15*(1/2), 3–16.

Goldstein, H. (May 1990). Strengths or pathology: Ethical and rhetorical contrasts in approaches to practice, *Families in Society,* 267–275.

Graybeal, C. (2001). Strengths-based social work assessment: Transforming the dominant paradigm, *Families in Society*, *82*(3), 233–242.

Staudt, M., Howard, M., & Drake, B. (2001). The Operationalization, Implementation, and Effectiveness of the Strengths Perspective: A Review of Empirical Studies," *Journal of Social Service Research*, *27*(3), 1–21.

Trotter, C. (1999). Don't Throw the Baby Out with the Bath Water—In Defence of Problem Solving, *Australian Social Work*, *52*(4), 51–55.

Tsang, N. M. (2000). Dialectics in Social Work, *International Social Work*, *43*(4), 421–434.

Conclusion

This chapter has reviewed the conceptual dilemmas and pragmatic steps of developing comprehensive, integrated case plans with clients. Particular attention has been given to reconciling conflicting assessment data and/or opposing theoretical points of view in the case planning process.

Concluding Reflection on Professional Education and Practice

Writing at the cusp of the ending of the 20th century and beginning of the 21st, Orosz (2000) cogently observed two important social trends moving in precisely opposite directions:

> The problems of people have been ever more complex and interconnected, while the scope of the academic disciplines and the professions has grown ever more narrowly differentiated. People have problems, the saying goes, but institutions have departments. (p. 80)

In conceptualizing and writing this book, I have been convinced more than ever of the accuracy of Orosz's insight. The university where I work has a graduate school of social work, a department of psychology, a graduate school of professional psychology, a college of education within which the counseling psychology and school psychology programs are located, and a law school. I have been fortunate to be involved in several interdisciplinary training grants with certain psychology and educational faculty colleagues (Kayser, 1995, 1997, 1999; Kayser & Linder, 1994; Kayser & Lyon, 1995, 2000; Linder, Robinson, Lyon, & Kayser, 1994; Lyon, Kayser, & Linder, 1997). This boundary-spanning training is the exception rather than the rule.

Despite a history of collaboration, students rarely venture beyond their own disciplinary boundaries. A few students seek flexible dual degrees, but at present there is no systematic cross-disciplinary training, even though graduates from each program likely will work with the same populations of clients, often in the same organizations or settings.

Surely the situation in my university is not unique. Greater collaboration among social work, psychology, education, law, medicine, and other human services disciplines will remain a hit-or-miss activity unless the very nature of professional practice and education across disciplines changes. A new century calls for new methods of practice and professional training.

Most helping professions continue to graduate students who lack coursework, practice experience, or supervision in learning how to work with others outside of their own discipline group. Two serious barriers to collaboration result from the current model of professional education and practice.

1. Education and training among the disciplines has increasingly become overspecialized to the point of myopia. McCroskey and Einbinder (1998) observe that

   > …university-trained professionals are too often narrowly-focused specialists, over-confident in their own expertise, unaware of all they do not know, unwilling to recognize the knowledge and strengths of clients and unable to effectively access help from outside of their own field of specialization. (p. 8)

2. Whatever learning about collaboration (if any) by professionals on the job or as students-in-training takes place largely because of individuals' own initiative and felt urgency to do so, not because of any educational standard or training requirement within the professions themselves—even when public policy or service delivery systems seek to develop coordinated, integrated service delivery systems of care (Friesen & Poertner, 1995; Hooper-Briar & Lawson, 1996). Thus, the concepts and skills of cross-disciplinary collaboration are not acquired as a core part of professional training but, rather, are picked up piecemeal or learned haphazardly.

In attempting to change the nature of fragmented services to clients, two promising developments emerged in the late 1980s and 1990s—*interprofessional practice* and *interprofessional education.* Interprofessional practice is characterized by a team approach to serving clients within an integrated, community-based, culturally competent, family-centered service delivery system (Berg-Weger & Schneider, 1998; McCroskey & Einbinder, 1998). Those who are being served are regarded not simply as "clients" or "patients" but, instead, as partners in co-designing the services. Leadership on teams is shared among the different professional groups, and team members actively use conflict and communication to arrive at cohesive, coordinated treatment plans. All members of the team assume mutual responsibility for every aspect of delivering high-quality care.

Interprofessional practice requires active communication, cooperation, and coordination among members of professional groups, recognizing that, when dealing with clients, their concerns frequently extend beyond and/or cut across the usual area of expertise held by any one profession (Zolnick et al., 1999). This requires professionals in each discipline to become informed consumers about the knowledge and skills in other disciplines while respecting the demarcations of expertise between and among the professional groups. Interprofessional practice requires that individuals are well grounded in their own professional knowledge base and also that they are committed to ongoing interactions with other disciplines to achieve a common vision in transforming programs and services to clients.

Interprofessional education was developed by leading universities, private foundations, and agencies of the federal government to create new methods of professional training that would better meet the changing nature of practice (Brandon & Meuter, 1995; Castro & Juliá, 1994; McCroskey & Eininder, 1998). Interprofessional education emphasizes linking public policy, clinical practice, and research outcomes on practice effectiveness to improve the health and welfare of at-risk populations. In this approach, professionals from different disciplines take a core set of courses together, some courses are cotaught by faculty from different professions, and groups of interns and trainees are placed together as a unit in a practicum agency, in which they receive discipline-specific supervision from a member of their own profession as well as supervision on their interdisciplinary team collaboration.

Achieving interprofessional education faces many institutional barriers to the advancement of faculty through promotion and tenure (where tenure still exists), which typically depends on faculty members' teaching and scholarly contributions to their own discipline, with little credit to contributions spanning the boundaries of knowledge and practice across disciplines. In addition, academic budgets are departmentally based, giving little reason for department directors or deans to forge collaboration with other units, because they would have to share control, personnel, and financial costs and resources with other departments.

In writing this book, my immediate objective was to provide an in-depth guide for referring professionals and students on how to incorporate psychologists' information into case planning decisions. I aimed to fill a gap in the knowledge base of social workers and members of other helping disciplines. The broader objective, however, is to contribute to the development of interprofessional education and practice. Despite the obstacles to interprofessional education mentioned above, I believe it is the way the future must go.

The first step in collaboration is to develop an exchange of information between professional groups (Brandon & Meuter, 1995). This book provides such an exchange, offering referring professionals essential information about psychological assessments and giving evaluating psychologists essential information about the case planning needs of professionals from other disciplines. I hope this book will nourish faculty members, students, supervisors, and referring professionals who hunger for greater collaboration among professional groups and disciplines and encourage them to make their contribution to this effort as well.

Referring and evaluating professionals need to become more *informed consumers* of each others' expertise and contributions to client care. To create effective case plans, professionals from different discipline groups need to develop a strong sense of trust, respect, and mutual collaboration. We need to have a working knowledge of one anothers' conceptual landscapes, basic terminology, types of expertise, forms of professional training, and scope of professional practice. In addition to deepening our own discipline-specific knowledge and expertise, helping professionals need to cultivate a greater appreciation for what we do not know.

Referring professionals from social work, education, law, corrections, and health/human services can make their best contribution to client care when each works together with evaluating psychologists, and vice versa, rather than working in isolation or at cross-purposes. Collaboration must become a core part of the education and training of all helping professionals.

Additional Resources

Readers who are interested in learning more about interprofessional education and practice may wish to consult the following resources:

Berg-Weger, M., & Schneider, F.D. (1998). Interdisciplinary Collaboration in Social Work Education. *Journal of Social Work Education, 34*, 97–107.

Bope, E., & Jost, T. (1994). "Interprofessional Collaboration: Factors that Affect Form, Function, and Structure," in R. Castro & M. Juliá's *Interprofessional Care and Collaborative practice* (pp. 61–69). Pacific Grove, CA: Brooks/Cole.

Brandon, R., & Meuter, L. (1995). *Proceedings: National Conference on Interprofessional Education and Training.* Seattle: University of Washington, Human Services Policy Center.

Castro, R. & Juliá's, M. (1994). *Interprofessional Care and Collaborative Practice.* Pacific Grove, CA: Brooks/Cole.

Friesen, B., & Poertner, J. (1995). *From Case Management to Service Coordination for Children with Emotional, Behavioral, and Mental Disorders: Building on Family Strengths.* Baltimore: Paul H. Brookes.

Hooper-Briar, K., & Lawson, H. (1994). *Serving Children, Youth, and Families Through Interprofessional Collaboration and Service Integration: A Framework for Action.* Oxford, OH: Danforth Foundation and Institute for Educational Renewal at Miami University.

Hooper-Briar, K. & Lawson, H. (Eds.) (1996). *Expanding Partnerships for Vulnerable Children, Youth, and Families.* Alexandria, VA: Council on Social Work Education.

Jivanjee, P., Moore, K., Schultze, K., & Friesen, B. (1995). *Interprofessional Education for Family-Centered Services. A survey of Interprofessional Interdisciplinary Training Programs.* Portland, OR: Portland State University, Research and Training Center on Family Support and Children's Mental Health, Regional Research Institute for Human Services, Graduate School of Social Work.

McCroskey, J., & Einbinder, S. (Eds.). (1998). *Universities and Communities: Remaking Professional and Interprofessional Education for the Next Century.* Westport, CN: Preager.

Zolnick, J., McCroskey, J., Gardner, S., de Gilbaja, M., Taylor, H., George, J., et al. (1999). *Myths and Opportunities: An Examination of the Impact of Discipline-specific Accreditation on Interpersonal Education.* Alexandria, VA: Council on Social Work Education.

References

A

Achenbach, T., & McConaughy, S. (2003). The Achenbach system of empirically-based assessment. In C. Reynolds & R. Kamphaus (Eds.), *Handbook of psychological and educational assessment of children: Personality, behavior, and context* (2nd ed., pp. 406–430). New York: Guilford.

Adesso, V., Cisler, R., Larus, B., & Hayes, B. (2004). Substance abuse. In M. Hersen (Ed.), *Psychological assessment in clinical practice: A pragmatic guide* (pp. 147–173). New York: Brunner-Routledge.

Ainsworth, M. (1982). Attachment: Retrospect and prospect. In C. M. Parkes & J. Stevenson-Hilded (Eds.), *The place of attachment in human behavior* (pp. 3–30). New York: Basic Books.

Ainsworth, M., Blehar, M., Waters, E., & Wall, S. (1978). *Patterns of attachment: A psychological study of the Strange Situation.* Hillsdale, NJ: Erlbaum.

Allen J., & Hollifield, J. (2003). Using the Rorschach with children and adolescents: The Exner comprehensive system. In C. Reynolds & R. Kamphaus (Eds.), *Handbook of psychological and educational assessment of children: Personality, behavior, and context* (2nd ed., pp. 182–197). New York: Guilford.

American Association of Mental Retardation. (1992). *Mental retardation: Definition classification, and systems of social support* (9th ed.). Washington, DC: Author.

American Educational Research Association, American Psychological Association, & National Council on Measurement in Education. (1999). *Standards for educational and psychological testing.* Washington, DC: Author.

American Psychiatric Association. (2000). *Diagnostic and statistical manual of mental disorders* (DSM-IV-TR)(4th ed.). Washington DC: Author.

American Psychological Association. (1992). *APA guidelines for providers of psychological services to ethnic, linguistic, and culturally diverse populations.* Washington, DC: Author.

American Psychological Association. (1994). Guidelines for child custody evaluations in divorce proceedings. *American Psychologist, 49,* 677–680.

American Psychological Association. (1997). *Services by telephone, teleconferencing, and internet.* Retrieved February 29, 2004, from www.apa.org/ethics/stmnt01.html

American Psychological Association. (1998a). *Guidelines for psychological evaluations in child protection matters.* Washington, DC: Author.

American Psychological Association. (1998b). *Rights and responsibilities of test takers: Guidelines and expectations.* Washington DC: Author.

American Psychological Association. (2002a). *Ethical principles of psychologists and code of conduct.* Retrieved September 23, 2005, from www.apa.org/ethics.html

American Psychological Association. (2002b). *Guidelines on multicultural education, training, research, practice, and organizational change for psychologists.* Retrieved July 26, 2004 , from www.apa.org/pi/multiculturalguidelines/homepage.html

American Psychological Association. (2002c). *Guidelines on psychotherapy with lesbian, gay, and bisexual clients.* Retrieved April 4, 2004, from www.apa.org.pi/lgbc/guidelines.html

American Psychology–Law Society. (1991). Specialty guidelines for forensic psychologists. *Law and Human Behavior, 15,* 655–665.

American With Disabilities Act of 1990, Pub. L. No. 101–336 (1990).

Anastasi, A. (1954). *Psychological testing.* New York: Macmillan.

Anastasi, A. (1995). *Psychological testing* (7th ed.). New York: Macmillan.

Angoff, W. H. (1971). Scales, norms, and equivalent scores. In R.L. Thorndike (Ed.), *Educational measurement.* Washington, DC: American Council on Education.

B

Bendor, S., Davidson, K., & Skolnik, L (1997). Strengths–pathology dissonance in the social work curriculum. *Journal of Teaching in Social Work, 15,* 3–16.

Benedek, T. (1970). Parenthood during the life cycle. In J. E. Anthony (Ed.), *Parenthood: Its psychology and psychopathology* (pp. 185–206). Boston: Little Brown.

Bergan, J. R. (1977*). Behavioral consultation.* Columbus, OH: Charles E. Merrill.

Bergan, J. R., & Kratochwill, T. R. (1990). *Behavioral consultation and therapy.* New York: Plenum.

Berger, R., & Kelly, J. (1995). Gay men: Overview. *19th Encyclopedia of Social Work* (Vol. 2., pp 1064–1075). Washington, DC: National Association of Social Workers.

Berg-Weger, M., & Schneider, F. D. (1998). Interdisciplinary collaboration in social work education. *Journal of Social Work Education, 34,* 97–107.

Bernstein, V., Campbell, S., & Akers, A. (2001). Caring for the caregivers: Supporting the well-being of at-risk parents and children through supporting the well-being of the programs that serve them. In. J. Hughes, A. LaGreca, & J. Conoley (Eds.), *Handbook of psychological services for children and adolescents* (pp. 107–131). New York: Oxford University Press.

Beutler, L., Wakefield, P., & Williams, R. (1994). Use of psychological tests/instruments for treatment planning. In M. Maruish (Ed.), *The use of psychological assessment for treatment planning and outcome assessment* (pp. 55–74). Hillsdale, NJ: Erlbaum.

Biringen, Z. (2000). Emotional availability: Conceptualization and research findings. *American Journal of Orthopsychiatry, 70,* 104–114.

Bloom, M., Fischer, J., & Orme, J. (1995). *Evaluating practice guidelines for the accountable professional.* Boston: Allyn & Bacon.

Bohman, J. (1996). *Psychology and sexual orientation: Coming to terms.* New York: Routledge.

Bombardier, C. (2000). Alcohol and traumatic disability. In R. Frank & T. Elliott (Eds.), *Handbook of rehabilitation psychology* (pp. 399–416). Washington, DC: American Psychological Association.

Bond, J. (1978). The psychologist's evaluation. In B. Schmidt (Ed.), *The child protection team handbook: A multidisciplinary approach to managing child abuse and neglect* (pp. 121–133). New York: Garland STPM Press.

Bootzin, R., & Acocella, J. (1988). *Abnormal psychology.* New York: McGraw Hill.

Bope, E., & Jost, T. (1994). Interprofessional collaboration: Factors that affect form, function, and structure. In R. Castro & M. Juliá (Eds.), *Interprofessional care and collaborative practice* (pp. 61–69). Pacific Grove, CA: Brooks/Cole.

Bowlby, J. (1969). *Attachment and loss: Attachment* (Vol. 1). New York: Basic Books.

Bracken, B., & Naglieri, J. (2003). Assessing diverse populations with nonverbal tests. In C. Reynolds & R. Kamphaus (Eds.), *Handbook of psychological and educational assessments of children: Intelligence, attitude, and achievement* (2nd ed., pp. 243–274). New York: Guilford.

Bradshaw. J. (2004, January/February). New Mexico rejects psychiatrists' push on RxP rules. *The National Psychologist, 13*(1). Retrieved February 27, 2008, from http://nationalpsychologist.com/articles/art_v13n1_1.htm

Bradshaw, J. (2005, May/June). New draft on training defuses RxP brohaha. *The National Psychologist, 14*(3). Retrieved February 27, 2008, from http://nationalpsychologist.com/articles/art_v14n3_1.htm

Brandon, R., & Meuter, L. (1995). *Proceedings: National conference on interprofessional education and training.* Seattle: Human Services Policy Center, University of Washington.

Brems, C. (2000). *Dealing with challenges in psychotherapy and counseling.* Pacific Grove, CA: Brooks/Cole Thomson Learning.

Bricklin, B. (1995). *The custody evaluation handbook: research-based solutions and applications.* New York: Brunner/Mazel.

Brodzinsly, D. (1993). On the use and misuse of psychological testing in child custody evaluations. *Professional Psychology: Research and Practice, 24,* 213–219.

Brown, V. (2002). *Child welfare: Case studies.* Boston: Allyn & Bacon.

Brown, R., & Macias, M. (2001). Chronically ill children and adolescents. In. J. Hughes, A. LaGreca, & J. Conoley (Eds.), *Handbook of psychological services for children and adolescents* (pp. 353–372). New York: Oxford University Press.

Burns, C. (2003). Assessing the psychological and educational needs of children with moderate and severe mental retardation. In C. Reynolds & R. Kamphaus (Eds.), *Handbook of psychological and educational assessment of children: Intelligence, aptitude, and achievement* (2nd ed., pp. 671–684). New York: Guilford.

Burns, B., Compton, S., Egger, H., Farmer, E., & Robertson, E. (2002). An annotated review of the evidence base for psychosocial and psychopharmacological interventions with children with severe disorders. In B. Burns & K. Hoagwood (Eds.), *Community treatment for youth: Evidence-based interventions for severe emotional and behavioral disorders* (pp. 212–276). New York: Oxford University Press.

C

Canino, I., & Spurlock, J. (1994). *Culturally diverse children and adolescents: Assessment, diagnosis, and treatment.* New York: Guilford.

Carey, K. B. (2002). Clinically useful assessments: Substance use and comorbid psychiatric disorders. *Behavior Research and Therapy, 40,* 1345–1361.

Carroll, K. M., & Rounsaville, B. J. (2002). On beyond urine: Clinically useful assessment instruments in the treatment of drug dependence. *Behavior Research and Therapy, 40,* 1329–1344.

Carter, B., & McGoldrick, M. (1988). *The changing family lifecycle: A framework for family therapy* (2nd ed.). New York: Gardner.

Cattell, R. (1940). A culture-free intelligence test: I. *Journal of Educational Psychology, 31,* 161–179.

Cattell, R. (1959). *Handbook of the culture fair intelligence test: A measure of "G."* Champaign, IL: Institute for Personality and Ability Testing.

Cavell, T., Ennett, S., & Meehan, B. (2001). Preventing alcohol and substance abuse. In J. Hughes, A. La Greca, & J. Conoley (Eds.), *Handbook of psychological services for children and adolescents* (pp. 133–159). Oxford: Oxford University Press.

Chandler, L. (2003). The projective hypothesis and the development of projective techniques for children. In C. Reynolds & R. Kamphaus (Eds.), *Handbook of psychological and educational assessments of children: Personality, behavior, and context* (2nd ed., pp. 51–65). New York: Guilford.

Cherpitel, C. (2000). A brief screening instrument for problem drinkers in the emergency room: The RAPS4. *Journal of Studies in Alcohol, 61,* 447–449.

Cloud, W., & Granfield, R. (2001). Natural recovery from substance dependency: Lessons for treatment providers. *Journal of Social Work Practice in the Addictions, 1*(1), 8–104.

Code of Federal Regulations, Title 42, Volume 1 (2002). *Confidentiality of alcohol and drug abuse patient records.* Washington, DC: U.S. Government Printing Office.

Comstock, D. (Ed.). (2005). *Diversity and development: Critical contexts that shape our lives and relationships.* Belmont, CA: Thompson Brooks/Cole.

Cooper, M., & Lesser, J. (2002). *Clinical social work practice: An integrated approach.* Boston: Allyn & Bacon.

Cowger, C. (1997). Assessing client strengths: Assessment for client empowerment. *Social Work, 39,* 262–268.

Cronbach, L. (1949). *Essentials of psychological testing.* New York: Harper & Row.

Crosson-Tower, C. (2001). *Exploring child welfare* (2nd ed.) Boston: Allyn & Bacon.

D

Dana, R. (1993). *Multicultural assessment perspectives for professional psychology.* Boston: Allyn & Bacon.

Dana, R. (Ed.). (2000). *Handbook of cross-cultural and multicultural personality assessment.* Mahwah, NJ: Erlbaum.

Davies, D. (1999). *Child development: A practitioner's guide*. New York: Guilford.

Davis, R. (2004). Five binge-drinking deaths just the 'tip of the iceberg.' *USA Today*. Retrieved October 7, 2004, from: http://www.usatoday.com/news/health/2004-10-07-binge-usat_x.htm

Dunn, L. (1987). *Bilingual Hispanic children on the U.S. mainland: A review of research on their cognitive, linguistic, and scholastic development*. Circle Pines, MN: American Guidance Service.

Dunn, L. (1988). Has Dunn's monograph been shot down in flames? Author reactions to the preceding critiques of it. *Hispanic Journal of Behavioral Sciences, 10,* 301–323.

Dupree, J., & Prevatt, F. (2003). Projective storytelling techniques. In C. Reynolds & R. Kamphaus (Eds.), *Handbook of psychological and educational assessments of children: Personality, behavior, and context* (2nd ed., pp. 66–90). New York: Guilford.

Dyer, F. (1999). *Psychological consultation in parental rights cases*. New York: Guilford.

E

Ebel, R. L. (1972). *Essentials of educational measurement*. Englewood Cliffs, NJ: Prentice-Hall.

Education for All Handicapped Children's Act of 1975, Pub. L. No. 94-142 (1975).

Emde, R., & Easterbrooks, M. (1985). Assessing emotional availability in early development. In D. K. Frankenberg, R. N. Emde, & J. W. Sullivan (Eds.),. *Early identification of children at risk: An international perspective* (pp. 79–101). New York: Plenum.

Ewing, J. (1984). Detecting alcoholism: The CAGE Questionnaire. *Journal of the American Medical Association*, 252, 1905–1907.

Ewing, J., Bradley, K., & Burman, M. (1998). Screening for alcoholism use CAGE. *Journal of the American Medical Association, 280*(22), 1904.

Eyberg, S., & Robinson, E. (1983). Dyadic parent–child interaction coding system: A manual. *Psychological Documents, 13* (Ms. No. 2582).

Eyde, L., Robertson, G., Krug, K., Roberston, A., Moreland, K., Shewan, et al. (1993). *Responsible test use: Case studies for assessing human behavior*. Washington, DC: American Psychological Association.

F

Field, T. (1991). Assessment of parent–child interactions. In C. Schaefer, K. Giltin, & K. Sandgrund (Eds.), *Play diagnosis and assessment* (pp. 401–415). New York: John Wiley & Sons.

Flanagan, D., & Ortiz, S. (2001). *Essentials of cross-battery assessment*. New York: John Wiley & Sons.

Forehand, R., & McMahon, R. (1981). *Helping the noncompliant child: A clinician's guide to parent training*. New York: Guilford.

Forehand, R., Peed, S., Roberts, M., McMahon, Griest, D., & Humphreys, L. (1978). *Coding manual for scoring mother–child interactions*. Unpublished manuscript, University of Georgia, Department of Psychology.

Frank, R., & Elliott, T. (2000). *Handbook of rehabilitation psychology*. Washington, DC American Psychological Association.

Friedman, R. (2001). The practice of psychology with children, adolescents, and their families. In J. Hughes, A. La Greca, & J. Conoley (Eds.), *Handbook of psychological services for children and adolescents* (pp. 3–22). New York: Oxford University Press.

Friesen, B., & Poertner, J. (1995). *From case management to service coordination for children with emotional, behavioral, and mental disorders: Building on family strengths.* Baltimore: Paul H. Brookes.

Frisby, K. (1998). Culture and cultural differences. In J. Sandoval, C. Frisby, K. Geisinger, J. Scheuneman, & J. Grenier's (Eds.), *Test interpretation and diversity: Achieving equity in assessment* (pp. 51–73). Washington, DC: American Psychological Association.

G

Gambrill, E. (1997). *Social work practice: A critical thinker's guide.* New York: Oxford University Press.

Gardner, R. (1983). *Frames of mind: The theory of multiple intelligences.* New York: Basic Books.

Gardner, R. (1993). *Multiple intelligences.* New York: Basic Books.

Geisinger, K. (1998). Psychometric issues in test interpretation. In J. Sandoval, C. Frisby, K. Geisinger, J. Scheuneman, & J. Grenier's (Eds.), *Test interpretation and diversity: Achieving equity in assessment* (pp. 17–30). Washington, DC: American Psychological Association.

Georgas, J., Weiss, L., van de Vijver, F., & Saklofske, D. (2003). *Culture and children's intelligence: Cross-cultural analysis of the WISC-III.* Amsterdam: Academic Press.

Gettinger, M., & Koscik, R. (2001). Psychological services for children with learning disabilities. In J. Hughes, A. LaGreca, & J. Conoley (Eds.), *Handbook of psychological services for children and adolescents* (pp. 421–435). New York: Oxford University Press.

Glutting, J., Watkins, M., & Youngstrom, E. (2003). Multifactored and cross-battery ability assessments: Are they worth the effort? In C. Reynolds & R. Kamphaus (Eds.), *Handbook of psychological and educational assessment of children: Intelligence, aptitude, and achievement* (2nd ed., pp. 343–374). New York: Guilford.

Goldberg, S. (1977). Social competence in infancy: A model of parent–infant interaction. *Merrill-Palmer Quarterly, 23,* 163–178.

Goldman, J., L'Engle Stein, C., & Guerry, S. (1983). *Psychological methods of child assessment.* New York: Brunner/Mazel.

Goldstein, H. (1990, May). Strengths or pathology: Ethical and rhetorical contrasts in approaches to practice. *Families in Society,* 267–275.

Gopaul-McNicol, S., & Armour-Thomas, E. (2002). *Assessment and culture: Psychological tests with minority populations.* San Diego: Academic Press.

Grant, B., Dawson, D., Stinson, F., Chou, S., Dufour, M., & Pickering, R. (2006). The 12-month prevalence and trends in DMS-IV alcohol abuse and dependence. *Alcohol Research and Health, 29*(2), 79–93.

Graybeal, C. (2001). Strengths-based social work assessment: Transforming the dominant paradigm. *Families in Society, 82*(3), 233–242.

Gray-Little, B., & Kaplan, D. (1998). Integration of psychological tests in clinical and forensic evaluations. In J. Sandoval, C. Frisby, K. Geisinger, J. Scheuneman, & J. Grenier's (Eds.), *Test interpretation and diversity: Achieving equity in assessment* (pp. 141–178). Washington, DC: American Psychological Association.

Guiterez, E., Parsons, R., and Cox, E. (1997). *Empowerment in social work practice: A source book.* New York: Thomson.

Gulliksen, H. (1950). *Theories of mental tests.* New York: Wiley.

Gutkin, T. B. & Curtis, M. J. (1982). School-based consultation: Theory and techniques. In C. R. Reynolds & T. B. Gutkin (Eds.), *The handbook of school psychology* (pp. 796–828). New York: John Wiley & Sons.

Gutkin, T. B. & Curtis, M. J. (1990). School-based consultation: Theory, techniques, and research. In T. B. Gutkin & C. R. Reynolds (Eds.), *The handbook of school psychology* (2nd ed., pp. 577–611). New York: John Wiley & Sons.

Guthrie, R. (1976). *Even the rat was white: A historic view of psychology.* New York: Harper & Row.

H

Haak, R. (2003). The Sentence Completion as a tool for assessing emotional disturbance. In C. Reynolds & R. Kamphaus (Eds.), *Handbook of psychological and educational assessment of children: Personality, behavior, and context* (2nd ed., pp. 159–181). New York: Guilford.

Hambleton, R., & Zensky, A. (2003). Advances in criterion-referenced testing methods and practices. In C. Reynolds & R. Kamphaus (Eds.), *Handbook of psychological and educational assessment of children: Intelligence, aptitude, and achievement* (2nd ed., pp. 377–437). New York: Guilford.

Harper-Dorton, K., & Hebert, M. (1999). *Working with children and their families* (Rev. ed.). Chicago: Lyceum.

Haynes-Semen, C., & Baumgarten, D. (1994). *Children speak for themselves: Using the Kempe Interactional Assessment to evaluate allegations of parent–child sexual abuse.* New York: Brunner/Mazel.

Health Insurance Portability and Accountability Act of 1996, Pub. L. No. 104–191 (1996).

Heinemann, A. (2000). Functional status and quality-of-life measures. In. R. Frank & T. Elliott (Eds.). *Handbook of rehabilitation psychology* (pp. 261–286). Washington, DC: American Psychological Association.

Hepworth, D., Rooney, R., & Larsen, J. (1997). *Direct social work practice: Theory and skills* (5th ed.). Pacific Grove, CA: Brooks/Cole.

Herrenkohl, E., Herrenkohl, R., Toedter, L., & Yanushefski, A. (1984). Parent–child interactions in abusive and nonabusive families. *Journal of the American Academy of Child Psychiatry, 23,* 641–648.

Herrnstein, R., & Murray, C. (1994). *The Bell Curve: Intelligence and class structure in American life.* New York: Free Press.

Hersen, M. (Ed.) (2004). *Psychological assessment in clinical practice.* New York: Brunner-Routledge.

Heubert, J. (2000). Graduation and promotion testing: Potential benefits and risks for minority students, English-language learners, and students with disabilities. *Poverty and Race,* 9, (pp. 1–2, 5–7). Washington, DC: Poverty and Race Research Action Council.

Hogan, T. (2003). *Psychological testing: A practical introduction.* New York: John Wiley & Sons.

Hood, A., & Johnson, R. (2002). *Assessment in counseling: A guide to the use of psychological assessment procedure* (3rd ed.). Alexandria, VA: American Counseling Association.

Hooper, S., & Baglio, C. (2001). Children and adolescents experiencing traumatic brain injury. In J. Hughes, A. La Greca, & J. Conoley (Eds.), *Handbook of psychological services for children and adolescents* (pp. 267–283). Oxford: Oxford University Press.

Hooper-Briar, K., & Lawson, H. (1994). *Serving children, youth, and families through interprofessional collaboration and service integration: A framework for action.* Oxford, OH: Danforth Foundation and Institute for Educational Renewal at Miami University.

Hooper-Briar, K., & Lawson, H. (Eds.) (1996). *Expanding partnerships for vulnerable children, youth, and families.* Alexandria, VA: Council on Social Work Education.

Horn, J., Wanberg, K., & Foster, M. (1990). *Guide to the Alcohol Use Inventory.* Minneapolis: National Computer Systems.

I

Individuals With Disabilities Education Act of 1995, Pub. L. No. 105-17 (1995).

Individuals With Disabilities Education Act of 2004, Pub. L. No. 108-446 (2004).

Ivey, A., & Ivey, M. (2003). *Intentional interviewing and counseling: Facilitating client Development in a multicultural society* (5th ed.). Pacific Grove, CA: Brooks/Cole.

J

Jayaratne, S., & Levy, R. (1979). *Empirical clinical practice.* New York: Columbia University Press.

Jensen, A. (1969). How much can we boost IQ and scholastic achievement? *Harvard Educational Review, 39,* 1–123.

Jensen, A. (1980). *Bias in mental testing.* New York: Free Press.

Jivanjee, P., Moore, K., Schultze, K., & Friesen, B. (1995). *Interprofessional education for family-centered services. A survey of interprofessional/interdisciplinary training programs.* Portland, OR: Portland State University, Research and Training Center on Family Support and Children's Mental Health, Regional Research Institute for Human Services, Graduate School of Social Work.

Jones, R. (Ed.). (1988). *Psychoeducational assessment of minority group children: A casebook.* Berkley, CA: Cobb & Henry Publishers.

Jordan, C., & Franklin, C. (1995). *Clinical assessment for social workers: Quantitative and qualitative methods.* Chicago: Lyceum.

K

Katz, L. (1985). *A practical guide to psychodiagnostic testing.* Springfield, IL: Charles C Thomas.

Kaufman, A. & Lichtenberger, L. (1999). *Essentials of WAIS-III assessment.* New York: John Wiley & Sons.

Kaufman, A., & Lichtenberger, L. (2002). *Assessing adolescent and adult intelligence* (2nd ed.). Boston: Allyn & Bacon.

Kayser, J. (1995). *Training curriculum for workshop on using psychological assessment information in child welfare planning.* Denver: Child Welfare Training and Research Project, University of Denver, Graduate School of Social Work.

Kayser, J. (1997). *Developing interdisciplinary teams and care management services at school-based health center: A training curriculum.* Denver: Department of Public Health and Environment, Colorado School-Based Health Center Initiative.

Kayser, J. (1999). *Developing university curricula for interprofessional education and collaborative practice: A working symposium.* Alexandria, VA: Council on Social Work Education.

Kayser, J., & Linder, T. (1994). *Developing cross-cultural competencies in service providers working with handicapped infants/toddlers and their families*. Denver: University of Colorado Health Sciences Center, Western Region Faculty Institute for Training, JFK Center For Developmental Disabilities,

Kayser, J., & Lyon, M. (1995). *The caseworker's quick reference to using psychological assessment information in child welfare planning*. Denver: University of Denver, Graduate School of Social Work, Child Welfare Training and Research Project

Kayser, J., & Lyon, M. (2000). Teaching social workers to use psychological assessment data. *Child Welfare, 79*, 197–222.

Kayser, J., Silver, J., & Lyon, M. (2001). From the frying pan into the fire: Three advocacy tales in child and adolescent mental health practice. *Reflections: Narratives of Professional Helping, 7*, 48–60.

Kissel, S., & Freeling, N. (1990). *Evaluating children for the courts using psychological tests*. Springfield, IL: Charles C Thomas.

Kline, P. (2000). *Handbook of psychological testing* (2nd ed.). London: Routledge.

Korman, M. (1974). National conference on levels and patterns of professional training in psychology: Major themes. *American Psychologist, 29*, 301–313.

L

Larry, P. et al. v. Wilson Riles et al. United States District Court, Northern District of California, Case No. 71-2270 RFP (1974–1979).

Lauer, J., Lourie, I., Salus, M., & Broadhurst, D. (1979). *The role of the mental health professional in the prevention and treatment of child abuse and neglect*. Washington, DC: National Center on Child Abuse and Neglect (DHEW Publication No. 79-30194)

Lazarus, A. (1981). *The practice of multimodal behavioral therapy*. New York: McGraw-Hill.

Lichtenberg, P., & MacNeill, S. (2000). Geriatric issues. In. R. Frank & T. Elliott (Eds.), *Handbook of rehabilitation psychology* (pp. 109–122). Washington, DC: American Psychological Association.

Lichtenberger, E., Mather, N., Kaufman, N., & Kaufman, A. (2005). *Essentials of assessment report writing*. New York: Wiley and Sons.

Lindaman, S., Booth, P., & Chambers, C. (2000). Assessing parent–child interactions with the Marshak Interaction Method (MIM). In K. Giltin-Weiner, A. Sandgrund, & C. Schaefer (Eds.), *Play diagnosis and assessment* (2nd ed., pp. 371–400). New York: John Wiley & Sons.

Linder, T., Robinson, C., Lyon, M., & Kayser, J. (1994). *Interdisciplinary leadership training project*. Washington, DC: U.S. Department of Education.

Lowenthal, B., Landerholm, E., & Augustyn, K. (1994). Three aspects of early childhood special education assessment: Family interviews, learning styles, and parent–child interactions. *Early Child Development and Care, 99*, 113–122.

Lyon, M., Kayser, J., & Linder, T. (1997). *The Center for Interprofessional Education and Research: Creating responsive and responsible services for vulnerable children, youth, and families*. Denver: University of Denver.

M

Mahoney, G., Spiker, D., & Boyce, G. (1996). Clinical assessment of parent–child interaction: Are professionals ready to implement this practice? *Topics In Early Childhood Special Education, 16*, 26–50.

Main, M., & Hesse, E. (1990). Parents' unresolved traumatic experiences are related to infant disorganized attachment status: Is frightened and/or frightening parental behavior the linking mechanism? In M. T. Greenberg, D. Cicchetti, & E. M. Cummings (Eds.), *Attachment in the preschool years; Theory, research, and intervention* (pp. 161–184). Chicago: University of Chicago Press.

Marschak, M. (1960). A method for evaluating parent–child interaction under controlled conditions. *Journal of Genetic Psychology, 97,* 3–32.

Maruish, M. (Ed.). (1994). *The use of psychological testing for treatment planning and outcome assessment.* Hillsdale, NJ: Erlbaum.

Matarazzo, J. (1990). Psychological assessment versus psychological testing: Validation from Binet to the school, clinic, and courtroom. *American Psychologist, 45,* 999–1017.

Mattessich, P., & Monsey, B. (1993). *Collaboration: What makes it work?: A review of research literature on factors influencing successful collaboration.* St. Paul, MN: Amherest Wilder Foundation.

Mayfield, D., McLeod, G., & Hall, P. (1974). The CAGE questionnaire: Validation of a new alcoholism instrument. *American Journal of Psychiatry, 131,* 1211–1223.

McCroskey, J. (1998). Remarking professional and interprofessional education. In J. McCroskey & S. Einbinder (Eds.), *Universities and communities: Remaking professional and interprofessional education for the next century* (pp. 3–24). Westport, CN: Preager.

McCroskey, J. & Einbinder, S. (Eds.) (1998). *Universities and communities: Remaking professional and interprofessional education for the next century.* Westport, CN: Preager.

McCullough, C. S., & Miller, D. (2003). Computerized assessment. In C. Reynolds & R. Kamphaus (Eds.), *Handbook of psychological and educational assessment of children: Intelligence, aptitude, and achievement* (2nd ed., pp. 628–670). New York: Guilford.

McDermott, J., Tseng, W., Char, W., & Fukunaga, C. (1978). Child custody decision-making. *Journal of the American Academy of Child Psychiatry, 17,* 104–116.

McMillen, J., Morris, L., & Sherraden, M. (2004): Ending social work's grudge match: Problems vs. strengths. *Families and Society, 85*(3) 317–325.

Medjuck, J. (Producer), & Reitman, I. (Director). (1984). *Ghostbusters* [Motion Picture]. Hollywood, CA: Columbia Studio.

Megargee, E. (2000). Testing. In A. Kazdin (Ed.), *Encyclopedia of psychology* (Vol. 8, pp. 47–52). Washington, DC: American Psychological Association.

Melton, G., Petrila, J., Poythress, N., & Slobogin, C. (1987). *Psychological evaluation for mental health professionals and lawyers.* New York: Guilford.

Melton, G., Petrila, J., Poythress, N., & Slobogin, C. (1997). *Psychological evaluation for mental health professionals and lawyers* (2nd ed.). New York: Guilford.

Mercer, J. (1979). *System of multicultural pluralistic assessment: Technical manual.* San Antonio, TX: Psychological Corp.

Merrell, K. (1994). *Assessment of behavioral, social, and emotional problems: Direct and objective methods for use with children and adolescents.* New York: Longman.

Miller, W., & Rollnick, S. (1992). *Motivational interviewing.* New York: Guilford Press.

Murray, H. (1943). *The Thematic Apperception Test.* Cambridge, MA: Harvard University Press.

N

National Association of School Psychologists. (1993). *Position statement on racism, prejudice, and discrimination.* Bethesda, MD: Author.

National Association of School Psychologists. (1997a). *Principles for professional ethics.* Bethesda, MD: Author.

National Association of School Psychologists. (1997b). *Standards for the provision of school psychological services.* Bethesda, MD: Author.

National Association of School Psychologists. (1999a). *Position statement on early childhood assessment.* Bethesda, MD: Author.

National Association of School Psychologists. (1999b). *Position statement on school psychologists' involvement in the role of assessment.* Bethesda, MD: Author.

National Forum on Interprofessional Education and Accreditation. (1998, May). *Summary of findings: Examination of the impact of discipline-specific accreditation on interprofessional Education.* Alexandria, VA: Council on Social Work Education.

National Institute on Alcohol Abuse and Alcoholism. (2006). National epidemiologic survey on alcohol and related conditions. *Alcohol Research and Health, 29*(2).

Nilsen, B. (1997). *Week by week plans for observing and recording young children.* Albany, NY: Delmar.

No Child Left Behind Act of 2001, Pub. L. No. 107-110 (2001).

Nunnally, J. C. (1978). *Psychometric theory* (2nd ed.). New York: McGraw-Hill.

O

Obert, J. (2002). *The matrix model of methamphetamine treatment.* Paper presented at Alcohol and Drug Abuse Division Conference, Pueblo, CO.

Ochoa, S. (2003). Assessment of culturally and linguistically diverse children. In C. Reynolds & R. Kamphaus (Eds.), *Handbook of psychological and educational assessment of children: Intelligence, aptitude, and achievement* (2nd ed., pp. 563–583). New York: Guilford

O'Connor, L. E., Esherick, M., & Vieten, C. (2002). Drug- and alcohol-abusing women. In S. L. A. Straussner & S. Brown, (Eds.), *The handbook of addiction treatment for women* (pp. 75–98). San Francisco: Jossey-Bass.

Orosz, J. (2000). *The insider's guide to grantmaking: How foundations find, fund, and manage effective programs.* San Francisco: Jossey-Bass.

Orton, G. (1997). *Strategies for counseling with children and their parents.* Pacific Grove, CA: Brooks/Cole.

Ownby, R. (1997). *Psychological reports: A guide to writing in professional psychology* (3rd ed.). New York: Wiley.

Ownby, R., & Wallbrown, F. (1983). Evaluating school psychological reports, Part I: A procedure for systematic feedback. *Psychology in the Schools, 20,* 41–45.

Ownby, R., & Wallbrown, F. (1986). Improving report writing in school psychology. In T. Kratochwill (Ed.), *Advances in school psychology* (Vol. 5, pp. 5–49). Hillsdale, NJ: Erlbaum.

P

Paliani, R. E. (1998, August). False negative. *Professional Counselor*, pp. 15–18.

Parents in Action on Special Education (PASE) v. Hannon, J. et al. Memorandum Decision No. 74c 3586, 1980. U.S. District Court for the Northern District of Illinois, Eastern District.

Parsons, R., Jorgensen, J., & Hernandez, S. (1994). *The integration of social work practice.* Pacific Grove, CA: Brooks/Cole.

Patterson, G. (1977). Naturalistic observation in clinical assessment. *Journal of Abnormal Child Psychology, 5,* 309–322.

Perlman, H. (1979). *Relationship: The heart of helping.* Chicago: University of Chicago Press.

Pinderhughes, E. (1989). *Understanding race, ethnicity, and power: The key to efficacy in clinical practice.* New York: Free Press.

Q

Quinn, K. (1992). The clinical evaluation for the juvenile court. In M. Kalogerakis (Ed.), *Handbook of psychiatric practice in the juvenile court* (pp. 37–45). Washington, DC: American Psychiatric Press.

Quinn, K. & Nye, S. (1992). Termination of parental rights. In M. Kalogerakis (Ed.), *Handbook of psychiatric practice in the juvenile court* (pp. 121–129). Washington, DC: American Psychiatric Press.

R

Rapp, C. (1998). *The strengths model: Case management with people suffering from severe and persistent mental illness.* New York: Oxford University Press.

Rehabilitation Act of 1973, Pub. L. No. 93-112 (1973).

Reynolds, C. R., Gutkin, T. B., Elliot, S. N., & Witt, J. (1984). *School psychology: Essentials of theory and practice.* New York: John Wiley & Sons.

Reynolds, C. R., & Kaiser, S. (2003). Bias in assessment of aptitude. In C. Reynolds & R. Kamphaus (Eds.). *Handbook of psychological and educational assessment of children: Intelligence, aptitude, and achievement* (2nd ed., pp. 519–562). New York: Guilford.

Reynolds, C. R., & Kamphaus, R. *Handbook of psychological and educational assessment of children: Intelligence, aptitude, and achievement* (2nd ed., pp. 519–562). New York: Guilford.

Riccio, C., & Hughes, J. (2001). Established and emerging models of psychological services in school settings. In J. Hughes, A. La Greca, & J. Conoley (Eds.), *Handbook of psychological services for children and adolescents* (pp. 63–87). Oxford: Oxford University Press.

Roberts, E., & DeBlassie, R. (1983). Test bias and the culturally different early adolescent. *Adolescence, 18,* 837–843.

Robertson, G. (2003). A practical model for test development. In C. Reynolds & R. Kamphaus (Eds.), *Handbook of psychological and educational assessment of children: Intelligence, aptitude, and achievement* (2nd ed., pp. 24–57). New York: Guilford.

Robbins, S., Chatterjee, P., & Canda, E. (1998). *Contemporary human behavior theory: A critical perspective for social work.* Boston: Allyn & Bacon.

Roggman, L., Boyce, L., & Newland, L. (2000). Assessing mother–infant interaction in play. In K. Giltin-Weiner, A. Sandgrund, & C. Schaefer (Eds.), *Play diagnosis and assessment* (2nd ed., pp. 303–339). New York: John Wiley & Sons.

Ryan, J. & Smith, J. (2003). Assessing the intelligence of adolescents with the Wechsler Adult Intelligence Scale-Third Edition (WAIS-III). In C. Reynolds & R. Kamphaus

(Eds.), *Handbook of psychological and educational assessment of children* (2nd ed., pp. 147–173). New York: Guilford.

S

Saari, C. (1989). The process of learning in clinical social work. *Smith College Studies in Social Work, 60,* 35–49.

Saleebey, D. (1996). The strengths perspective in social work practice: Extensions and cautions. *Social Work, 41,* 296–305.

Saleebey, D. (1997). *The strengths perspective in social work practice* (2nd ed.). New York: Longman.

Saleebey, D. (2002). *The strengths perspective in social work practice* (3rd ed.). Boston: Allyn & Bacon.

Samuda, R. (1998). *Psychological testing of American minorities: Issues and consequences* (2nd ed.). Thousand Oaks, CA: Sage.

Sandler, A., & Hatt, C. (2004). Mental retardation. In M. Hersen's (Ed.), *Psychological assessment in clinical practice: A pragmatic guide* (pp. 321–345). New York: Brunner-Routledge.

Sandoval, J. (1998). Testing in a changing world: An introduction. In J. Sandoval, C. Frisby, K. Geisinger, J. Scheuneman, & J. Grenier's (Eds.), *Test interpretation and diversity: Achieving equity in assessment.* Washington, DC: American Psychological Association.

Sandoval, J., Frisby, C., Geisinger, K., Scheuneman, J., & Grenier, J. (Eds.). (1998). *Test interpretation and diversity: Achieving equity in assessment.* Washington, DC: American Psychological Association.

Sandoval, J., & Irvin, M. (2003). Legal and ethical issues in the assessment of children. In C. Reynolds & R. Kamphaus (Eds.), *Handbook of psychological and educational assessment of children: Intelligence, aptitude, and achievement* (2nd ed., pp. 58–78). New York: Guilford.

Sapp, M. (2002). *Psychological and educational test scores: What are they?* Springfield, IL: Charles C Thomas.

Sattler, J.M. (1988). *Assessment of children* (3rd ed.). San Diego: Jerome M. Sattler.

Sattler, J. (1998). *Clinical and forensic interviewing of children and families: Guidelines for mental health, education, pediatric, and child maltreatment fields.* San Diego: Jerome M. Sattler.

Sax, G. (1997). *Principles of educational and psychological measurement and evaluation* (4th ed.). Belmont, CA: Wadsworth.

Schmidt, B. (Ed.). (1978). *The child protection team handbook. A multidisciplinary approach to managing child abuse and neglect.* New York: Garland STPM Press.

Searcy, J., & Baldwin, V. (1998). An annotated bibliography: Interprofessional education and training, and education issues, health care issues, social service issues, integrated services, plus bibliographies. Monmouth, OR: Western Oregon University, Teaching Research Division.

Seligman, L. (2004). *Diagnosis and treatment planning in counseling.* New York: Kluwer Academic/Plenum.

Sharma, S. (1986). Assessment strategies for minority youth. *Journal of Black Studies, 17,* 111–114.

Shirk, S. (2001). The road to effective child psychological services: Treatment processes and outcome research. In J. Hughes, A. La Greca, & J. Conoley (Eds.). *Handbook of psychological services for children and adolescents* (pp. 43–59). Oxford: Oxford University Press.

Shulman, L. (1999). *The skills of helping individuals, families, groups, and communities* (4th ed.). Itasca, IL: Peacock.

Shulman, L. (2006). *The skills of helping individuals, families, groups, and communities* (5th ed.). Belmont, CA: Thomson Brooks/Cole.

Smith, D. (2000). Parent–child interaction play assessment. In K. Giltin-Weiner, A. Sandgrund, & C. Schaefer (Eds.), *Play diagnosis and assessment* (2nd ed., pp. 340–370). New York: John Wiley & Sons.

Solomon, M. (1973). A conceptual, developmental premise for family therapy. *Family Process, 12,* 179–188.

Staudt, M., Howard, M., & Drake, B. (2001). The operationalization, implementation, and effectiveness of the strengths perspective: A review of empirical studies. *Journal of Social Service Research, 27*(3), 1–21.

Straussner, S. L. A., & Attia, P. R. (2002). Women's addiction treatment through a historical lens. In Straussner, S. L. A. & Brown, S. (Eds.), *The handbook of addiction treatment for women* (pp. 3–25). San Francisco: Jossey-Bass.

Substance Abuse and Mental Health Services Administration (SAMHSA) (2007). *Results for the 2006 National Survey on Drug Use and Health: National findings* (NSDUH, Series H-32; Publication No. SMA 07-4293.) Rockville, MD: Office of Applied Studies, Department of Health and Human Services.

Sue, D. (1980). *Counseling the culturally different: Theory and practice.* New York: John Wiley & Sons.

Suen, H., & French, J. (2003). A history of the development of psychological and educational testing. In C. Reynolds & R. Kamphaus (Eds.), *Handbook of psychological and educational assessment of children: Intelligence, aptitude, and achievement* (2nd ed., pp. 3–23). New York: Guilford.

T

Tafoya, T. (1992, April 29). *Keynote address.* Paper presented at the Emerging Perspectives: Drug And Alcohol Interventions With People of Color conference: Denver: University of Denver, Graduate School of Social Work.

Terman, L. (1922). *Intelligence tests and school instruction.* Yonkers-on-the-Hudson, NY: World Books.

Teyber, E. (2006). *Interpersonal process in therapy: An integrative model* (5th ed.). Pacific Grove, CA: Thompson Brooks/Cole.

Thorpe, J., Kamphaus, R., & Reynolds, C. (2003). The Behavior Assessment System for Children. In C. Reynolds & R. Kamphaus (Eds.), *Handbook of psychological and educational assessment of children: Personality, behavior, and context* (2nd ed., pp. 387–405). New York: Guilford.

Timken, D. (2001). *ADHD approved evaluation instrumentation for substance-using adults.* Denver: Colorado Department of Human Services, Alcohol and Drug Abuse Division.

Trotter, C. (1999). Don't throw the baby out with the bath water—In defence of problem solving. *Australian Social Work, 52,* 51–55.

Tsang, N. M. (2000). Dialectics in social work. *International Social Work, 43,* 421–434.

Tulsky, D., Saklofske, D., Chelune, G., Heaton, R., Ivnik, R., Bornstein, R., Prifitera, A., & Ledbetter, M. (Eds.). (2003). *Clinical interpretation of the WAIS-III and WMS-III*. San Diego: Academic Press.

Tulsky, D. Saklofske, D., & Ricker, J. (2003). Historical overview of intelligence and memory: Factors influencing the development of the Wechsler Scales. In D. Tulsky, D. Saklofske, G. Chelune, R. Heaton, R. Ivnik, R. Bornstein, A. Prifitera, & M. Ledbetter (Eds.), *Clinical interpretation of the WAIS-III and WMS-III* (pp. 7–41). San Diego: Academic Press.

U

U.S. Department of Health and Human Services (1994). *Treatment of opiate addiction with methadone* ([SMA 94-2061]). Rockville, MD: Author.

U.S. Department of Health and Human Services (2000). *Substance abuse treatment for persons with child abuse and neglect issues* ([SMA 00-3357]). Rockville, MD: Author.

U.S. Department of Health and Human Services (2002). *Navigating the pathways: lessons and promising practices in linking alcohol and drug services with child welfare* ([SMA] 02-3639). Rockville, MD: Author.

V

Valencia, R., & Suzuki, L. (2001). *Intelligence testing and minority students: Foundations, performance factors, and assessment issues*. Thousand Oaks, CA: Sage.

van de Vijver, F. (2003). Methodology of combining the WISC-III data sets. In J. Georgas, L. Weiss, F. Van de Vijver, & D. Saklofske (Eds.), *Culture and children's intelligence: Cross-cultural analysis of the WISC-III* (pp. 265–276). Amsterdam: Academic Press.

Van Dorsten, B. (Ed.). (2002). *Forensic psychology: From classroom to courtroom*. New York: Kluwer Academic/Plenum.

W

Wanberg, K. (2000). *User's guide to the adult substance use survey: The North Carolina normative group*. Arvada, CO: Center for Addictions Research and Evaluation.

Wanberg, K. W., & Milkman, H. B. (1998). *Criminal conduct and substance abuse treatment*. Thousand Oaks, CA: Sage.

Weaver, J. (1984). *Testing children: A reference guide for effective clinical and psychoeducational assessments*. Kansas City: Testing Corporation of America.

Wechsler, D. (1991). *Wechsler intelligence scale for children—3rd ed*. New York: Psychological Corp.

Weis, L., Suklofske, D., & Prifitera, A. (2003). Clinical interpretation of the Wechsler Intelligence Scale for Children—Third Edition (WISC III) Index Scores. In C. Reynolds & R. Kamphaus (Eds.), *Handbook of psychological and educational assessment of children: Intelligence, aptitude, and achievement* (2nd ed., pp. 115–146). New York: Guilford.

Werthman, M, (1995, September/October). A managed care approach to psychological testing. *Behavioral Health Management*, pp. 15–17.

Whiston, S. (2000). *Principles and applications of assessment in counseling*. Belmont, CA: Brooks/Cole.

Wicks-Nelson R., & Israel, A. (1997). *Behavior disorders of childhood* (3rd ed.). Upper Saddle River, NJ: Prentice Hall.

Wicks-Nelson R., & Israel, A. (2006). *Behavior disorders of childhood* (5th ed.). Upper Saddle River, NJ: Pearson/Prentice Hall.

Winters, K., Newcomb, M., & Fahnhorst, T. (2004). Substance-use disorders. In M. Hersen (Ed.), *Psychological assessment in clinical practice: A pragmatic guide* (pp. 393–408). New York: Brunner-Routledge.

Wodrich, D. (1997). *Children's psychological testing: A guide for nonpsychologists* (3rd ed.). Baltimore: Paul H. Brookes.

Wodrich, D., & Kush, S. (1990). *Children's psychological testing: A guide for nonpsychologists* (2nd ed.). Baltimore: Paul H. Brookes.

Wolber, G., & Carne, W. (1993). *Writing psychological reports. A guide for clinicians.* Sarasota, FL: Professional Resource Press.

Wood, K. (1978, November). Casework effectiveness. A new look at the research evidence. *Social Work*, pp. 437–458.

Y

Yalom, I. (1980). *Existential psychotherapy.* New York: Basic Books.

Yalom, I. (1989). *Love's executioner and other tales of psychotherapy.* New York: Basic Books.

Yalom, I. (2002). *The gift of therapy: An open letter to a new generation of therapists and their patients.* New York: HarperCollins.

Young, N. K., Gardner, S. L., & Dennis, K. (1998). *Responding to alcohol and other drug problems in child welfare.* Washington, DC: Child Welfare League of America.

Z

Zimmerman, I., & Woo-Sam, J. (1973). *Clinical interpretation of the Wechsler Adult Intelligence Scale.* New York: Grune and Stratton.

Zolnick, J., McCroskey, J., Gardner, S., de Gilbaja, M., Taylor, H., George, J., et al. (1999). *Myths and opportunities: An examination of the impact of discipline-specific accreditation on interpersonal education.* Alexandria, VA: Council on Social Work Education.

Zuckerman, E. (1995). *Clinician's thesaurus: The guidebook for writing psychological reports* (4th ed.). New York: Guilford Press.

Zuckerman, E. (2000). *Clinician's thesaurus: The guidebook for writing psychological reports* (5th ed.). New York: Guilford Press.

Name Index

305

Subject Index